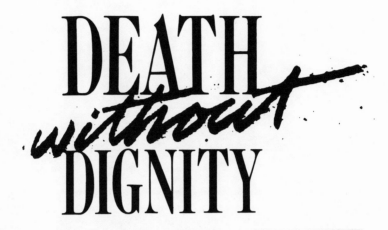

DEATH without DIGNITY

The story of the first nursing home corporation
indicted for murder.

BY STEVEN LONG

Foreword by Elma L. Holder
The National Citizens' Coalition for Nursing
Home Reform.

★

TexasMonthlyPress

Texas Monthly Press, Inc.
P.O. Box 1569
Austin, Texas 78767

A B C D E F G H

Library of Congress Cataloging-in-Publication Data

Long, Steven, 1944–
   Death without dignity.

   1. Autumn Hills Convalescent Centers (Texas City, Tex.)—Trials, litigation, etc.   2. Trials (Murder)—Texas—Galveston.   3. Breed, Elnora.   4. Aged—Texas—Texas City—Crimes against.   5. Nursing home patients—Texas—Texas City—Abuse of.   I. Title.
KF224.A9L66   1987   345.73'02523   86-30070
ISBN 0-87719-062-3   347.3052523

Text design by Don Crum

CONTENTS

To my mother, who nursed my father to a peaceful death

FOREWORD

This book will join a library of investigations about serious problems in our nation's nursing homes documented over the last thirty years. The story is especially important because it provides the public with a close human account of one of the most significant set of events in nursing home reform history—the investigation and litigation charging a nursing home corporation and its officials with criminal acts against its residents.

For the first time, in a sustained public forum, a fundamental question was asked and explored: Does day-to-day neglect, over an extended period of time, turn into abuse; and does the resulting abuse, over an extended period of time, cause premature death? Is this called murder? Other critical questions follow: Who is actually responsible, and how will this person or persons ever be held accountable?

Understandably, this case attracted widespread attention from the nursing home industry, government officials and consumer advocates. For those who have advocated nursing home reform for many years, myself for at least twenty, the lack of verdict in the trial the *State of Texas* v. *Autumn Hills Convalescent Centers, Inc.*, is painfully telling. Even in the face of tremendous evidence of neglect and abuse of vulnerable, ill and disabled persons in nursing homes, we are not yet ready to hold anyone responsible or accountable. Except for the victims involved—the residents, family members and close friends, and other eye-witnesses such as honest and caring staff and regulatory inspectors—it is too easy for us to forget, or to diminish or negate such unthinkable pain and suffering as described in this book. Unlike the residents and those closest to them in nursing homes, we can all escape to the comfort and freedom we have living in the broader community.

As you read through these chapters, you may come to realize that, in many ways, our nursing home system is set up to permit or foster neglect and, even abuse, of residents. Because we have had such difficulties with nursing homes, we have become tolerant of very low standards of care and accountability. We are grateful if a facility is clean and attractive and provides basic services. We often accept minimal conditions because, at least, "things are better than they used to be—or things could be a lot worse."

This case is one of those which is horrendous enough to shake us up and remind us that major problems still abound in nursing homes. In fact, practically any problem ever surfaced in a nursing home was uncovered in the investigation of Autumn Hills. My organization, the National Citizens' Coalition for Nursing Home Reform, for the last ten years, has received regular calls from families, nursing home staff, regulatory officials and others who describe these continuing problems that affect the quality of care of residents.

Nursing homes do not employ enough licensed nursing staff to give the residents the specialized, individualized care and services they need and deserve. Even licensed nursing staff often lack the skills needed to provide geriatric care or to train and supervise other workers.

Perhaps the most revealing aspect of poor care in nursing homes is how little we care about the workers who are employed to provide most of the services and direct, hands-on-care for residents. Although we are fortunate that so many nurse aides care deeply about the residents and show it in the care they provide; there are few incentives for aides to do their best or for them to dedicate themselves to work in nursing homes. Aides are not usually given the full orientation and training they need. They are poorly paid and have few benefits. Their tasks are often extremely difficult, tiring, unattractive, and emotionally and physically draining. They are often ridiculed or mistreated by confused, unhappy or disturbed residents, or by family members or co-workers. Their supervisors often lack the time for them and the skills necessary to help them improve their work. Many facilities lack the proper equipment and sufficient supplies needed to provide good care. It is common for facilities to be short on staff; so, many times, aides simply cannot complete the services needed by the residents to whom they are assigned.

Aides seldom receive the public recognition they deserve for their important work. Little wonder the turnover for nurse aides, and other nursing home personnel, is so high. Clearly, this turnover results in a discontinuity in care which is also detrimental to the residents and other staff.

Why do these conditions exist? Owners, administrators and other management staff in nursing homes make the decisions which foster poor conditions for workers. We cannot expect high quality care for residents when these conditions exist. In fact, we begin to understand why neglect and abuse of residents occurs. But poor quality nursing care is only part of the problem.

Beyond basic skilled nursing services, our nation's elderly in nursing homes need much more that they do not receive. It is unusual to find regular rehabilitative services provided by trained professionals such as physical therapists, occupational therapists, speech and communication therapists. Emotional and social support services are needed by residents from trained social workers, uncommon in nursing homes. Critical mental health services for residents, families, and nursing home staff are rarely available. Even resources for activity programs are usually meager and do not support the variety and level of activities needed by the residents.

The Autumn Hills case highlights another serious issue in nursing homes—physician services are often missing or extremely poor. As exposed in these chapters, doctors are not usually held accountable for their poor services, neglect or even abuse of residents they verbally claim as "their" patients. The situation surrounding medical care in nursing homes is so poor it often seems hopeless to turn around. Specialized geriatric training for nurse practitioners and physicians assistants is often promoted as one of the answers to assure that basic health care is given to residents. Still, the public must demand good services and accountability from the medical community.

Contrary to the complaints about "over-regulation" of nursing homes by some of the officials in the Autumn Hills Corporation, our regulatory system at the state and federal levels is often weak and ineffectual. The system is in desperate need of support and strength. Public outcry and another important legal case, *Smith* v. *Heckler* have exerted the pressure necessary to influence the government to take a long, hard look at its regulatory system since the late 1970s. Additional Congressional action persuaded the government to contract with the Institute of Medicine of the National Academy of Sciences to conduct an indepth study of nursing home regulation beginning in 1983. In March 1986, IoM released its important study, *Improving the Quality of Care in Nursing Homes.* The Committee that conducted the study called for fundamental changes in the regulatory system. It concluded, "There is a broad consensus that government regulation of nursing homes, as it now functions, is not satisfactory because it allows too many marginal or substandard nursing homes to continue in operation."

The government is currently modifying its survey system to be able to detect actual quality care delivery, instead of "paper compliance," to standards. This is a step in the right direction; but the government is not providing the increased resources that are needed to make the fundamental changes called for explicitly in the IoM study. More funds and programs are needed to provide quality training for surveyors so that they can become better monitors and enforcement agents. Survey teams must be composed of experienced professionals who can determine actual patterns of care and document evidence which can stand up in court as needed. Enforcement mechanisms must be developed and implemented.

Perhaps if the regulatory system had been operating for the full benefit of nursing home residents, the Autumn Hills case would never have reached the stage which required the vast amount of time and money expended by the State of Texas and the Autumn Hills Corporation. Better the money had been available to be spent on improving services for the elderly residents in Texas nursing homes and bolstering the state survey agency.

Still, we can be thankful that there are potential checks on the system when it fails—when people care enough to use them. One such person was attorney David Marks, whose dedication to pursuing justice regarding one nursing home in Texas cannot be overlooked and must not be underestimated. Mr. Marks, and all the people who helped and supported him, advanced the possibility of future, system-wide nursing home reform. Regulatory agencies and future prosecutors who take on nursing home issues will benefit from the extensive development of this case, some of which is described in this book.

I would be remiss if I did not review the public's role in nursing home reform. As a public, we too, have tremendous unmet responsibilities to pursue quality and accountability in America's nursing homes. The conditions described in the proceedings against Autumn Hills are inexcusable. Because such problems continue to exist throughout the country, we cannot ignore them. We must take action against those who neglect and abuse our elderly loved ones and friends. The general caring we all express must be turned into direct action which can be expressed in several ways:

- Regular visitation with nursing home residents; providing personal and social contacts to promote quality of daily life as well as quality care

- Regular nursing home visits to monitor the care delivered, and to advocate for better care directly with nursing home staff, owners and administrators

- Active recognition of the importance of the work of all nursing home staff, with support for action to improve their working conditions

- Volunteer work with the local and state long-term care ombudsman program, with support for action to strengthen and expand such programs in every community

- Support for new federal and state laws and regulations to provide the direction and guidance needed for delivery of quality care and to assure strong enforcement measures when needed

- Support of state and federal regulatory personnel as the public servants entrusted with monitoring and enforcement of laws and regulations; as well as support for action to hold them accountable when they do not perform their responsibilities to the public

Most of us know that there are models of high quality nursing home care throughout the country. Since I visited the facility in 1968, I have personally used Golden Acres, the Dallas Home for Jewish Aged, as one of my models. We must use these best models to guide in our reform activities. It is prudent to work with progressive nursing home industry representatives and nursing home staff for the improvements needed—in individual nursing homes and in the nursing home system.

But, most importantly, this books reminds us that we must ac-

knowledge and support any special action—such as litigation—
that is taken to assure accountability when the system fails. More
of us must follow David Marks's leadership, to take action to determine who is actually responsible when residents are victimized and
suffer. Who makes management decisions which can eventually
lead to neglect, abuse and even premature death?

When nursing home owners apply for licensure and certification
to receive state and federal reimbursement for their services, they
voluntarily sign a contract with the government. Through this public contract, they obligate themselves to maintain, at least, the minimal standards developed by public regulatory agencies. Too often,
nursing homes receive public monies without fulfilling their con-
tracts. We must use every public forum to seriously question how
nursing home care is financed; who is qualified to receive the
money; and, how this tax money is actually spent. As concerned
citizens and taxpayers, we must not shy away from the responsibility to hold individuals accountable for poor or selfish management
decisions which deprive the elderly of the care they need, no
matter what the individual's professional title or community reputation or standing.

This book, *Death Without Dignity*, should reinforce our commitment to achieve the fundamental changes needed to assure quality
care and life for all our nation's nursing home residents. The special
sensitivity with which Steven Long describes the lives and deaths
of two Autumn Hills residents, Elnora Breed and Edna Mae Witt,
has surely helped strengthen my own personal commitment.

Elma L. Holder, Executive Director
National Citizens' Coalition for Nursing Home Reform
1424 16th Street, N.W., Suite L-2
Washington, D.C. 20036
(202) 797-0657

ACKNOWLEDGMENTS

When I began the project of writing about the events that happened in Texas City during 1978, I was a novice regarding the law, nursing care, medical care, and the particular ailments of the aged. I am no longer a novice. The following people have given unfailingly of their time and knowledge to assist me in the task of writing a book about nursing home abuse and neglect. They have also given me much needed advice on the complexities of how a team of Texas prosecutors attempted to bring a final measure of dignity to those who died at Autumn Hills Nursing Home and of how a stout team of defense attorneys represented their clients to the best of their considerable abilities.

David Marks, who brought the case to the attention of the nation, has assisted me greatly in understanding the difficulties with which he lived for eight years. Tom Sartwelle and Gail Friend have provided me with scores of documents and medical records without which the book could not have been written. Roy Minton and Charles Burton were open and honest and took time out from their busy trial schedule to educate me about the case over several delightful dinners.

Judge Don B. Morgan has been a wonderful teacher about the law and the strategies of the lawyers. Besides that, he was unfailingly open with me while the case was still in trial. No reporter could ask for more. He became a close and trusted friend.

Gene Lucas, president of Gal-Tex Hotel Corporation, arranged for my delightful stay at San Antonio's elegant Menger Hotel. My heartfelt thanks!

Dr. Thomas R. Cole and Dr. William J. Wineslade of the Institute for the Medical Humanities at Galveston's University of Texas Medical Branch read the manuscript and gave me great encouragement to keep going.

The national press was on hand for many phases of the trial; however, a stalwart group of reporters for six months became the Autumn Hills Press Club. They were Sheila Allee of the Associated Press, Renee Haines of United Press International, Jimmie Woods of the *Houston Post*, and Lynelle King, a freelance writer. All of them helped fill in the gaps. In Galveston, Steve Olafson of the *Houston Post* and Kevin Moran of the *Houston Chronicle* helped me untangle the web of the early years of the Autumn Hills case. Also, thanks to Jim Guidry and Vandy Anderson of KGBC radio for saving much needed wire copy for my files and to Teri Crook of the *Galveston Daily News*, who was kind enough to copy her clips for me.

J. Curtiss Brown, Jr., and the staff of *In Between* magazine did a great job when I was away from the office. I could not have completed the project without their patience and support.

I owe a great debt of gratitude to Michael Barryhill and Chad Gordon, who wrote a superb story on the case for *Houston City* magazine. It functioned like a road map of the early days of the case.

Many thanks to Sam and Martha Levine, who stored and protected countless floppy discs for long months.

M. T. "Bujo" Waddell of Galveston College struggled through a chapter of my disjointed syntax. I especially thank Irvin Power, a much better writer than I, who read the entire manuscript on a computer screen. If the book reads well, it is largely because of him.

Special thanks go to Scott Lubeck of Texas Monthly Press for taking a risk on an author's first book. Scott had the foresight to see that nursing home problems are probably here to stay, and he saw the Autumn Hills case as the tip of the iceberg. Anne Norman at Texas Monthly Press continued to encourage me to keep going when times got rough. She also told me when to take a much needed rest.

Finally, thanks to my wife, Peggy, and my daughter, Michelle, who allowed me a year off from washing dishes. They, above anyone else, cracked the whip and kept me going.

INTRODUCTION

On September 10, 1986, jury selection began in one of the most remarkable criminal trials in American jurisprudence. In *State of Texas* v. *Autumn Hills Convalescent Centers, Inc.*, a corporation and five of its executives were accused of murder. The case was six years old before it reached the jury. The trial lasted six months, and the approximate cost to the state and the defendants was a staggering $4 million.

At issue in the case was whether the defendants had willfully caused the death of an 87-year-old black woman named Elnora Breed in a Texas City, Texas, nursing home. Also mentioned in the indictment were sixty other nursing home residents whom the State of Texas accused the corporation of abusing and neglecting. Most died, the state said, because of conditions in the home in 1978, the year that prosecutors had targeted for their case.

The Autumn Hills case is but the most celebrated in a long list of investigations into the growing industry of long-term care for the elderly. On Capitol Hill, both the United States Senate and the House of Representatives have held long and exhaustive investigations into elder abuse and neglect. It appears that the problem is not getting better and is only getting worse.

America is aging. The baby-boom generation will begin to engulf the nursing home industry in the same impressive numbers that have engulfed every other phase of American life. With the graying of a generation used to the good life will come the stark reality of dying, probably alone, possibly abused, and almost certainly neglected. The system simply will not be able to keep up with the numbers it will have to deal with.

Autumn Hills in Texas City was better than some nursing homes and worse than others. Despite the problems of a turnover rate in personnel during 1978 of one thousand percent, some loyal and caring employees stayed on staff. They were simply overwhelmed.

This book does not pretend to have an answer to the problems facing the nursing home industry or the next generation of its residents. I have attempted to clearly portray the story of a monumental legal case and the lawyers who fought it. In doing so, I have also told the story of what can go wrong in an environment where the recipients of care are often totally dependent on the care givers, as dependent as infant children.

The book is largely taken from hundreds of hours of trial testimony by eyewitnesses and experts, from medical and nursing records, recollections of attorneys, and observations of the players in a drama acted out before the bar of justice. I have attempted to portray the characters as they were: emotional, jocular, grim, fallible, angry, happy, egotistical, humble, brilliant, simple, callous, cold, and, above all, concerned.

Portions of the book are a tale of horror, a nightmare, Halloween in real life. Those portions will not be pleasant reading; however, rotting flesh, stale urine, dried feces, and physical abuse are pleasant only to a sick few. But the book also holds out the hope that the Autumn Hills case will change things for both the residents of nursing homes and nursing home owners, that this industry will care as much about human misery as it does about the bottom line.

Galveston, Texas
June 2, 1986

CHAPTER ONE

The caravan of cars and a U-Haul truck left the Gulf Freeway at LaMarque, Texas, and slowly moved down the blacktop road toward nearby Hitchcock.

A funeral procession in reverse, they turned off the farm-to-market road and slowly moved down a smaller road to the gates of the cemetery. As they went through they passed monuments to Galveston's recent past: W. L. Moody, the financier; Rose Maceo, the gangster; and Congressman Clark W. Thompson, intimate of presidents and Moody's son-in-law. But the procession did not go to the graves of the rich and famous; it went to the graves of lesser beings, in search of clues to a mystery that had been building for seven years.

The cemetery covered several acres, sloping toward a bayou filled with placid waters, waters that gave sustenance to stately oaks covered with Spanish moss and to towering pines, waters that gave this part of the Texas coast a lusciousness analogous to southeastern Louisiana. An alley of oak trees in the cemetery could have led to a plantation house carefully maintained for the hordes of tourists who come to those places, had this not been Texas and had this not been a cemetery.

There were much older cemeteries in Galveston County. On Galveston Island alone the abodes of the dead occupied a large portion of the city's limited geography. In those places lay the original pioneers of Texas, Austin's colonists, Texas revolutionaries, Civil War dead, victims of plagues brought on by the lowly mosquito, which the coast had in such abundance, and the dead of several hurricanes, not the least of which was the 1900 Storm, which killed perhaps seven thousand people, Poles, Italians, Serbians, Germans, Scots, Englishmen, Irishmen, former slaves, and their offspring.

On the mainland there were older cemeteries too. In Dickinson, for example, was a lovely plot in an Anglican churchyard that held the remains of settlers of the pine-wooded town that sprang up along Dickinson Bayou after Gail Borden built a sugar mill there in the 1830s. In this cemetery were the earthly remains of stalwart souls who had built their homes on fields filled with arrowheads. The Dickinson cemetery was older to be sure; it was right in the middle of town, and when the state built the highway to Houston, the crews were careful not to disturb the graves near Trinity Episcopal Church. Before the Gulf Freeway (I-45) was built, some had met their maker in the Dickinson cemetery. On weekends, the highway would be jammed with automobiles going to the beach or to the casinos in Galveston. More than once, a Houstonian with too much whiskey in his belly crossed the Dickinson Bayou bridge but did not negotiate the steeply banked curve on the north side by the cemetery. The oak trees by the highway showed the scars of wrecks of forty years ago. The wrecks didn't disturb the residents of the churchyard. The oaks had stood guard.

The old cemeteries ran out of room after a century of interment. Along the Gulf Freeway, the Catholics built a cemetery on the prairie, Forest Park of Houston found profit in building permanent housing near the banks of Clear Creek, and a Galveston undertaker found that a wooded tract of land along a meandering bayou north of the small bedroom community of Hitchcock increased the size of his bank account. This was the new cemetery, the fashionable one that suddenly began to fill with the populace of the recent past. In this place lay the remains that the cortege was seeking.

May 25, 1985, was one of those balmy days that presage the sweltering heat to come. The temperature reached a high that day of only 82, but there was no wind, and few clouds disrupted the constant beam of the sun. It was a welcome relief to the handful of people in the cortege, who had weathered two winters of record cold, despite their macabre task. They were outside, out of their offices in a beautiful place. They were alive and they felt it.

The line of vehicles moved slowly through the paved streets of Galveston Memorial Park to a sunlit meadow. In the meadow, there were no tombstones, just small markers set in the earth. The line stopped a few yards away from the place they were seeking, a small plot of ground perhaps four feet by eight feet. Next to that plot was a large orange tractor with a scoop attached to its front: a backhoe, the modern grave digger, the twentieth century's answer to the sweat of man. The passengers in the vehicles of the cortege emerged, dressed as if they were going to a softball game, horseback riding, or fishing. The solemnity of a funeral procession did not exist on this day. There was business to be done, and the cemetery was the place to do it.

David Marks, former Galveston County assistant district attorney and now, as much out of self-defense as anything else, a special assistant attorney general, wore a baseball cap. At 33, Marks could have been anything but the obsessed prosecutor his enemies claimed him to be. He had a grim expression on his face as he approached the grave. He had suffered to get to this point, not in a physical way, but suffered nonetheless. Marks looked at the other passengers emerging and walking slowly to the gravesite.

Tom Sartwelle, a Fulbright and Jaworski lawyer, was also in casual clothes, and he would abide no interference from Marks on this mission. Sartwelle was old money, the Houston establishment in a big way, a throwback to when Houston was not the petrochemical capital but just a cow town. His family owned the Port City Stockyards, a Houston institution despite its move to an isolated spot on Highway 36 north of Sealy, Texas. Marks's enemy was Sartwelle, whom another lawyer had described as a "prick by reputation." He was the kind of lawyer who generated tons of paper. On this case it was said that the paper generated by Sartwelle filled six offices at Fulbright and Jaworski's Houston office. Sartwelle's penchant for masses of paper coincidentally translated into thousands of billable hours for his firm.

Gail Friend also walked across the sunny meadow to the small plot. She too had done her time on the case, working at Fulbright and Jaworski as a nursing consultant while she also attended law school. Sartwelle described her as a workaholic. At 44, she had the credentials for a task like this. She had taught nursing at a Texas university. Friend was dressed for the day in pants—prim, yet cool and casual, the attire a schoolteacher might wear for a barbecue at the principal's house.

Also in the group were the doctors, who would, with a little luck, make this day worthwhile for one side or the other. These professionals were the hired guns on whose testimony might hang the fate of a whole host of people, none the least of whom were the accused.

The small sunlit plot that all of the assembled group were seeking belonged to Edna Mae Witt, a Galveston woman who had died in 1978. The funeral had been conducted by Broadway Funeral Home, the more ethnic of Galveston's three "white" funeral homes. Here, Hispanics, Italians, and other Southern Europeans spent their last days above ground in a white stucco building at the foot of Broadway, the street that bisects the city of Galveston. The rest of the Broadway's clients were lower-middle-class whites who either couldn't afford the silk-stocking funeral parlors or were friends of the family that owned the Broadway. Of that family, Broadway Joe Termini, as he is affectionately called by some Galvestonians, was at the cemetery that day to oversee the exhumation of his former client. Termini was dressed in jeans and a blue and white striped shirt. He was prepared to get dirty, for he had hands-on work to do.

As the group approached the small plot of earth, another cluster of workers began their task. Cameramen with video equipment got into position to record the day's proceedings, and four still photographers snapped photos as if they were paparazzi.

The tractor moved forward, lowered the backhoe, and began to remove the earth that had covered the remains of Edna Mae Witt for seven years. With each load, the assemblage strained to get their first glimpse of the top of the vault containing the casket. Finally, a scraping sound could be heard as the cold steel of the earth mover met the concrete of the burial vault. When all of the earth was removed from the top of the vault, two men, one black, the other white, began a more primitive method of unearthing the dead. With long-handled shovels, the men stood atop the vault and cut a low trench around the lid. Finally, enough earth was removed so that chains could be attached to the covering. This done, the grave of Edna Mae Witt was ready to be opened.

As the lid of the crypt was removed, the crowd moved closer to get a glimpse of what to most of them was a first-time experience. Bright sunlight glinted off the lid of a white coffin buried only two feet below the surface of the ground. The crowd moved closer still as the engine of the orange tractor was stilled and the two men attached chains to the silver handles of the snow-white casket. When their work was done, again the serenity of the cemetery was broken by the sound of the engine as it lifted the coffin from the earth. It dangled in the air out of place and time, then was lowered to the ground. Edna Mae Witt would not sleep in peace this day. Broadway Joe supervised the men as they moved the coffin in workaday fashion to the waiting U-Haul truck, which had seen much service moving the possessions of Galveston County families from apartment to apartment, from rent house to rent house. At this funeral-in-reverse there were no flowers, no mourners, no delicate handling of the late beloved. Instead, there was only work to be done and little time for the niceties reserved for the family of the deceased.

The dead are the last bastion of segregation in Texas and most of the rest of the South. In Galveston County, there are three black funeral homes. Blacks are even segregated in their final resting place in cemeteries scattered around the Island and on the prairies of the mainland, kept in often less well-maintained facilities than their white brethren.

The cortege again was on the move, just down the road from the fashionable cemetery to one of these less well-kept places, a sun-drenched postage-stamp-sized piece of the world where lay the remains of Elnora Breed. Again, the cortege parked near the gravesite and the passengers left their cars. Again, the orange tractor with the scoop on the front was waiting to do its morbid work. Again, they surrounded the grave. This time they were immune to their initial misgivings, for they had seen the exhumation of Edna Mae Witt and they knew what to expect. Witt had come up in a pristine white coffin; there was a fitting finality about the thing, respectable, the kind of container appropriate for their own grandmothers.

Again the tractor did its work, and the two men, one black and the other white, climbed atop the lid of the vault and dug the necessary trench. Again chains were attached to the lid of the vault, then to the tractor, which revved its engine as the chains became taut. Again the lid of the vault swung up and over the grave, then over to the side. But this time, unlike at the fashionable cemetery, something was amiss. They found the casket of Elnora Breed in the grave all right, but it was floating in a chasm filled with water. The casket had an old-fashioned shape, a lid with sloping sides, and a long, flat surface running from end to end. On top of that long, flat surface was a deposit of mud. Elnora Breed had been buried in a grave that was below the shallow water table of Galveston County.

It is not uncommon for a Galveston County grave to fill with water. Especially on the Island, after one of the city's frequent floods, caskets sometimes float themselves to the surface, displacing the soft sand that covers them. As in Louisiana graveyards, many Galveston graves are above the ground, in granite tombs that keep out the elements and intruders. The practice was much more common in the nineteenth century, when Victorians almost made a cult of death.

At the end of Elnora Breed's wet grave was a low tombstone, lovingly placed there by her family to mark the spot for posterity. If anyone cared to find the place where Elnora Breed rested a century hence, all he had to do was look, for on the stone was chiseled in oversized letters one word, "Breed."

The two men approached the grave and began the distasteful task of placing the chains around the casket. They seemed reluctant to place their hands in the water that filled the oblong hole. Finally, with obvious misgivings, they attached their triangular chain to the casket and, assured that their work was done, moved away from the spot. Again, the orange tractor tensed its mechanical muscles and began to lift the casket, which looked almost golden in the sunlight reflected from the water. It did not seem to want to leave the grave, no matter how much the power of modern machinery tried to remove it. At last the water released its hold, and the casket swung free and into the air. As it did so, water poured from the casket back into the grave. The casket seemed to be drawn back to the grave as it tilted, then crashed headfirst back into the pit, depriving Elnora Breed of her last vestige of dignity. The crash caused the lid to open, and the assemblage—hard, cold, businesslike, as they were—recoiled from the grave. They had not expected this. Opening the grave of Edna Mae Witt had been so pristine, so white, so clean.

Again, the two men went to the grave, but this time they simply got more men and removed the upright casket from the grave and laid it on the ground. Broadway Joe approached the casket in a manner befitting his trade and opened it slowly. Then one of the doctors approached and used a wooden stick to rummage around the interior of the thing as a person would if he had lost a watch in the garbage. As he stooped to retrieve some of Elnora Breed's remains, there hung from the casket lid tattered fragments of the cloth liner that had looked so nice to the family in the funeral home. It hung in wet strands, like a Hollywood attempt to portray spiderwebs in a vampire movie. But this was no movie; this was real life, or rather real death, and death was all around. Gail Friend, the Fulbright and Jaworski lawyer who was also a nurse and had seen her share of putrefaction, put her hand to her face. Plastic lid holders remained in the eye sockets of the skull. The pathologist lifted the head of Elnora Breed from the open casket and held it up, like a medieval executioner might after his work was done. Elnora Breed had an unusually small skull, and there were wisps of fine white hair still attached. The horror of what had been her final years continued.

A few bones were removed, examined, and placed back in the casket. One of the doctors asked Sartwelle if he thought "taking it in" would be worthwhile. Sartwelle was reluctant to do so, but Marks insisted, and the casket that had glimmered golden in the sun was placed unceremoniously in the back of the U-Haul truck. Marks and the prosecution team had believed that an autopsy would be an exercise in futility. The young attorney general had studied body preservation, casket quality, the whole macabre science of the undertaker's art. He had little expectation that in Breed's type of casket and the bottomless vault there would be anything left. Now, exposed, the remains were in such a state after seven years below the water table that it was doubtful anything could be found that would be beneficial to either side. Yet, Marks felt that the damage had been done, the rest of Elnora Breed disturbed, the quiet of death interrupted. At the very least, Marks believed, the remains must be professionally examined in a laboratory, not in an open casket with a wooden stick.

On October 22, 1979, a young Texas prosecutor named David Marks moved into a new office space next to a window in the Galveston County Courthouse. A more experienced prosecutor had left the office, and the desk next to the window was the first movement of any sort in the young man's career as a prosecutor. For a year as a misdemeanor assistant to Galveston County district attorney James Hury, Marks had tried every case that came his way in order to gain courtroom experience. The work of the misdemeanor prosecutor is the lowest rung on the legal ladder for a lawyer. Yet handling the petty crimes that the foibles of man put upon the legal system gives a young lawyer the kind of trial experience that will serve him well in later years, particularly if he is interested in criminal defense work or in representing plaintiffs in civil lawsuits. David Marks was a trial lawyer, a colt lately out of the stables of South Texas College of Law in downtown Houston.

Marks had come to Galveston after the experience of a year of practice with a veteran Houston attorney. Marks had taken the job with Hury but had not really wanted it. He was ambivalent during the interview, experiencing no white knuckles. He was not desperate for the job. But Hury put him to work. Marks had grown up in Port Arthur, Texas, the son of an engineer in the burgeoning petrochemical industry of the Golden Triangle of Beaumont, Port Arthur, and Orange. The boy had been the skinny kid at Port Arthur High School, a kid who was also overshadowed by overachiever siblings: a brother who went to Dartmouth and Oxford and a sister who would become a pediatric neurologist. "While my sister and brother were doing those things that would serve them well later in life, I was screwing off," Marks would say. Marks was too small and thin to excel in sports, although he did play Little League baseball.

His family was drawn from the melting pot of America. A grandfather had come to this country from Germany. His name was Haas, and when he first stepped foot on these shores, an immigration inspector promptly couldn't pronounce the name. The government man asked the young immigrant what he wanted to be called, so the family story goes. All the youth had been thinking about across the Atlantic was the money he had in his pocket, so he blurted out "*Marks*" to the man. From that time forward, "Marks" was the family name in America.

Young Marks assimilated into the melting pot, married, and raised a family. A couple of generations later, the family was on the Texas coast, and the product was David Marks, his brother, and his sister. Their father was a Jewish engineer, a thin man who had grown up in Dallas and who carried the North Texas accent with him to the coast. Their mother was an Arkansas Baptist who had been valedictorian of her high school class.

Young David Marks managed to make his way through grade school, then high school, then tenaciously through the University of Texas as a psychology major. He graduated and entered business school but got bored. Finally, he applied to every law school he could think of but, because of low grades, had to settle on South Texas. Marks had no idea what to expect from law school, yet from the first day he adapted to the new terminology, the new way of thinking, and the majesty of the law. He took a job at the Harris County Courthouse as a bailiff during the daytime and attended classes at night. In the courtroom, the young bailiff watched experienced trial lawyers practice their art and learned their tricks. At night he put those tricks to work for him in argument classes. He boasts that in those sessions, he consistently led the rest of his class. The skinny kid from Port Arthur was developing into a member of that unique institution, the Texas Bar.

Marks was moving up in his profession, being recognized by his superior for doing his job well. James Hury, district attorney of Galveston County, was shorthanded and was also aware that Marks had received offers to work elsewhere. Marks was good. He had put first offenders, particularly DWI defendants, in jail, almost unheard of in the late seventies. Hury promised Marks that he would move to the felony division. Marks took the opportunity to mention to his boss that he had discovered an interesting file. Hury had heard of the Autumn Hills file before, and here was a young prosecutor who was showing promise, a man who might someday be entrusted with more serious cases, cases significant to the very fiber of society, felony cases that could send people to the penitentiary, or even worse. Hury said that Marks could pursue the file.

As Marks looked over his new space, he moved books around, shuffled files, and even thumbed through some of those files. Behind some out-of-date law books he found a file, one inch thick, dusty, old, and unused, the file he had told Hury about. The file seemed to relate to a medicaid fraud investigation from the year before. In it he had found a report from the Texas Department of Human Resources alleging that a Texas City nursing home named Autumn Hills had defrauded the state and federal governments of $63,000, mainly by padding its payrolls.

Marks also found state nursing home inspection reports from the Texas Department of Health. In those reports, a state inspector noted that the Texas City home had had double the death rate of three comparable nursing homes during a ninety-day period. An unusually high number of Autumn Hills patients were developing large decubitus ulcers, commonly known as bedsores, and many of them were allegedly developing infections from the large sores. The report went on to say that the patients had been allowed to lie in their own bodily wastes, their own urine and feces. The connection seemed natural. Were the patients of Autumn Hills dying because of infections caused by nursing care? Marks suspected that they were.

As Marks continued reading he became increasingly outraged, increasingly fascinated by the dormant file he had found in his new office. The young prosecutor learned that some of the Autumn Hills patients had suffered from severe weight loss and malnutrition. He was later to believe that at least ten of them had, at one time or another, been placed on a starvation diet.

A nursing inspector noted that in February 1978 she had made a routine visit to the Texas City facility. She had seen the emaciation of some patients, some who lost weight not because of disease but because of inadequate nutrition. The inspector, Paulette Miller, wrote to the Autumn Hills administrator that "it appears that the residents are starving."

Elderly people are subject to falls, and standard nursing practice usually requires that the fall be reported to a physician and that the nurse assume that a bone may be broken. Yet Autumn Hills nurses, Marks believed, often did not make such reports to either the doctors or the families of the patients.

Many people in a nursing home can't get out of bed to care for their basic needs because they are too old, too ill, or have some disability such as paralysis or blindness. To such people, the lifeline and the communications link to the outside world to summon critically needed service is the call button next to the bed. Marks learned that state inspectors had found that this critical link was often out of the reach of bedfast patients.

As Marks read on, he learned that medications prescribed by physicians were routinely not given, or if the prescriptions had been given, the patient's chart did not show that the work had been done. He also learned that medical records had sometimes been falsified, according to the state inspectors, to cover such omissions. An especially damning allegation was that a physician's signature stamp had possibly been routinely used on the patients' charts by the administrator. Did that constitute practicing medicine without a license? What if the stamp was used to begin or to discontinue treatments?

David Marks began to wonder why the district attorney's office hadn't paid more attention to the file. Was it because a nursing home case was so alien to the normal work of the office that there was nobody available to handle the task? This was no armed robbery, no common rape, no burglary; nor was it illegal gambling or prostitution. But was it a more subtle crime? Marks at least knew that a 1977 law had made it illegal for a nursing home owner or employee to fail to report abuse or neglect.

Marks learned that state inspectors charged that Autumn Hills did not have adequate linen for the residents. Even worse, the state inspectors said that the home did not have adequate medical supplies on hand. Had the supplies been on hand, information in the file indicated, the place was so understaffed that personnel would have had scant time to administer them.

By this time Marks was beginning to have a feel for the way Autumn Hills was run, but could these inspectors be off base? Everybody has a bad day. Did the state team catch the facility on a bad one of its own? A good prosecutor learns to read between the lines when someone is charging that another has violated the law. Was there animus here? Such thoughts quickly become second nature to a young lawyer. Marks was no different, and those thoughts raced through his head as he read on. Yet, as he read, he wasn't surprised to see that the state inspectors said that Autumn Hills nurse's aides had not been properly trained and that patients had been improperly and without authorization tied to their beds and wheelchairs.

The inspectors cataloged a litany of pain and suffering. Two patients broke their hips because of inattention. An aide forced one of them to walk on the broken joint even though the patient cried out in pain. Both patients died from complications possibly relating to their injuries. Another patient got thirsty during the day and attempted to call an aide to bring her water. No aide came, and the patient made her way to the hall and found a cleaning cart. On the cart was a container of toilet bowl cleaner, which she drank from. Ten days later she died. An autopsy did not show burns to her throat and stomach, but the pathologist believed that the event contributed to her death. It was against regulations to leave such dangerous materials unattended in the hallways where elderly patients often wander.

Marks's horror and indignation reached a climax that day as he continued to thumb through the abandoned file and came upon a photograph of an 88-year-old woman named Rosa Whited. She had been brutally beaten by an aide, who later confessed to the incident. Such things were unthinkable to Marks. He wanted to know more, but mainly he wanted to know why the information in the file had not been pursued.

The following day, Marks bought a large amount of butcher paper and took it back to the courthouse. He attached it to the blank walls of the office he had just vacated. There he began to chart what he had learned. The habit of charting cases would be a hallmark of his style in years to come.

As time went by, Marks thought less and less of the case as fraud and more and more of it as corporate murder. Could he, a lowly misdemeanor prosecutor, convince his boss that the case of Autumn Hills deserved more attention than it was getting? He looked out the window of his third-floor office and considered his options. He also increasingly wondered what this case was doing in the misdemeanor division.

Marks was to continue his examination of the dusty file for the next few days, calling people, inspectors, anyone who might shed more light on the matter for him. Among those he called was a nursing home inspector named Betty Korndorffer whose reports were a prominent part of the file. She was the wife of Galveston County medical examiner William E. Korndorffer. Betty Korndorffer was reluctant to talk to Marks. She had faced enough grief from Autumn Hills. "No way do I want to talk to you," she told the young prosecutor. Marks admits that he had to threaten Betty Korndorffer with a subpoena before she would cooperate. They soon became fast friends, sharing an obsession to bring to justice people who they had come to believe were murderers.

After the subpoena threat, Korndorffer came to Marks's office in the Galveston County Courthouse, walked through the door, gave him a briefcase full of records, and turned to leave. Thus began three years of work between Marks, the green young lawyer and Korndorffer, the nurse who had high standards and expected her peers to adhere to those standards.

In Korndorffer's records, among others, were charts showing the final days of Edna Mae Witt and Elnora Breed, who had suffered at Autumn Hills before finally they had no more suffering left in them.

Marks continued his quest for information. He talked to anyone who had any information at all that would shed some light on what had happened at Autumn Hills. His work went on after his February 1980 promotion. For the next fourteen months he continued to prosecute felony cases for the county, but his thoughts turned again and again to Autumn Hills and the case he began to believe he could make against the nursing home. As he learned more about Autumn Hills and the nursing home industry, as he talked to experts in the field, he began assembling a team of volunteers who believed that something should be done. The case began to grow, and Marks needed help. He did not get that help from his boss, James Hury, who thought there was little to the case, so little in fact that he had not prosecuted the aide who had allegedly beaten Rosa Whited. Hury told Whited's daughter, who had come to his office demanding action, that a pattern of persistent abuse would have to be proven. Later Hury told *Houston City* magazine that he had decided not to prosecute because the victim was not mentally competent to testify, even though the photo of the severely beaten old woman would have been strong testimony to a jury in itself.

James Hury told Marks that he should leave the Autumn Hills case in the misdemeanor section or turn it over to the special crimes section, a division that had been created, according to Marks, as a vehicle for the office to receive grant money. Marks requested that the case be moved to special crimes, but he and his ragtag team of volunteers continued to pursue Autumn Hills. Marks also enlisted the help of investigators and inspectors from a handful of state agencies. By the early spring, Marks had garnered an impressive amount of information, which he hoped would soon be ready for presentation to a grand jury.

A decubitus ulcer is a bedsore. Marks learned the term as he investigated events at Autumn Hills. He further learned that bedsores can progress through four stages unless they are treated with proper medical and nursing care. Marks did not know that only in the early seventies had these sores been seriously studied and finally "staged." During stage one, a reddened, warm, and tender area appears on the skin in thirty minutes or less. In stage two, ischemia develops if pressure continues 2 to 6 hours. It takes at least 36 hours for such an ulcer to disappear. As the bedsore progresses to stage three, a pus formation emerges and begins to crust over.

Finally, a patient is in real trouble when the ulcer reaches stage four. At that point, the sore has gone through to muscle or bone. Depending on the location of the sore, it can contribute to the death of a patient. For example, if the patient develops a large stage four bedsore on the back, because of the closeness to the bowel, bodily fluids can be lost. Furthermore, a large bedsore can become deep, open, and ugly, with decomposing flesh around its circumference. It is not uncommon for these large ulcers to be more than four inches in diameter with a hollow center more than one inch deep, exposing the bone.

As Marks learned more about bedsores, he came to believe that as Autumn Hills patients lay in their own waste, a direct line of infection was provided by the gaping wounds. He also learned that as much as one cup of bodily fluids per day could drain from a single sore, possibly more than that if the ulcer was in a critical area such as the back. Marks's theory that the disproportionately large number of bedsores on Autumn Hills patients was their cause of death solidified and eventually became his deep-seated conviction. He later compared the track record of the Texas City facility with a National Institute of Health study of bedsores in nursing homes. His calculations indicated that Autumn Hills patients suffered from six to seven times as many bedsores as did patients in the NIH study. He began to believe that an epidemic of bedsores had existed at the Texas City nursing home.

Bedsores happen when a person is confined to bed and either won't turn himself or is unable to turn himself. Unless the patient is turned every two hours, the sores are likely to develop at pressure points such as the shoulders, buttocks, hips, and heels. The sores develop most often on older people, whose skin is just not able to take as much punishment as the skin of young people, although bedsores can and do afflict people of all ages. Blood flow to the affected areas is cut off, causing tissues to sometimes die from the inside out. Older patients often have poorer circulation than younger patients. To compound matters, older patients' skin is sometimes frighteningly thin, as thin as tissue paper.

If a patient who is unable to control his bladder and bowels (nurses and doctors call this an incontinent patient) is allowed to lie in his own waste, the problem of the weakened skin is compounded. Especially dangerous to an incontinent patient with an open bedsore is neglect. Should that person defecate and be allowed to lie in his own waste, massive infection and septicemia (blood poisoning) can occur, spreading through the patient's vital organs. Death can quickly follow through failure of any one of those organs. Marks learned that during most of 1978, such inattention appeared to be the rule at Autumn Hills, not an occasional nursing exception.

By the fall of 1980 James Hury, the D.A., requested that the young prosecutor either get indictments or leave the case. For the past year Marks had spent every evening and every weekend working on the case, interviewing witnesses, studying data, talking to experts. It was time to move. Autumn Hills attorney Carol Vance was pressing Hury either to take the case to the grand jury or let his people go. Marks would not give up. A grand jury was assembled by state district judge Ed Harris, a former liberal Democratic member of the Texas Legislature. Marks took the case to it. As Marks presented his findings to the grand jury, its interest grew and members of the body became caught up in the case, so caught up, in fact, that they spent six months listening to witnesses and viewing physical evidence such as photographs of Autumn Hills patients suffering from purulent bedsores. A few of the jurors wept; one left the grand jury room of the Galveston County Courthouse to vomit. Finally, in March 1981, what was to become known in the press as the first Autumn Hills grand jury returned 23 indictments charging that Autumn Hills Convalescent Centers, Inc., and eight named high managerial employees of the corporation had committed murder by not providing adequate nursing care and other essential services to patients Edna Mae Witt, Betty Cappony, Elnora Breed, Freedie Mae Larsen, Frank Coss, Alberta Welcome, Fannie Burns, and Laura Bell Johnson.

In an eleventh-hour report, the grand jury issued a stinging rebuke to district attorney James Hury and his staff. They said that "there was a lack of secrecy on the part of the office personnel regarding the subject of our investigation. The subject was often the topic of public conversations, in the hallways, offices, and elevators.

"We feel that the District Attorney, James Hury, should have shown an interest in our Grand Jury. More specifically, Mr. Hury should have been more cooperative with our investigation, freeing up his assistants from other duties instead of throwing up obstacles along the way (i.e., consistently having the Assistant District Attorney in charge of this investigation scheduled for trial when we were attempting to question witnesses). There should have been some support, even minimal, in clerical, legal, and any other areas from the District Attorney and his staff."

The frustration the grand jury felt and the extent to which their investigation was hampered by Hury's lack of support were evidenced next in the report thanking then attorney general Mark White for "support in these areas, particularly the eleventh-hour clerical support this evening."

More stinging still, the grand jury leveled a personal criticism at Hury: "We feel that there should be more concern on the part of the District Attorney himself, for cases of this nature being presented and for Grand Jurors that give up time and money to serve. Acknowledgment of a grand juror's presence is conducive to better relations with the community. . . . The District Attorney's support could have eliminated many of these problems."

The grand jury thanked assistant district attorney David Marks, the principal force behind the investigation and the individual whom Hury had kept in trial throughout the term, as well as attorney general investigator Robert F. Carlisle and his "eleventh-hour helpers." The jurors also thanked Texas Department of Health nursing home investigators Betty Korndorffer and Paulette Miller and others from that department.

Finally, the grand jurors recommended

to the people of the state of Texas who have friends and relatives in nursing homes that they not forget them, that they work to be sure these elderly people are given the best of care.

We would also like to recommend that permanent financial penalties be assessed against the nursing homes that are in violation of state and federal standards and that state and federal standards be tightened. We would like the state legislature to develop more stringent laws which will impose more serious criminal sanctions against those who use, abuse, and neglect the elderly.

We recommend that a complete investigation be conducted into the workings of the State Department of Health, from the administrator in Austin to the low man on the totem pole.

We recommend that doctors involved in abuse or neglect be investigated and severely penalized for their actions or lack of actions in this horror story.

James Hury was boxed in. He had to live with the Autumn Hills case. Furthermore, he had to live with David Marks, who states that he had nothing to do with the grand jury report. He also says that although he didn't help frame the stinging criticism that the twelve grand jurors shot at the district attorney, the report shaped the future course of the case. Hury could not easily dispose of *State of Texas* v. *Autumn Hills* or of David Marks either.

Outside the grand jury room *Houston Post* reporter Steve Olafson had maintained a vigil. After midnight, the grand jurors began to leave. Judge Harris, a political enemy of James Hury, emerged with some of the grand jurors. He saw Olafson and instructed one of the jurors to give the reporter a copy of the report. The following day, the critical report was front-page news and Hury was in a rage.

The district attorney was surrounded by reporters in the corridor of the Galveston County Courthouse, and he invited them into his office for an impromptu press conference. Olafson describes Hury as being "purple" with rage. To the reporters, the district attorney charged that two grand jurors who had supported his opponent in a past election were playing politics. He also denied that he had put up roadblocks to the investigation.

More than one and a half years later, almost every single expert directly involved in the state's investigation leading to that first set of indictments signed affidavits stating that Hury not only had impeded progress in the case but, even more damning, had also had no knowledge of the details of the case whatsoever.

The cortege moved again over the sunbaked blacktop road, carrying the white casket and the somewhat wet and mud-covered gold one in the U-Haul truck. Again the procession wound onto the Gulf Freeway, this time in the opposite direction from its journey at eight that morning. The vehicles left the highway and proceeded toward Texas City, passing the College of the Mainland and its spartan campus. In the distance the smokestacks of Texas City belched their fumes into the bright sunlight with white smoke, brown smoke, and pitch-black smoke going almost straight up in the still air.

As they neared the old highway that had once carried holiday travelers from Houston to Galveston during another era, the vehicles again left the road and pulled up to a small building near the county hospital. They had reached the office of Galveston County medical examiner William E. Korndorffer, husband of state nursing home inspector Betty Korndorffer. He was about to see for himself what his wife had been talking about when she brought her personal horrors home from work.

The room was small, with two autopsy tables at right angles to each other. Elnora Breed's open casket lay next to one of them. Doctors walked to the casket and began to lift the bones of Elnora Breed, one by one, out and away from their resting place and place them on the table. As each bone came to rest on the table, it made a metallic noise. Most of the clothes had decomposed, as had the flesh of Elnora Breed, yet remarkably, panty hose still covered her lifeless legs and had to be removed before those bones too could take their place on the table. The bones that the doctors placed side by side began to take the shape of a human skeleton.

Tom Sartwelle and Gail Friend, the Fulbright and Jaworski lawyers, were dressed like the medical experts they were, Friend in surgical greens and Sartwelle in blues. Mike Guarino, the Galveston County district attorney, was also dressed in blues as he watched the doctors do their work. Guarino didn't speak much; neither did David Marks as they looked at Elnora Breed, one of the two hundred people that Marks now believed had been killed by Autumn Hills.

Away from the metal table where lay the now headless skeleton of Elnora Breed, at a small shelf near a sink, one of the doctors was sawing off the top of her small, blackened skull. As he removed the cranium, people in the room strained to see if there was anything left of the brain. There was, but it was useless for any pathological analysis. The autopsy requested by Sartwelle to prove that his clients were innocent of causing the death of Elnora Breed had come to nothing.

A small sheet three feet square was brought out and placed next to the metal table. One by one, the bones were placed on it until finally they were all within its confines. Gail Friend walked over to the sheet and stared at the remains of the woman whom her clients were accused of having killed. Friend was solemn, almost reverent, as she gazed for one last time at what had once been another woman who had spent her time on earth. She was also checking the bones one last time for evidence of cancer.

As Gail Friend had her final look at Elnora Breed, the intact body of Edna Mae Witt was rolled into the small room and the attention of the group was immediately riveted in the direction of the corpse. As the body came to a stop in the small room, the eyes of Marks and Guarino were drawn to the face of the woman. What looked to them like a tear rolled from the left eye down the cheek of Edna Mae Witt. Marks felt a wave of emotion as he gazed on the face of the woman whom he had come to know so well. Condensation had formed much as it does on a windowpane in a hot room on a cloudy day. The body in the grave had been cool; on a muggy May day natural things happen, though strange nonetheless. The woman in the white casket with silver handles was perfectly intact. Sartwelle knew that with an intact body, under the microscope, his experts might be able to destroy the state's allegations that Edna Mae Witt had died of septicemia contracted through bedsores as she lay in urine and feces, or better still they might prove his theory that the woman had died of cancer. There was an almost ghostly image before the assembled lawyers and doctors. Before them lay a woman dressed in white, with white hair, white skin, a white so all-encompassing that it could have been a wedding day. For seven years, Edna Mae Witt had lain in the ground of Galveston Memorial Park on the sunbaked meadow surrounded by tall pines and bordered by a stately oak alley. Broadway Joe and his men had done their work well.

Sartwelle and Friend quickly approached the body, hoping that this time their quest for information would be fulfilled. Behind them, almost timidly, were Guarino and Marks. Emotion showed on the face of Marks as he looked at the lifeless woman, whose most prominent feature was an unusually high forehead. At death she was 78 years old and mourned by thirteen grandchildren. Marks had come to know the patients of Autumn Hills almost as if they were alive. He knew their families too, such as the two daughters of Edna Mae Witt: Agnes Buxton, a large, outgoing woman, and Maxine Anonsen, a tiny wisp of a woman. He knew that the families of the patients of Autumn Hills were being affected in different ways. He, in particular, knew that the family of Edna Mae Witt still mourned the woman lying before him, who was about to be stripped of what dignity had been left to her in death after the supreme indignity of her final days.

The body was measured and weighed. The clinical details of the autopsy were about to begin as the doctors noted that Edna Mae

Witt was 61 inches in height. When the pillow, which had spots of mildew on it, was removed, the head stayed in the same position, stiff, erect. With practiced precision, someone called for scissors to cut the strings holding the shroud in place around her body. Someone thought of untying them, and the clothing was removed as the doctors and photographers now surrounded her body, examining the hands, the feet, and a lesion on the ear. The right hand had suffered either massive ulceration or was beginning to decay. Remarkably, after seven years in the grave, the skin was still supple. The foot showed a bedsore. Finally, after the superficial examination of the front of her body was completed, Edna Mae Witt was rolled on her side and the nightmare of her final days was revealed.

After seven years in the grave, the body had flattened out to fit the hard bottom of the casket, yet all of the features of a human body were intact. The back was covered by small lesions, which were distinctly different from the moles that were also present. On the lower back the doctors could see a large bedsore four inches across with a hole in the center occupying at least half that space. A finger covered by a rubber glove was inserted into the ancient sore, and crusty matter that had once been packing was removed. The doctors now had short rulers with which they measured the wound. They measured the depth of the sore to a full inch, as the two teams of photographers snapped photos. The prosecutors hoped later to use the photographs in court to prove that Edna Mae Witt had died of massive septic shock. The defense photographers sought to validate Sartwelle's contention that she had been well cared for by Autumn Hills.

Edna Mae Witt and Elnora Breed led lives like most people's. They were once young, with the hopes and dreams young people cherish. They grew up, courted, and fell in love. They married and seasoned into adulthood during the Great Depression. They both saw two world wars come and go. Edna Mae Witt raised a family; Elnora Breed chose to spend her life alone with her husband and the children of her siblings. Finally, both women reached the age when the body begins to fail, although Elnora was still mowing her lawn with an old-fashioned push mower at the age of 86. The certainty of the ending came to them slowly, through little failings, small breakdowns, until finally they had to be hospitalized. At last, after there was no more the hospital could do, they were sent to the warehouse, Autumn Hills, to be given the minimum care allowed by law until they died.

CHAPTER TWO

On any given day there are about 1.5 million elderly Americans in the country's 14,000 nursing homes. Generally, they are the weak, unwanted castoffs of a nation moving too fast for them to keep up. They are too sick, too poor, or just too old to cope with the modern world. The average nursing home patient is an 82-year-old female (women outnumber men three to one) who has lost her spouse (nine out of ten of these women have no living mate) and is very dependent. Almost all of the residents of nursing homes need assistance in bathing. Seventy percent need help getting dressed, half must be helped in being toileted, one third must have help in eating, and forty percent have trouble controlling their bowels or bladder.

These inhabitants seldom come to a nursing home out of choice. They are sent there by a physician because the hospital has found that it can do no more for the patient or because the patient has run out of government eligibility for funds with which to pay room and board, or they are sent there by a family that is unwilling or unable to care for the loved one at home. Unfortunately for the nursing home patient, few leave. Only one in five of these patients will return home. Some will be lucky enough to be transferred to a hospital, but most die in the nursing home, some because abuse or lack of care has hastened their death.

The population of the United States is rapidly aging. This graying of America is accelerating at a rapid pace, and in a relatively short time the baby-boom generation born shortly after World War II will confront the health care industry with astronomical numbers. More immediately pressing are the demands the parents of that generation will shortly make on an already overcrowded and underfunded nursing home industry. The people most often needing institutional care are those 85 years of age and older. The U.S. Census Bureau estimates that this group will more than double from 1980 to the year 2000. In sheer numbers, there will be more than 5.1 million Americans over 85 by the turn of the century. As medical science continues to make progress in extending life by quantum leaps, the numbers of those needing nursing home care could be greater still.

The federal government, faced with ever spiraling health care costs, has instituted a new system for paying medicare costs. Instead of paying for actual costs of services provided during a hospital stay, the system pays a fixed amount based on the diagnosis of the patient's illness. This policy is known as DRG, short for "diagnosis related group." Recent studies by the General Accounting Office conclude that patients are being released "sicker and quicker" than under the old system. What this means to the already overcrowded nursing homes is that they are dealing with a much more ill and more dependent group of patients than ever before. It also means that the industry owners are apt to see a boom in profits in coming years.

Studies conducted by Congressman Claude Pepper's subcommittee on health and long-term care (under the Select Committee on Aging) show that of the elderly lost in confinement to an institution,

seventy percent may be denied the simple right to complain out of fear of retribution and therefore remain silent in the face of abuse and neglect. Seventy percent may be denied the choice of what and when to eat, when to wake up or go to sleep, and what to wear. Forty-five percent may be denied the basic right to privacy. Forty-five percent may be denied the right to maintain personal possessions; many are the victims of frequent thefts. Forty percent may be the victims of verbal abuse; 35 percent may be denied adequate and appropriate medical and nursing care; 25 percent may be denied the right of freedom of movement, being the victim of unnecessary physical and chemical restraints or simply not being allowed to leave his or her room; 20 percent may be denied a safe and clean living environment; 20 percent may be denied the right of freedom of speech, assembly, and religion, by being denied access to visitors, ready access to a telephone, and access to religious services. Fifteen percent may be the victims of physical or sexual abuse.

The Pepper study only confirms what critics of nursing homes have been crying out for years. In almost all of the studies, isolated cases from around the nation are pointed out as evidence that abuse and neglect occur on a broad scale. Some fear that the abuse and neglect are institutionalized within the system itself.

Dr. Richard Campbell is pastor of Houston's Central Congregational Church. His parish is in an area of the city that is rapidly being revitalized by young professionals, but a substantial number of elderly people still come to his church every Sunday. Campbell is also a gerontologist who is active in a Texas nursing home reform group and is on the board of the National Citizen's Coalition for Nursing Home Reform. Campbell, an angry man, says that the situation in nursing homes makes him "revert back to my Marine Corps language."

Campbell tells of a parishioner who, while confined in a nursing home, was placed on a stool in a shower with a cap pulled over her head. A nurse's aide turned on scalding water and said, "I'll show you who's boss." Campbell's parishioner was lucky; she lived through the ordeal.

The paster points out that there is a national shortage of beds in nursing homes. It is easy, he says, for the all-powerful administrator to tell a family member, "If you don't like it, get out of here." Campbell says, "That's not so easy when there is nowhere else to go." He continues to say of his group, "The system is what is wrong. We stopped looking at things on a case-by-case basis and began to look at the whole system."

That system is built around the nurse's aide. A recent National Academy of Sciences report states that as much as 90 percent of the care of an elderly, often ill nursing home patient is carried out by an aide who is typically poorly educated and has little or no nursing experience. As a group, nurse's aides are among the most poorly paid Americans, often making only minimum wage. For this, the aide is expected to perform backbreaking labor under conditions that would make most people retch. It is no wonder, then, that the turnover of aides averages 110 percent nationally. At Autumn Hills during 1978, there was a 1000 percent turnover in personnel.

Typically, an aide's routine duties are to bathe patients or assist them in bathing, care for the patients' hair and nails, feed or assist the patients in eating, assist patients in toileting (including cleaning up after incontinent patients have soiled themselves), recording each patients' food intake, taking and recording patients' temperature, pulse, and respiration rate, assisting patients in dressing and undressing, and assisting patients in walking or pushing wheelchairs. The aide is also expected to clean the rooms and make the beds. In many nursing homes, aides are expected to do a lot more than that, duties for which they are unqualified.

A 1983 Institute of Medicine study cited in the report prepared by Pepper's subcommittee showed that nurse's aides were "preparing and administering oral medications, suctioning patients' throats, inserting indwelling catheters, counting apical pulses, and suctioning patients' noses."

Pamela James was a nurse's aide at Autumn Hills, where her mother, a licensed vocational nurse at the nursing home, got her a job. Her previous work experience after high school was as a waitress at a fast-food restaurant. The pretty, heavyset black woman had no previous medical training. She worked on the skilled side of the nursing home, where the patients most in need of care were housed.

During orientation, conducted by another aide, Pamela was shown how to comb a patient's hair, shown how to pick up a patient, shown how to make beds, how to feed a patient, and other fundamental tasks ordinarily expected of a nurse's aide. The young aide "had never taken a vital sign in my life." Worse still, she said, "I didn't know how to read a thermometer or take blood pressure" when she came to work there.

Pamela James liked to watch TV. She liked to watch her soap operas every day from eleven to one. She got plenty of opportunity to keep up with the daily television dramas at Autumn Hills. In trial testimony she said that one day she was caught by the director of nursing but was not scolded for neglecting her patients or threatened with being fired. She said she was simply told not to let the administrator of the nursing home catch her. The director allegedly told her to "make sure that you act like you are doing something."

On the other hand, Carol Josey was an experienced aide when she came to Autumn Hills, having worked in hospitals. After only eleven months, Josey, a conscientious woman, left the Texas City home out of frustration. She told of one veteran Autumn Hills aide who refused to learn to take vital signs even after the director of nursing attempted to teach her how to accomplish the simple task. The aide instead found it more convenient to find a vacant bed, lie down, and take a nap.

As often as not, eyewitnesses said, the halls of Autumn Hills were deserted. Patients' relatives came to see their loved ones and never found a busy corridor, such as would normally be expected in a hospital or health care environment. Others complained that they never saw an aide enter the room to care for their family member. Worse still, when an aide was needed and a family member went for help, frequently there was no one to be found and the caring family member became the care giver.

It wasn't that the aides were lazy. On the contrary, the aides at Autumn Hills were overworked. Most of their morning was spent washing linen, which was perpetually in short supply. One aide was in charge of the linen supply in the washroom. Pamela James noticed that the aide would often have the laundry "scattered out," or separated, for the aides "she wanted to get it," the ones she liked. Patients were forced to sleep on filthy sheets because of the pecking order in the laundry room.

Some patients did receive some care, but there simply weren't enough aides to go around. Feeding patients who couldn't feed themselves was a particular problem because it took so long for the aides to wash the linens. After the morning washing was done, the aides received instructions from the nurses. According to Pamela James, "The nurses would tell us who we were supposed to feed. . . . We would go back and feed the ones that needed to be fed." Some of the aides rebelled at the constant overwork. James said, "They knew a patient needed to be fed, but they wouldn't go in there."

One patient in particular was fortunate enough to have her son come almost daily to feed her. Pamela James noticed that "when he didn't come, some of the aides would get mad and say that he should have come to feed her." On those days the woman, like many of the other patients in Autumn Hills, went hungry.

Other patients went hungry for another reason. Ensure is a food supplement often given to patients as an addition to their regular diet or through nasal gastric tubes to patients who are too weak to feed themselves or who are semiconscious or comatose; it comes in liquid or powder form. Autumn Hills was in constant short supply of the dietary supplement. From December 8, 1977, to November 20, 1978, physicians had ordered a total of 10,828 units of Ensure for patients, but Autumn Hills purchased only 6810 units, leaving a shortfall of 4018. For some patients, Ensure was the only food they had. When the Texas City nursing home ran out of Ensure, staff members would dash to a local discount store or to small Cedar Pharmacy in nearby LaMarque to pick up the needed supply. During every month from December 1977 to November 1978, the Ensure supply was dreadfully short. By May 1978 the facility had 65 percent less Ensure than had been prescribed by physicians. In August, 41 percent; September, 48 percent; October, 43 percent; and November, 48 percent.

On some days the facility was completely out of Ensure, if doctors' prescriptions and Autumn Hills purchase orders are to be believed. In May 1978, Autumn Hills patients went 22 days without Ensure; August, 14 days; September, 15 days; October, 16 days; and November, 20 days, according to David Marks's studies.

The young district attorney began to learn of the chronic shortage of Ensure during the early phases of his investigation. He assembled a team of student nurses led by a geriatric dietitian to conduct a study of Autumn Hills practices in ordering the dietary supplement. As they compiled their results, Marks strengthened his theory that greed had been the motive for murder in the Texas City nursing home. He believed that even though Ensure bought from the manufacturer, Ross Laboratories, was only 28 cents per can and the savings on the shortfall of almost a year's supply would be comparatively modest, that savings spread through a chain of seventeen nursing homes could be substantial for the bottom line, perhaps fatal for the residents.

The Pepper subcommittee's white paper primarily concerned itself with the violation of constitutional rights of elderly patients "lost in confinement." In cases cited from all across the country, the committee published examples of neglect and abuse. None of the examples cited in the report happened at Autumn Hills, yet they were a fair sampling of the type of thing that happens in the industry of which that facility was a part. The report reinforced data found in past studies of nursing home abuse and neglect and cemented those findings that illustrate that the problem is a national issue. The survey examined seven basic rights. The following excerpts from the report give examples of violations of those rights.

The right to complain and seek redress of grievances

One Ombudsman from a Rocky Mountain state noted that family members told him not to investigate conditions in a home where their mother was being fed only twice daily and that nearly seven hours elapsed before aides cleaned the mess she made from a bowel discharge. They loved their mother but were unable to care for her at home. With that State having 99% of its nursing home beds occupied, they were afraid that eviction of their mother from this home where her rights were being abridged would mean that she would have no place to go.

A western state source said that residents in one of that State's facilities were afraid to complain about conditions. Those who had complained in the past had their rent raised until they could no longer afford to live there.

A spokesman from a Pacific coast state observed that retribution can take many subtle forms. "If you know the people around you have the power to bring you a warm meal or serve yours to you late, when it's cold, and can get you to the bathroom on time or let you sit in your own waste, and turn you gently or with roughness, you soon learn not to make too many complaints.

The right to make basic personal choices

A midwestern state official commented that few residents of facilities in that state have any personal rights. Very frequently the decision making process is signed over, via the homes, to family members and other "reasonable people."

In one southern state, two homes routinely roused residents from bed between 4:00 and 4:30 a.m., and required them to go to bed between 5:00 and 5:30 p.m. These hours did not fit the normal sleep cycle of most residents, and they conflicted with visiting hours and other activities.

Clients in a western state nursing home were not allowed to turn on the lights in their rooms after dark. Also, the residents, once put to bed, were required to remain there until breakfast. The living room television was .set on a specific channel selected by the owner, and no suggestions for variation were entertained.

Sometimes, denial of the right to make choices seems almost trivial: no sugar and cream for coffee at one home in Kentucky, a television was turned off promptly at 9:00 p.m. at a facility in Michigan. However, officials surveyed believed that such small factors—having the freedom to choose food and clothing, and hours of TV viewing and wakefulness—are critical to an individual's emotional well-being. Denial of these rights can produce in the resident a feeling of loss of power, which frequently translates into mental or physical illness.

The right to privacy

A woman, seeking a possible home for her mother, came upon a deplorable situation in a New Mexico facility. Through a wide open door, in plain view from the hallway, she could see an elderly woman, totally nude, tied to a portable potty chair. This woman was crying out for help. When the hall nurse was asked about the situation, she replied that they always stripped the lady down because she made such a mess of things.

A respondent from a middle Atlantic state noted that privacy in many of that State's institutions is a scarce commodity. Areas for private conversation are almost nonexistent and in some homes, even married couples are not permitted to sleep together. At those places which do allow this privilege, privacy is at a minimum and the residents are subjected to snide remarks and other harassment by staff.

The right to maintain personal possessions

An 82-year-old woman in an Illinois nursing home received 12 cotton housedresses and three pairs of slippers as Christmas gifts from her daughter and grandchildren. Within a month the clothing had all been taken away. In a letter to the Subcommittee, the daughter told us this was the fourth time this had happened at the facility. When the nursing home management was approached by family, their complaint was ignored.

In a New England state, a woman who had worked for over 30 years and who enjoyed a liberal pension suffered two broken hips at the age of 88. An acquaintance arranged for her to be placed in an unlicensed boarding home. Within two weeks, the owners had either forged the victim's name to checks or had forced her to sign over $2,300 in checks to them. The investigation revealed that the woman was purposely overmedicated in order to keep her in a stupor. It was later found that her generous holdings in stocks and bonds had also been misappropriated.

The right to freedom from verbal abuse

A comment from a southern state was that residents are viewed as the property of the nursing home. It is not looked upon as unusual when a resident is addressed in an abusive or patronizing way by staff.

The owner of a New Jersey nursing home was heard shouting at a resident, "You don't like it here? Get out!"

The operator of a New Mexico home told an 88-year-old resident, "Your son is never going to take you out of here, no matter what. You're stuck here."

The right to adequate and appropriate medical and nursing care

A respondent from a southern state said that overmedication is a commonly used restraint. All too frequently, drugs are used to replace the lack of staff. A sedate resident requires much less care than an alert one.

A source from an east coast state told of a frail elderly woman who was put in a tub of scalding water and never checked on, even though she screamed and was severely burned. After being removed from the tub, the woman was wrapped in sheets to conceal the burns and was never given treatment. She died from the burns.

In one southern state facility, a drug was administered an additional four weeks after the patient's physician prescribed the medication to end. The patient survived, although with temporary side effects.

The right to freedom of movement

A response from a Rocky Mountain state mentioned several homes which have policies that clearly state, "We won't tolerate wanderers." Obviously anyone walking the halls for whatever reason might be charged with this "offense."

Five senior citizens were found locked in the basement of a board and care facility. The basement was lit by two light bulbs and the people were fed two meager meals daily. They were coerced into signing over their Social Security checks to the proprietor. The basement smelled of urine and there were cockroaches all over.

A source in one midwestern state said that doctors have great power and can freely legislate a resident's mobility. "If a patient wants to go across the street to the K-Mart, (a doctor's) permission is frequently required."

The right to a clean and safe living environment

An unlicensed New England board and care home was closed when officials found five elderly persons living in filth there. The home was littered with decaying food and dog urine and feces, and the temperature was about 55 degrees.

Health and safety problems are an all-too-common occurrence. In a northern state, the kitchen of a nursing home was being painted. Unfortunately, no drop cloth was used. Personnel saw paint spattering onto food but were told to serve it anyway.

The conditions to which residents of one home in a middle Atlantic state were subjected were nothing less than wretched. Visitors found one woman covered with her own excrement and no nurses or aides nearby. Improper turning of this resident meant that within two months of admission her foot was eaten to the bone by a bedsore.

The right to freedom of speech, assembly, and religion

Residents in one home in a western state have phone access, but it is far from private—the phone is located in the noisy dining room, next to the ice machine.

Mail delivery in some homes in one southern state is irregular. Mail often sits at the main desk or nurse's station for more than a week. It is frequently opened, even if labeled "personal."

Residents of one nursing home on the west coast are not allowed to "visit" with each other during the time when meals are served.

At one facility in the midwest, even silent grace at meals is forbidden. So are half-hour Bible tapes provided by a local clergyman.

The right to freedom from physical or sexual abuse

A nursing home on the Atlantic coast found it hard to have time to feed all its patients, and so many went without proper nourishment. One 66-year-old Alzheimer's patient died due to malnutrition and dehydration. (At the time of her death, she weighed 61 pounds.) The death certificate cited cardiac arrest as the cause.

A Pacific coast source tells of an elderly woman who was told that if she did not have sexual relations with the home operator, she would never see her family again. In another case at that home, an operator decided to teach an incontinent resident a lesson by taking him into the back yard, undressing him, and spraying him with a blast from a garden hose.

James Hury was not confident of Marks's ability to get a conviction in the case, and Marks was not confident of Hury's commitment to the case. Marks had managed to obtain indictments of the Autumn Hills corporation and eight Autumn Hills employees or former employees. They were corporate vice president for operations Ron Pohlmeyer, the corporation's director of nursing (in nursing home lingo, "nursing consultant") Mattie Locke, and Cassandra Canlas, Phyllis Daulong, Ann Wright, and Mary Wagner, all of whom had served at one time or another as director of nursing for the corporation. Also indicted were Marie Ritchie and Virginia Wilson, who had both served as administrators for the Texas City nursing home.

If found guilty, each defendant could face a prison sentence of from 5 to 99 years. The corporation would face a maximum fine of $20,000 for each of the six indictments, or $40,000 compensation for each personal injury caused, or twice the amount of money gained by committing the felony.

James Hury had never seen a case so complex. Marks believed that Hury was paralyzed by his fear of the case. In fact, Hury had been quoted in the local newspaper as saying that the Autumn Hills case was "scary as hell." He was not in the district attorney's office to make law or to set legal precedents. He viewed his job for what it was, to put into prison people who were not safe to leave on the streets. Besides, Hury had a budget to work under, and such a case would be extremely costly to prosecute.

Hury thought about the case and could not convince himself that Marks could prove that the deaths at Autumn Hills were caused by inadequate care. Marks, on the other hand, felt that Hury didn't know enough about the case to make any kind of decision whatsoever. Deaths in nursing homes are nothing unusual, and Marks would have to prove that the deaths were caused by neglect and inadequate care rather than from the multiplicity of illnesses that had caused the patients to be institutionalized in the first place. Furthermore, Marks would have to prove that high company officials, both at the Texas City nursing home and at the corporate headquarters in Houston, knew that Autumn Hills policies were producing grave consequences for the people under their care. Finally, Hury knew that the defense would attempt to show that Pohlmeyer, a former state inspector himself, had instructed the Texas City staff to clean up their act, to fix whatever was wrong at the facility.

Hury expected that the Autumn Hills defendants would use the standard war-crimes argument, that they had just done what they were told. Down the corporate chain of command, the easy thing to say was "I was just following instructions."

Marks clearly was not charging the workers at Autumn Hills, the aides who were responsible for the day-to-day, hour-to-hour care of the patients, with the crimes. It was his belief that the poor care provided at the Texas City facility was corporate policy. He had learned of a bonus program, based on profits, that the administrators and Pohlmeyer participated in. Marks was convinced that the patients had received poor care because of the bonus program, because small savings here and there would result in more profits for the corporation, which ran seventeen such operations. Scrimping on Ensure, for example, was just one way of improving the year-end bonuses. Costs cut by administrators ended up in their own pocketbooks after monthly meetings where the bonuses were allegedly paid from stacks of $100 bills.

In early June 1981, Marks planned to bring the charge of felony murder against the defendants, in addition to the first grand jury's indictment for murder by omission. The felonies the defendants were alleged to have committed were theft of medicaid funds and tampering with official state records. Marks hoped to show that by committing those felonies, high Autumn Hills officials had knowingly omitted essential parts of daily patient care. He believed that he could prove that as a result of such omissions, several patients had died. Marks believed that the omissions were not simple negligence, because the Texas City nursing home had been repeatedly warned by state inspectors and, on several occasions, sanctions had been taken by the state against the home. Marks intended to prove greed as the company's motive for murder.

Heat on Autumn Hills was coming from all sides, and the corporation began to fight back. As early as March 1978, Autumn Hills vice president Ron Pohlmeyer and Autumn Hills nursing consultant Mattie Locke attempted to pressure state officials. The two paid a call on the Houston office of Gene Daniels, nursing inspector Betty Korndorffer's superior, to complain that Korndorffer shouldn't be inspecting their facilities. Daniels, of the now defunct state Department of Public Welfare, said, "They went over their strong objections to Mrs. Korndorffer's acting as an inspector of their nursing home. They claimed she had some grudge against the nursing home." He said that the alleged grudge stemmed from Korndorffer's two-year stay at the nursing home chain's Friendswood, Texas, facility where she had been director of nursing. Korndorffer asserted that she never intended to hold the job at Friendswood so long and simply wouldn't make the long drive to the corporate headquarters in Houston anyway.

According to Daniels, they accused her of fabricating some of the findings, which resulted in a "vendor hold" after a February 1978 inspection. When a nursing home is placed on vendor hold, federal and state funds are withheld until inspectors give the home a more favorable report. Daniels pressed the two officials but could get no information proving that Korndorffer's findings were not true. He then pointed out to the two officials that the inspection team, of which Korndorffer was only a part, "suspected that the facility was not staffing as the nursing home was reporting to us." The team had found several instances when no licensed nurse was on duty at Autumn Hills. The report confirmed suspicions that the state inspectors had held for some time.

Daniels knew the Autumn Hills style in a tight situation with the state. "Most of the conversation centered around their desire for me to remove Mrs. Korndorffer from their facility. In the past, this had been a tactic of Mr. Pohlmeyer and Mrs. Locke and the nursing home chain: they tried to personalize it, make it into some kind of personal vendetta. My decision was not to remove Betty Korndorffer unless they gave me some better evidence," Daniels told *Houston City* magazine.

Autumn Hills fared better with state legislators. Corporate officials approached two powerful members of the Texas Legislature to intervene with the Texas Department of Health. Representative Bill Heatley of rural Paducah (more than four hundred miles to the north of Galveston County) chaired the committee that controlled the purse strings of the health department, and Senator Chet Brooks of urban Pasadena headed the committee that oversaw health care legislation in the Texas Senate. These friends of the nursing home industry applied pressure on Dr. Robert Bernstein, who caved in and removed Betty Korndorffer as inspector of the Autumn Hills Texas City facility. Brooks says that he didn't know the name of the inspector in question or even that Korndorffer was a woman. He says that Bob Gay, president of Autumn Hills, "or one of the administrators called me and claimed that there was some harassment going on, that there had been an exit interview in which one of the team had cursed the staff [at Autumn Hills] and stormed out. Whenever we get a call like that we follow up. I called Dr. Bernstein and asked him to look into the situation. We get calls like that all the time, and we try to follow up."

Bernstein, a critic of nursing home abuse and neglect, told reporters that Betty Korndorffer was one of the state's best employees. He also said that twice, in 1978 and 1980, he had been on the verge of decertifying Autumn Hills when Texas legislators intervened. Furthermore, Bernstein said that the Galveston County grand jury had been late in issuing indictments in the Autumn Hills case because he had turned over two cases to the local district attorney's office in 1978.

The Texas Senate sits in the East Wing on the second floor of the native-granite state capitol building of Texas. In the relatively small but luxurious room, 31 desks face the podium, which is presided over by the lieutenant governor, the second-highest officeholder in the state. The individuals who sit at those desks receive a meager salary of $600 a month, which is grudgingly granted to them by the voters of the state of Texas. That salary belies the real power they exercise over state government for their constituents and sometimes for their benefactors.

Chet Brooks was first elected to the House of Representatives in 1963. He had been real estate editor with the *Houston Post*, but he had political ambitions. In 1966 Brooks was elected to a newly created Senate seat, which he has held since that time. In 1982 he became one of the two deans of the Senate. As in Washington, this position of seniority carries considerable weight with a senator's colleagues, and maybe even a little more than that with state bureaucrats.

Unlike the majority of the Texas Senate, Brooks is not a lawyer; he is a full-time politician and sometime businessman. At fifty, he has graying black hair behind a receding hairline and a full mustache and looks like a riverboat gambler. His clothes don't help the image either. No matter how hard Brooks tries to dress well, he looks more like a gangster in a B movie than the picture of decorum that Texas politicians attempt, sometimes successfully, to portray to the electorate. Despite his appearance, he manages to get reelected every four years and at times has been an extraordinary legislator. Through early talent and accumulated seniority, Brooks became chairman of the powerful Senate Human Resources Committee, which oversees nursing home legislation in the upper house.

Among Brooks's more outstanding achievements was his cosponsorship, with three other senators, of Senate Bill 9, which was an outgrowth of a ten-day special session of the Texas Legislature in 1977 after the hue and cry for nursing home reform in the state had reached a pitch that Governor Dolph Briscoe could not ignore. The legislation requiring nursing home owners and employees to report abuse and neglect was passed; however, the legislature neglected to include provisions that would cause the forfeiture of a facility's license if such abuses consistently reoccur. The law imposed misdemeanor penalties, with a fine of $200 for the first offense and $100 for subsequent offenses. It also made violators subject to a civil penalty of not less than $100 nor more than $500 for each violation. The law simply did not anticipate the wholesale abuse and neglect in nursing such as Marks believed had happened at Autumn Hills.

Brooks does not deny that he has known Gay for a long time though. Neither does he deny that Gay and Houston oilman and real estate developer George P. Mitchell, a 20 percent stockholder in Autumn Hills, both have contributed to his campaigns. Of Gay he says, "I knew him from another business. I think that I first met him when I was still real estate editor at the *Post*."

Mitchell and Gay also go back a long way, and their relationship is a warm one. Gay's wife was a secretary in the Houston developer's small office in the early days. In fact, Gay built a beach house in a Galveston resort development that Mitchell had founded. Over the years Gay and Mitchell became fast friends and business associates.

State Representative Bill Heatley benefited handsomely. The powerful longtime member of the Texas House of Representatives received a $3500 legal fee for his efforts on behalf of the nursing home. Such loyalty to a politician does not go unrewarded, particularly when the politician is as adroit at surviving as Heatley. A Texas Democratic county chairman described the late legislator as the classic good ol' boy, who was at his best when he was killing legislation. That same politician said, "The lobby went out of its way to help him, and he had a long memory." Brooks confirms that Heatley intervened on behalf of Autumn Hills.

Brooks was not content to intervene with only a call to Bernstein. After a team of nursing specialists recommended decertification of the nursing home in the spring of 1980, he sent his own inspector, an assistant, to Texas City for an on-site inspection. The assistant was not a medical specialist qualified to inspect health care facilities. The aide to Brooks was a former deputy United States marshal who was on his committee staff to investigate. Autumn Hills was soon out of hot water, temporarily.

David Marks had failed for the time being. The young assistant district attorney saw months of work crumbling before his eyes as it was discovered that the set of indictments he had tried so hard to obtain, which the holdover grand jury had worked on until midnight and typed themselves with the help of the attorney general's office, were not sufficient from a technical standpoint to hold up. With his heavy caseload, Marks did not have the time to prepare the documents meticulously. He had, in fact, only three days from the time the grand jury voted the indictments until the end of their term. In that period, he had to research the law, draft the document, and then interpret it for the jurors. Murder by omission is a rare doctrine in the criminal justice system; rarer still is corporate murder by omission. Some parts of the indictments were still handwritten, and worse, in one case the names of a victim and a defendant were transposed as the jurors worked toward their midnight deadline on March 31, 1981.

Marks could easily have waited for the next scheduled grand jury to convene. He feared, however, that in the interim the case would be forgotton and become another dusty file for another small-time misdemeanor prosecutor. Marks told Hury that the state should withdraw the indictments and go to work on another, more comprehensive set immediately.

Marks needed help. Hury called friends, lawyers who might know of someone whose knowledge of criminal law was such that he could draw the complex indictments needed to send the Autumn Hills defendants to jail. He finally found former Texas Court of Criminal Appeals judge Jim Vollers. Marks and Vollers spent the next three months researching the law, looking for an airtight way to make the indictments stick. Nobody had ever done such a thing. Corporate murder by omission just hadn't been tried anywhere else.

A second grand jury was convened and went to work the following month on additional evidence Marks had developed. He now had an investigator, provided by Hury, who had been stung by the previous grand jury's criticism. Finally, at the end of three months, the citizens of Galveston County issued a massive 1200-page indictment against Autumn Hills Convalescent Centers and the same eight high managerial officials who had originally been indicted. This time, the charge was felony murder, of the same eight patients that had been named in the first flawed indictments.

A scramble began in the nursing home industry and in the Autumn Hills defense. The nursing home's lawyer, former Harris County district attorney Carol Vance, was fired from the case and replaced with the law firm of Minton, Burton, Foster, and Collins of Austin, then famed for its successful defense of Texas House Speaker Billy Clayton in a trial resulting from an FBI sting operation. The nursing home industry also rallied to the aid of one of its own (Bob Gay had once been president of the state organization) and issued a public statement through the president of the Texas Nursing Home Association, Sidney Rich. He said, "The unheard-of theory of 'murder by fraud' involving persons far removed from the scene . . . is extremely disturbing. This extremely dangerous doctrine, which should be of concern to all citizens, could grow to destroy this nation's entire health care system and is a great threat to all professionals and everyone else involved in any segment of that system."

Rich was right. The indictment of Autumn Hills sent shudders through the entire health care industry, but the ones who shuddered most were those in the nursing home industry. That industry had spent good money to forestall just the kind of unfortunate event that had happened to the Houston corporation. Through its political action committee, NHAPAC, from 1978 to 1980 the industry had contributed $244,000 to Texas politicians in the hope of receiving favorable treatment. It had contributed more than $50,000 to members of four key legislative committees whose work directly affected the nursing home industry. That such a thing as happened to Autumn Hills could occur to one of its own was unthinkable.

CHAPTER THREE

Elnora Bell grew up with her seven brothers and sisters. She grew to be a thin young woman who was ready to tackle the world around her. Like most young people, she fell in love. She married a young man named Robert Breed. Elnora shared with her husband a life of respect that came from clean living and hard work. By 1950, Elnora was 59 years old. She had weathered life well. The woman who had once been the young girl on the coastal prairie now had beautiful long gray hair. Her father Frank Bell's farm had been passed to her and her siblings, and they lived on it, although what remained was now in town and Bell Drive ran through it.

Elnora Breed settled into old age gracefully. Robert died and left her a widow. She refused to give up the hard work and cleanliness that had been a part of her very being since childhood. Even after she was well into her eighties, every Monday she still insisted on boiling dirty clothes in a big iron pot because nothing less would get the clothes clean enough to meet her high standards. A woman of the nineteenth century, she still used a rub board although she owned a washing machine. Her sister Ruth, who lived across the street, as well as her nieces, attempted in vain to get her to use it. When the wash was done, Elnora would carry the sheets to the clothesline while Ruth, whom people often mistook for her twin, would help "hang the sheets together."

The proud old woman also did her own shopping when the need arose. Her health was good despite two close calls with cancer, which had been surgically removed. Her health was so good, in fact, that into her early eighties she insisted on mowing her lawn with an old-fashioned push mower. "We told her that she shouldn't be pushing a lawn mower," Ruth says, but she ignored her family and kept on pushing. In her yard Elnora planted flowers, for she had grown up with them on the prairie. She also remained active in her church and attended circle meetings regularly.

Most of all, Elnora loved her family. On Bell Drive it was good that she did, because she was surrounded by descendants of Frank Bell. Every night Aunt Elnora would insist that the family get together and play dominoes. She had a passion for dominoes, and to the consternation of some of the family, including Ruth, she usually won.

The family loved the aunt also. They looked in on her from time to time to make sure that she was managing to get along by herself. Thus it was when they found her by the side of her bed on the floor. Time had finally taken its toll on Elnora, who had run through the fields, who had laughed, who had loved, who wouldn't give up. She was felled by a stroke.

Elnora had always been a practical woman. Unlike others she knew, the old woman with the long gray hair had provided for her old age. She was prepared to pay for her own care and had made arrangements with her sister Ruth to handle her financial affairs should she be incapacitated. She would not be a charity patient, as so many others she knew were. Ruth had the checkbook. Elnora was assured in her mind that good care would be provided for her until she passed from the earth.

Others of Elnora's generation, and a lot of them younger than she was, could not care for themselves any longer. These people, many of whom had followed the oil to Southeast Texas, were now old; some of them were sick, many were dying. They had come of age when America was still innocent, when Texas still had vestiges of the frontier. In their youth, they had seen bearded Civil War veterans walking the streets, heard stories of the great cattle drives told as if they had just happened. They had seen the demise of the horse and buggy. They had driven the Model T and the Model A. They had seen the Great Depression and survived it. They had suffered through two world wars, Korea, and Viet Nam. They had watched man land on the moon on television, a miracle, considering that for many electric power was still a newfangled luxury.

What was happening to these people in Texas City and Galveston and Hitchcock and Dickinson was also happening all across the nation. They were growing old.

The legislative battle was fierce. The powerful American Medical Association (AMA) and its allies the American Hospital Association and the American Nursing Home Association were staunchly opposed to national health insurance, and they put together a formidable lobby in Washington. Health care for the elderly was not a new concept. Theodore Roosevelt had made the idea a part of the Progressive party platform during his ill-fated third-party run for the White House. Yet the coalition did not lose a legislative battle until 1950, when an Old Age Assistance program was passed by the Democratic Congress, allowing aged people on welfare to apply state and federal funds to their medical costs. The new legislation did little for those not on the dole. Although those people could meet day-to-day living expenses, they could not cope with the sudden high cost of being sick.

The American Federation of Labor and the Congress of Industrial Organizations merged in 1955, forming the AFL-CIO, and the AMA and its friends for the first time faced a formidable lobby on the other side. Again, the medical lobby was defeated with the passage of a new Social Security benefit for permanently disabled persons past fifty. Although it provided a relatively minor benefit, the program proved to be a smashing success, and shortly thereafter the age limit was removed.

Legislative skirmish followed legislative skirmish, but a strong friend of the elderly was coming of age in the Senate. John F. Kennedy, the rich young solon from Massachusetts, latched onto the issue of health care for the elderly. When he was elected president in 1960, proponents of what was now called medicare felt that they had a real chance to provide help for the aged.

The year 1962 was looked upon by many in the administration and in the Congress as the year for medicare, yet Kennedy was distracted by foreign policy problems such as the Bay of Pigs incident, the building of the Berlin Wall, a meeting with Khrushchev, and increasing communist involvement in Laos. The country was also going through a minor recession, and the Congress turned its attention to antirecession measures.

The following year brought other pressures on the young president, such as civil rights problems in the South, the nuclear test ban treaty, and an omnibus tax reform bill. In the House of Representatives, the Ways and Means Committee did manage to meet for further hearings on medicare by mid-November. The hearings were going well and things were looking good for medicare when the chief council for the committee rushed into the room and whispered something into the ear of Chairman Wilbur Mills. The chairman turned pale and announced to the committee that the president had been shot. The hearing was adjourned.

A ground swell of emotion followed Lyndon Johnson into the White House following Kennedy's death in Dallas. The former Senate majority leader had been one of the most able men ever to serve in Congress. He put the experience he had gained from men such as House Speaker Sam Rayburn to good use and passed the laws Kennedy had supported but could not get enacted when he was alive. Practically the entire Kennedy program became law under Johnson's careful manipulation of his former colleagues on Capitol Hill. In the summer of 1965, medicare, which helped pay the medical expenses of the middle-income elderly, and medicaid, which helped with medical expenses of the indigent poor, became law and revolutionized health care for the aged. It also revolutionized the medical industry in time as opportunists realized that a profit could be made from the system.

A direct beneficiary of the new laws was the nursing home industry, which had fought so hard with the AMA against passage of federal health care reform measures. Before the passage of medicare and medicaid, nursing homes in this country were little more than a cottage industry of mom-and-pop operations, with little corporate ownership whatsoever. "Old folks' homes" with often vacant rocking chairs sitting on the front porch showed little promise of profit to Wall Street investors or banks interested in safe energy and real estate loans. When the federal government guaranteed payment of medical costs for a huge segment of society, all of that changed. No matter how small the guaranteed payment was, smart operators could find a way to make a profit. The government didn't run out on its bills or die before they could be paid, and its checks didn't bounce.

Robert E. Gay may not have been such an opportunist, but at age 38 he was looking for a profitable business. He turned to nursing homes just in time to get in on the ground floor of the new federally subsidized industry. In 1963 he purchased a nursing home on Janish Street in Houston. This home became the first in what was to grow into a chain of seventeen nursing homes with 1910 beds. By December 31, 1980, all but two of those beds were contracted out to the medicaid agency as medicaid beds. Gay's nursing homes, Autumn Hills, would certainly take patients who could pay for their care out of their own funds, such as Elnora Breed, but what kept the wheels turning and the cash register ringing were federally subsidized patients such as 78-year-old Edna Mae Witt.

Edna Mae Witt was a native Galvestonian. She was born a scant five months before the 1900 Storm devastated the island city. Her daughter Agnes Buxton describes her as "a unique mother who raised five children through the Depression." After the death of her husband, Edna Mae moved in with her daughter Maxine Anonsen who worked in the daytime at D&M Poultry on Broadway. At lunch, Maxine would come home and check on her mother, eat with her, and then go back to work.

Edna Mae would sit, watch TV, play with her grandson, and crochet. She didn't confine herself to a chair; she was up and around. Agnes Buxton remembers that "she was a great one to tell the past and remember." She also says that "she liked the attention of all of the family." The elderly woman also enjoyed going on trips with the family. No matter how small the trip was, it was important that Grandma was along.

A relative says that Edna Mae, like many older people, enjoyed being in the hospital. Medical records indicate ten admissions in the last ten years of her life. She had suffered from minor bouts with arthritis, high blood pressure, and gout but was in generally good health, according to her family. At one point she crocheted an afghan for her Galveston doctor.

Edna Mae Witt was a large woman. She enjoyed home cooking and maintained a good appetite. In the evenings, Agnes Buxton would come around the corner to her sister's house and check on her mother. The three of them, sometimes with grandchildren around, would often eat dinner together. Like her mother, Agnes is a large woman, but her sister Maxine is small and almost birdlike.

In the summer of 1978 things began to change with Edna Mae Witt. She could not sleep, and at night when Maxine would get home from work, her mother would insist on talking long into the night. Mrs. Anonsen became exhausted working all day and then talking to Edna Mae until the early morning hours. Finally she asked for help from the rest of the family. Edna Mae had reached the point most old people dread; she had become a burden on her children, although she may not have known it.

Edna Mae Witt was moved to the mainland in early August to live with her son Charles, a dispatcher for the Yellow Cab Company, and to give Maxine Anonsen a rest from caring for her mother. By August 7 she was running a fever, and she was admitted to Galveston's St. Mary's Hospital, run by the Sisters of Charity, a Catholic order of nuns who had been working on the island since the mid-nineteenth century.

Mrs. Witt stayed in St. Mary's 22 days and, according to her daughters, was recovering nicely. She ate well, sat up in a chair, lost no weight, even though she was suffering from a urinary tract infection; the catheter that had been placed in her was removed and she was able to use a bedpan. When it came time for her release from the hospital, her doctor told the daughter Maxine Anonsen, "Let's give her a couple or three months in a nursing home to get her strength back."

The sisters and the brother had been arguing as siblings do, little things really, yet at one point the arguing was so robust that Charles was asked to leave the hospital. Agnes and Maxine attempted to get their mother into Turner Geriatric Center, a private nursing home next to the Moody House, a fine retirement home run by the Methodist Church on Galveston's beachfront. In the meantime, someone had ordered flowers for their mother, yet the flowers couldn't be delivered to St. Mary's. The florist called the sisters, asking where to deliver the flowers because Edna Mae wasn't in St. Mary's.

Agnes Buxton and Maxine Anonsen found from the hospital that their brother had moved their mother to an unfamiliar nursing home on the mainland. It was called Autumn Hills, and it was near his house in LaMarque, a community adjacent to Texas City. Edna Mae Witt was in room 22.

CHAPTER FOUR

The nursing home industry in America is a big, strapping business, and with the graying of America's baby-boom generation in coming years it can only get much bigger. Across the country, after the passage of medicaid, entrepreneurs like Bob Gay jumped on the federal bandwagon and rode that buggy to millions of dollars in profit. Before buying his first nursing home, Gay was employed along with thousands of others at Tenneco. In his spare time, he bought real estate, remodeled the buildings, and sold that real estate at a profit.

Gay bought his first nursing home in 1963, and then another the next year. With the exception of 1966 and 1967, Bob Gay acquired nursing homes annually until 1978, when his chain totaled seventeen facilities, including six that Gay did not own outright but leased. The chain stretched from Beaumont in deep East Texas to Giddings, near Austin in Central Texas.

Each of the nursing homes in what came to be called Autumn Hills Convalescent Centers, Inc., was a fairly independent operation with a great deal of authority vested in the on-site administrator. As a result, the quality of care varied from home to home in direct relationship to the quality of each administrator. In the Texas City facility, occupancy in 1980 ran at 98 percent of the 120 available beds. From a business standpoint, Gay was pleased with the performance of the home.

A nursing home often consists of two distinct types of sections: an intermediate care facility that houses patients who are able to provide a portion of their own care and need only minimum nursing and medical attention, and a skilled care facility that houses patients who need considerably more medical and nursing attention. In 1980 the facilities in the Autumn Hills chain were preponderantly devoted to skilled care. Of the 1908 beds in the seventeen homes, 1452 were devoted to skilled care patients; only 456 were for intermediate care. In the Texas City home, the 120 beds were divided evenly between the two focuses of care.

There is one excellent reason why operating a skilled care facility is preferable—from a business standpoint—to operating an intermediate care facility. A 1980 medicaid agency study of 1978 cost reports revealed that of the 227 facilities reviewed by the agency and its auditing firm, the skilled nursing facilities were collecting $31.95 a day for each patient and the intermediate care facilities were being paid only $24.77 a day. (In ICF-II facilities, where even less care is required, an even smaller return of $21.76 was reported.) That $7.18 difference offered far greater flexibility for manipulating costs in a skilled care facility than in intermediate care homes. In that light, Autumn Hills' preference for skilled care facilities is completely understandable.

Bob Gay is a small nursing home operator compared with the giant conglomerates in the field, and Autumn Hills Convalescent Centers is a small, closely held corporation alongside, for example, the nation's largest operator of nursing homes, Beverly Enterprises. A New York Stock Exchange report by Standard and Poor's on September 18, 1985, described Beverly Enterprises this way: "Through an aggressive acquisition program, Beverly Enterprises has grown to be the largest publicly held owner/operator of long-term health care facilities, with over 910 facilities and 102,000 beds located throughout the U.S. and Canada. Beverly also has interests in retirement living and congregate care projects, home health care services, and durable care medical equipment."

A 1983 investment report said of Beverly,

The graying of America is good news for this company. The number of people over age 75 is growing. By 1990, there probably will be more than 11 million people in this age bracket, compared with less than 10 million a few years ago. Beverly, the leading provider of nursing home care, surely will benefit from this trend. This age segment is the company's primary source of patients.

Competition isn't likely to pose a problem. Most small nursing home chains are suffering, despite occupancy rates exceeding 95 percent industrywide. Government regulations combined with inadequate Medicare and Medicaid reimbursement rates are crimping their profits. Beverly is one of only a handful of companies that can afford to expand internally or through acquisitions under these unfavorable market conditions. This company has economics of scale and avenues of finance that are not available to others in the industry.

Standard and Poor's summarized the company by noting,

Beverly Enterprises is an operator of skilled and intermediate care nursing homes. The company has expanded its operations significantly in recent years through a vigorous acquisition program. As of May 1, 1985, the company operated 914 nursing centers with 102,563 beds, located in 44 states, the District of Columbia, and Ontario, Canada. The company also provides special services such as care for the mentally troubled elderly and the developmentally disabled.

Of the total homes operated, Beverly owned 449 facilities with 48,800 beds, leased 435 units with 51,056 beds, and managed 30 facilities with 2,707 beds. . . . The average occupancy at the company's facilities in 1984 was 90 percent (88 percent in 1983).

In 1984 Beverly received 65 percent of its revenue from the federal government. The other 35 percent came primarily from private sources. From 1982 to 1984 Beverly acquired 535 facilities, or 56,479 beds. Such growth has not damaged Beverly's reputation as a well-run company. From 1980 to 1984 Beverly more than tripled the book value of its stock, while doubling its earnings, and has paid a dividend since 1979.

Beyond its nursing home properties, Beverly operated 107 home health care agencies, 39 retirement living facilities, 24 durable medical equipment outlets, and 20 pharmacies. Standard and Poor's notes that in July 1985, Beverly "and Shimizu Construction Co. Ltd. of Tokyo signed a letter of intent to establish a joint venture for the development of retirement living projects in Japan." It also notes that in 1985 Beverly agreed to acquire 42 more nursing homes with 4461 additional beds. In 1984 Beverly generated $1.42 billion in revenues, with 65 percent of that figure paid in federal and state dollars. The company's long-term debt amounted to slightly more than $1 billion.

What is intriguing about the nursing home explosion is the way hard-nosed institutional investors have jumped into the field, bringing a massive influx of capital and reaping impressive gains. Some 74 percent of Beverly's stock is held by institutions; 3 percent is held by Hospital Corporation of America. Wall Street, for the best of all reasons, likes Beverly Enterprises.

By 1978 Bob Gay's nursing home chain had total assets of almost $9 million. Autumn Hills Convalescent Centers had current assets of $1.7 million, but unfortunately it also owned liabilities of $1.8 million, according to an October 1982 audit prepared for Congressman Claude Pepper's House committee by the General Accounting Office (GAO) of the United States government. The federal auditors discovered that the Autumn Hills chain was inflating patient costs by 34 cents a day for each patient, usually by charging unallowable costs to government agencies.

The report to Pepper also cited a 1978 audit for the State of Texas, which had disallowed $139,150 in costs being passed on to the taxpayers by Autumn Hills. The costs included $8238 in personal travel expenses; $3490 in fees for professional services rendered to other business interests; $20,575 for personal use of motor vehicles; $1110 for dues and subscriptions; $36,606 for employee meals, gifts, and parties; $8432 for radio and billboard advertising; $41,093 for interest on personal loans and purchases, including development of a site for expansion and the purchase of bank stock; $12,198 for an employee salary spent on nonnursing-home interests; $4730 for donations and director's fees; and $2678 for miscellaneous items.

The 1980 GAO audit found that although Autumn Hills had mended its ways to some degree, more than $6000 was spent on personal travel, another $2000 on professional service fees, more than $1700 on personal use of motor vehicles, and $2336 for a life insurance premium on a spouse not employed by the company. The audit also found that Autumn Hills was still spending $2357 on interest on personal loans and $1692 for employee time not spent on nursing home business. Although GAO disallowed items totaling only $20,319 in 1980, Autumn Hills had already attracted the microscopic scrutiny of the Galveston County district attorney's office.

Among the costs that the government found had been passed on to the taxpayer were trips to Manila, Vancouver, and New York. The professional service fee covered the cost in 1980 of preparing an income tax return for an affiliated partnership consisting of the three Autumn Hills owners. Government auditors said the insurance premium was for minority owners and a spouse who were not employed by the company. Furthermore, auditors found that Autumn Hills had purchased the company's automobiles, instead of leasing them, and most of the vehicles were allegedly used by members of Bob Gay's family.

The 1980 GAO audit also tagged another $118,410 in expenses that, because of vague language in Texas medicaid agency regulations, were questionable but could not be officially disallowed. Auditors said, "The $49,758 we estimated as entertainment includes $34,758 for employee lunches, dinners, and drinks, $8,469 for employee and vendor Christmas parties, $1,623 for an employee picnic, and $4,908 for various other items, including flowers and liquor for employees. These costs were reported to the Medicaid agency as home office advertising and promotional costs and allocated to the 17 company facilities as administrative costs. . . . The same types of costs, as well as costs for a hunting lease and tennis club membership, were included in the 1978 audit report. [The auditing firm hired by the state] and the Medicaid agency agreed at that time that most of the items were unallowable. They did, however, allow the cost of one Christmas party as an employee fringe benefit."

Autumn Hills' response to the government auditors is revealing. "The company," the response made clear, "expects its senior management team to conduct business under whatever circumstances it deems appropriate. The business lunch in the Houston area is a useful as well as traditional way to conduct business. The conclusion of a morning business conference with lunch is a convenient way to wrap up the conference. Additionally, the business luncheon is an opportunity to see people, on a more ready basis, whom the management must transact business with, whereas it might be several days before a conference could be scheduled by either party to the luncheon at their respective offices."

Autumn Hills also justified spending taxpayer money for parties because, in the opinion of top company management, the parties indirectly served patient care.

The Company has for a number of years held an annual holiday season party in December at a public facility for the purpose of bringing together all of the employees of the company in order for the President to provide a report to the employees on matters affecting the management of the respective health care facilities, as well as present awards to various members of the health care facilities' staffs for achievement as determined by several professional affiliations of the company. The party is an opportunity to provide a discussion of ideas as to patient care and management of the homes, as well as provide a re-emphasis of the Company's commitment to the professional delivery of health care to the patients. The job of providing health care is one which requires dedication and care and professional diligence which the company believes its employees discharge. Accordingly the Company believes that the inclusion of the cost of the holiday season party is properly included in the cost report and does disagree to the disallowance of the amount of $4061.11.

The party given annually at (the president's) house serves patient care indirectly in that it serves to focus on acknowledging the contribution of all of the employees of the company as well as vendors to the company. The affair gathers together the central office people as well as all those from the health care facilities who can attend, together with a selective list of vendors, during a period where it is appropriate to acknowledge the contributions of those who serve the company well.

Accordingly, the Company does not agree to the disallowance of the amount of $4,299.62 which it deems to be the approximate cost of the 1980 party.

Autumn Hills executives also argued that a company picnic served patient care.

The company believes that an annual picnic is necessary and vital to the furtherance of the company's purpose for being in the business of providing patient care to those requiring it.

The picnic serves as a morale booster to the employees of the Company and the time together at the picnic allows those present to exchange ideas (cross fertilization) about effective patient care as well as overall management of the individual health care facilities. The fact that the Company codes the expenditures to advertising and promotion does not preclude the inclusion of such an expenditure into the cost report as the company is of the opinion and judgment that such affairs benefit the Company's basic purpose of providing indirect patient care. The Company does not agree to the disallowance of $1,622.77.

Autumn Hills justified its purchase of flowers and liquor this way: "The Company believes these items are benefits to the employees."

The auditors also questioned legal fees from 1980. Some $9588 was paid to attorneys in applying for certificates of need and obtaining land for possible additional nursing homes in Houston, Galveston, and LaMarque.

Auditors also considered $59,064 in life insurance premiums questionable. "Both the owner and spouse work at the Company's central office, but the insurance policies in question name both the Company and insureds' spouse as beneficiaries."

Consultant fees were also questioned by the auditors, even though the fees were paid to owners who had unquestionable expertise in their fields. One owner receiving fees was a physician who was paid to "determine what the chain's medical position should be." The other was Houston oilman and developer George P. Mitchell, ranked one of the fifteen wealthiest men in the United States in 1983. Mitchell "was to provide business management expertise," the company said in justifying the outlay. The physician-owner was Mitchell's brother-in-law.

Auditors also found costs not reported to the medicaid agency, costs revealing of the inner workings of the corporation. Among the most interesting of those outlays was $4334 in penalties for late payment of mortgages, $2000 in director's fees, and a portion of Gay's salary. The GAO report also noted,

> In addition to the above, the owners of Autumn Hills, through a partnership related to Autumn Hills through common ownership, contributed $6,500 from 1978 to 1980 to the Nursing

Home Administrators Political Action Committee of Texas, Inc. The partnership spent an additional $2,500 reimbursing two individuals, including one of the owners, for their contributions to the committee. This $9,000 was not included in the home office costs reported to the State Medicaid Agency.

Autumn Hills owns a nursing home in Houston that it does not operate but leases to another corporation. This corporation's officers and directors consist of the Autumn Hills principal owner, his wife, and his son.

The GAO audit also found through incorporation data that Autumn Hills was doing business with companies owned by current and former stockholders of Autumn Hills Convalescent Centers or their family members. Among those companies was Fort Crockett Investors, a partnership consisting of current and former Autumn Hills owners, which also owned a Cleveland, Texas, nursing home leased and operated by Autumn Hills. Another such company was Hyde Park Service Corporation, "currently a defunct subsidiary of Autumn Hills." Hyde Park, the GAO report said, was a chain of funeral homes purchased from Gay. Also on the list were Ashford Bank, where Gay was on the board of directors; Designs by Joyce, "a miscellaneous home furnishings supplier" owned by Gay and his wife; and Lifecare Corporation, headed by Gay, his wife, and his son, which also operated a nursing home leased from Autumn Hills. Only the relationship with Designs by Joyce was disclosed to the state medicaid agency.

The GAO audit questioned two items that related to the Autumn Hills facility in Texas City: $2538 in excess building depreciation and $1014 for employee meals. Significantly enough, the report also noted that a medicaid agency caseworker had reported delays in making refunds from the patient's trust fund to discharged patients or the survivors of deceased patients.

Finally, the GAO found that Autumn Hills did not have a sufficient number of nurses on duty to meet state and federal regulations. It concluded,

The Autumn Hills Texas City nursing home has a history of not complying with Medicaid standards for nurse staffing. On numerous occasions over the three-year period from 1978 to 1980, the home failed to have a sufficient number of nurses on duty to provide the level of nurse staffing required by Medicaid standards. According to our analysis for three selected months in 1980, the required number of nurses were available only about two thirds of the time. In our opinion, the frequency of nurse shortages raises questions about the level of nursing care provided Texas City home residents. Further, the Company has little financial incentive to hire temporary nurses to meet the standards. The State of Texas does not reduce payment rates when its staffing requirements are not met.

In November 1982 Gay wrote to Congressman Pepper and the regional office of the GAO protesting the audit findings regarding staffing. He argued that in 1980 the facility was in fact overstaffed, and he asked that the audit be reopened.

In 1983, before the United States Senate Special Committee on Aging, Michael Zimmerman of the GAO summed up the agency's findings: "The major area of concern I have with these relatively significant amounts of questionable cost is that the money was apparently not being spent on patient care."

Combined income statements of Autumn Hills Convalescent Centers for 1978 show the company reported a profit of $235,308. In 1979 Autumn Hills showed a profit of $242,855. In 1980, a loss of almost $10,000 was reported. In 1978 Autumn Hills had revenues of $12,201,047; in 1979 revenues totaled $14,761,670, and in 1980 revenues totaled $16,715,988.

On November 20, 1979, one year to the day after the death of Elnora Breed, David Marks and members of the Galveston County Sheriff's Department moved against Autumn Hills in Texas City. Employees to this day call Marks's actions the Gestapo raid. Whatever the tactic is called, Marks seized Autumn Hills records that provided a bonanza of information useful to his investigation of the nursing home and the court case he was building. Sartwelle and the other Autumn Hills attorneys would later charge that the raid was patently illegal and violated due process.

State investigators also subpoenaed corporate records from the home office of the corporation, which revealed even more than the GAO audit for Congressman Pepper. The federal audit was concerned primarily with how Autumn Hills dispersed medicare and medicaid funds. Marks was far more interested in whether Gay and his associates were profiting from the misery of the Autumn Hills patients Marks believed had been murdered in 1978. Sorting through the mountain of material now in their hands, Marks and his team began to unveil what was to them a compelling picture of profiteering, profiteering that David Marks was convinced had contributed directly to the untimely deaths of 58 patients in Texas City.

Marks learned that Autumn Hills Convalescent Centers had been deeply in debt during 1978, the year that state inspectors first discovered that the Texas City facility was not exactly a health spa. Marks also learned that the corporation had to borrow consistently to meet its payroll. The state frequently withheld medicaid funds when inspectors found poor care, which—along with Gay's wheeling and dealing—led to the cash flow problems, according to Howard Johnson, a medicaid fraud auditor and investigator with the Texas attorney general's office. The corporation either took out or renewed small loans ranging from $25,000 to $40,000 sixteen times from January to November 1978.

Johnson also determined from his audit that in 1978, Gay received $523,433 in salary and benefits, including payments and repairs for five cars and a motor home. Two of the vehicles were used by Gay's children and two by his wife, in addition to his personal transportation. The automobile fleet included a Cadillac and a Mark V Lincoln Continental. For those two cars, the tab during the eleven months of Johnson's audit allegedly totaled $7252.

Autumn Hills also paid more than $2000 for a deer lease for Gay to use during the state's fall deer hunting season. Gay and his family were also well traveled that year. Johnson found that the Gays went to Vancouver, British Columbia, and to Colorado at Autumn Hills' expense. Johnson also found that Gay charged the company $1600 for medical bills and more than $38,000 in insurance premiums for himself and his wife. Unfortunately, the state had not completely done its homework. Gay had signed personal guarantees for the company's debt, and in the event of his death, the insurance would have protected his estate.

The corporation also made payments benefiting other businesses owned by Gay. Johnson asserted that Autumn Hills bought a $150,000 certificate of deposit for Gay, who used it as collateral for a $200,000 loan to pay off debts in another venture.

A whopping $700,000 in interest was paid on mortgages on the nursing homes. The company had expanded rapidly, and much of the payment total made went toward interest on those mortgages.

In 1978 Bob Gay was living the American dream. His company had cash flow problems, to be sure, but he was still president and principal owner of a chain of seventeen nursing homes and an owner of several other businesses. He maintained a house in the Woodlands, the posh residential city north of Houston that his friend George Mitchell had created from a pine forest. He was making more than $105,000 when his salary and perks were totaled. His future was generally regarded as secure; his knuckles were not white and his palms did not sweat when he faced a banker across a desk. He was able to enjoy his hobby, sailing, which was a diversion from the day-to-day management of his interests. He had a staff that he trusted to handle the trivial and mundane tasks he had earned the right to pass on to others. No one, least of all Bob Gay, could have believed that he would see his fiefdom crumble, and that he would be indicted for murdering the residents of one of his nursing homes.

Elnora Breed had no reason to believe that she would die lying in her own excrement with maggots devouring the rotting flesh of her sores as she slipped toward death. Nor did Edna Mae Witt have any reason to believe that she would lie in her own waste as the acrid sting of urine pierced her gaping flesh for hours without help or relief. She told her daughters of the pain. Pearl Creighton could not have known that she would lie in the same position on her back for days and develop fourteen bedsores that never received proper care, care she was entitled to expect and that her government was paying to see she received. Frank Coss did not know that at the end of his life his genitalia would be allowed to swell to the size of a volleyball or that his hands would rot. But all those horrors and more plagued Autumn Hills in 1978.

The patients of Autumn Hills had for the most part chosen to live out their lives on the Texas coast. Many had chosen to end their days in the tank town of Texas City. But surely none chose the end that they endured at Autumn Hills. They had been promised a better finale than that. Thanks to Social Security, they were supposed to conclude their lives with more dignity than their ancestors had found. They had been promised—and had believed—that with medicare and medicaid they would be secure from overwhelming medical debt as they lived out the winter of their lives.

What they had not been told was that they would be caught up in a government-created free enterprise system that allowed ambitious men to make what, to the elderly inhabitants of Autumn Hills in Texas City, would be unimaginable profits for providing a minimum amount of care—and often less than that.

The elderly of Autumn Hills were, in a sense, society's castoffs. Their ranks included the poor, the unwanted, the excess baggage of humanity. Critics of David Marks charge that the families of the Autumn Hills dead are as guilty in what happened there as any company executive. Those critics overlook—or ignore—the fact that some Autumn Hills patients had outlived their families or had no family to begin with. Many of the children of Autumn Hills patients were themselves too aged and ill to care for a parent. Certainly, there were families who were callous to the needs of their elders, yet was that reason for the home itself to abandon them?

One of the least attractive sides of corporate America is the nursing home industry. What was once a cottage industry of old folks' homes, whose most noticeable common characteristic was pristine lines of vacant rocking chairs on a long front porch, has become a giant, usually profitable business in which limiting costs is a critical key to handsome bottom lines. In the boardroom, care for Grandmother's bedsore is sometimes reduced to a line item in a budget that must be reduced to please stockholders and secure the keys to the executive washroom.

If the attorney general's audit of Autumn Hills is accurate, then the nursing home would have shown a handsome profit had Gay taken only the $100,000 salary that he publicly claimed and had he not gone from one venture to another building his company. Yet Autumn Hills Convalescent Centers is not a publicly held corporation, and in 1978 there were only three stockholders. Unless the stockholders complain, in a closely held corporation almost anything is acceptable practice. Gay did nothing different from what hundreds of other small businessmen do. But unlike others, Gay's business was the relief of human misery.

Shortly after the first Autumn Hills indictments were handed down by the holdover Galveston County grand jury, the Texas Department of Human Resources released the findings of its own study. The department reported that 839 nursing home cost statements filed with the agency showed a pacesetting 33.8 percent return on equity for nursing home owners. In comparison, oil companies showed a 22.9 percent return, Texas banks reported 15.3 percent, natural gas companies showed a 14.7 percent profit, fast-food operations reported 14.4 percent, and retailers showed 12.2 percent.

When those figures were released, Dell Hagen, then president of the National College of Nursing Home Administrators, complained that the numbers were artificially high. Hagen, part owner of a Tyler nursing home, said the profit figure was enlarged by poorly run homes that cut corners on staff and food to save money.

CHAPTER FIVE

Maxine Anonsen and Agnes Buxton were worried about their "Mama," Edna Mae Witt, as they crossed the two-mile causeway that connects Galveston Island with the mainland. Their mother was in a strange place, Autumn Hills Nursing Home, in a strange town, Texas City. Galvestonians born on the Island—B.O.I. is the popular abbreviation—have a particular disdain for the newer communities across the narrow bay that separates the Island from the rest of Galveston County. Galvestonians prefer the pristine sea air to the often noxious odors emitted by the belching smokestacks of Texas City's petroleum refineries. Conversely, Texas Citians tell outsiders that all they smell is money.

When the florist called Maxine and Agnes, the two sisters were flustered. They had been trying to find a residence for their mother since her doctor suggested she be placed in a nursing home for a few months to get back on her feet. They were shocked to learn that she had been placed in Autumn Hills without their knowledge. After all, hadn't Mama lived with Maxine for the last ten years? She had lived with their brother Charles for only five days before entering St. Mary's Hospital in Galveston.

For a Galvestonian, mainland communities are difficult. Galveston is a city whose streets are laid out with geometrical precision, numbered streets running north and south, lettered streets running east and west. An enterprising early land salesman had even multiplied the available lots by establishing half streets—Avenue O 1/2 lies between Avenues O and P, for instance—on the south side of Broadway to the beachfront. People who live on Ave-

nue P 1/2 are fond of shocking newcomers by telling them, "I only
have to go a half block to P."

So Island natives find the maze of suburbs surrounding the mainland communities exasperating. There is no order that resembles
the squared-off precision of Galveston's streets. Maxine Anonsen
and Agnes Buxton, as would most other Galvestonians of their generation, faced locating Autumn Hills with some trepidation. They
stopped and asked directions when they reached LaMarque, and
even then they had trouble finding the nursing home, which was a
short distance from College of the Mainland, a community college
enthusiastically funded by local voters a few years earlier.

When the two women walked through the front door, their nos-
trils were immediately assaulted by the rancid stench of stale urine.
Agnes later remembered the odor as "so strong it would take your
breath away." There was little activity in the place, but the two
women didn't notice. Their thoughts were on their mother, suddenly confined to a strange place.

The two sisters walked to room 22, where their mother and her
roommate, Minnie, lay in bed. The daughters immediately noticed
that their mother was wet, and that a pool of urine soaked the floor
under her bed. But Edna Mae Witt was alert. This did not surprise
Maxine and Agnes, since their mother had been recovering nicely
in St. Mary's Hospital, a place that was one of her favorites. Like
many of her age, Edna Mae Witt loved to go to the hospital, where
she was pampered and fussed over. But Edna Mae didn't like Autumn Hills. She begged her daughters to take her home.

Maxine was used to her mother's maladies. She had nursed Edna
Mae at home when things got out of hand. "She had a busted vein,
arthritis, and gout," Maxine remembers today. "I would soak her in
Epsom salts," a routine that endured throughout the years they
lived together.

Though Maxine and Agnes were perplexed that Charles had put
their mother in the nursing home without telling them, and though
their mother wanted to go home, they managed to quiet Edna
Mae's fears for the evening. But they returned to Galveston determined to bring their mother back to the Island and familiar surroundings. Edna Mae needed the loving care of her daughters, and
they in turn did not want their mother in a strange place in a
strange town in a urine-soaked bed.

The following night, the two sisters returned to Autumn Hills, remembering the tedious route from the night before. Again they were assailed by the permeating reek of urine as they entered the building. They soon found out why. When they entered room 22, they found their mother soaked with her own urine. As Agnes later described it, "She was all wet, even under the pad." They asked their mother if she had tried to call a nurse or an aide and were told, "I tried to ring the bell, but nobody answered."

Agnes lifted her mother's outer sheet and found the bed sheet covered to the outer edge with rings of dried urine and soaking wet in the center. Maxine was appalled at the condition of the linen. Agnes snatched up the bed buzzer and rang for an attendant. But no one responded, and after waiting nearly twenty minutes, she went to the nurse's station down the hallway and asked for sheets to change the bed herself. At the nurse's station, she was directed to a cart farther down the hall, where she found laundered sheets. Maxine and Agnes then bathed their mother, the first bath Edna Mae Witt had received at Autumn Hills. The women received no assistance from any of the staff.

Agnes went into the small bathroom, which served her mother and her mother's roommate and the two patients in the adjoining room, looking for a bedpan. In the bathroom she was appalled to find a stainless steel bedpan stained from frequent use and containing dried feces. She scrubbed the bedpan with hot water for a long time until it was usable. There was only one bedpan for the four patients in the two-room suite.

Agnes Buxton returned to Autumn Hills night after night to care for her mother, increasingly aware that the staff of the nursing home was providing little, if any, necessary care. Each night, Agnes bathed her mother alone, since Maxine was herself ill and did not want to expose their mother to further possible contamination. Each night, Agnes found the bed wet, with dried rings from earlier urinations on the sheets.

In most hospitals, the hallway is a continuous tremor of activity. Nurses and aides are in seemingly perpetual motion caring for patients, passing out medications, serving food, water, and soft drinks, taking vital signs, adjusting bedclothes, and repositioning the patients to avoid the bane of long confinement, bedsores. In Autumn Hills, Maxine and Agnes could see from the door of their mother's room that the hallway was usually deserted. The only activity was in the nurse's station down the corridor. Day after day, the two women saw nothing that resembled the health care they had seen in St. Mary's Hospital.

Evenings when she arrived, Agnes sensed that something was missing, almost unnoticeable, but gone nevertheless. As she scanned the room, she discovered that the bed buzzer, which had been of little use to Edna Mae in summoning nurses or aides, had been removed from her mother's bedside. Maxine found her mother lying in her own urine.

"Mama, why are you wet?" Maxine asked. "Why didn't you ring your bell?"

"They won't come when I ring the bell, Maxie. I finally had to use the bed. I kept ringing it, and someone came in and took it away," Edna Mae answered her daughter.

Both Agnes and Maxine were furious about the care their mother was receiving. They repeatedly complained to the staff of Autumn Hills but soon learned from other families that "if you complain, it is going to be harder on your mother."

As the first week went on, they learned something else. On arriving each night, they would find their mother lying flat on the bed, in the same position they had left her in the night before. They never saw any Autumn Hills staff member come to their mother's room to turn her or roll up the bed, and they never saw their mother placed in a geriatric chair.

Maxine and Agnes usually arrived at the nursing home at dinnertime. Aides would bring trays to each patient's room, and to Edna Mae's room as well, yet the aides did not roll up the bed or attempt to feed their mother or even see that she was fed, this large woman who loved to eat. According to Maxine, "they would just bring in the tray of food and sit it down and leave."

On weekends, the two sisters were able to come to their mother during the day. On the first weekend of Edna Mae Witt's stay at Autumn Hills, Maxine and Agnes learned what was standard fare for the patients' lunch. On their mother's plate was a peanut butter and jelly sandwich on stale bread. Next to it sat a tiny glass of milk. For dessert she was offered "three or four pieces of fruit cocktail in a bowl." Edna Mae "was not used to that kind of food," her daughters say. All of her life Edna Mae Witt had been a hearty eater. Her daughters began bringing food to the nursing home each evening, and according to Agnes, "she ate it all."

The sisters brought personal supplies to their mother and placed them in the small cabinet by the bed. In that cabinet they also placed clothes, bedclothes, robes, and her slippers from home. Convinced that the nursing home diet was not fit to eat, they also placed food in the cabinet. The next night, the sisters would find clothes and food gone. Again they complained at the nurse's station, but to no avail. They repeatedly brought food but soon learned that nothing was safe from disappearance at Autumn Hills.

The bathroom was never cleaned either. Each evening, Maxine and Agnes found the single bedpan encrusted with feces. They dutifully washed the bedpan again and again. They also found the water pitcher always empty. Each day, they filled it, hoping that the water would last until they returned. But it made little difference. Aide Pamela James remembers, "Many a time a patient asked for water and a nurse would walk right out of the room." Other times she found that the water in a patient's pitcher had thickened. "It was real slimy. It was slowly coming out. I knew they hadn't washed the pitchers and glasses."

Neither of Edna Mae's daughters ever saw their mother receive any skin care. And Agnes Buxton saw her mother given only one blood pressure pill—but never any other medication—during her entire stay at Autmun Hills. Maxine Anonsen's recollections of that period are identical: she never saw her mother receive medications or skin care, never saw her mother turned, never saw an aide wash or give water to Edna Mae Witt during the long hours she spent with her mother at Autumn Hills.

Edna Mae had fine skin, soft to the touch and well cared for. Her skin began to break down from the constant contact with urine. Just one week after the admission of her mother to Autumn Hills, Maxine Anonsen again came to the room and again found her mother lying in her own urine. She lowered the sheet and turned Edna Mae on her side and found a bedsore on her lower back.

"Mama, what's that on your bottom?" Maxine asked.

"I don't know, Maxie. What is it?" Edna Mae answered.

"Does it hurt, Mama?" the daughter asked.

"Oh, it burns so," the mother answered.

"Mama, has anybody tended to this?" Maxine questioned her mother.

"No, Maxie," Mrs. Witt answered, crying. "I want to go home. Please take me home, Maxie."

Deeply concerned, Maxine went to the nurse's station to report her discovery to the on-duty nurse. "They said that they had seen it; they said that they were going to tend to it."

Autumn Hills nurse's aides quickly became familiar with Edna Mae Witt. They dreaded handling her because she was a large woman and difficult to turn, although her daughter Maxine, a fairly small woman, later said that she could turn her mother alone. Pamela James, the aide who loved soap operas, was herself a large woman, and she would not turn Edna Mae without help. "It took two people to turn her and four people to get her out of bed," James remembers. And where bathing was concerned, James says that if "I couldn't get someone to help me, I wouldn't do it."

James remembers that she was poorly trained when she came to Autumn Hills. She knew that other aides were similarly ill-trained for their jobs. When James first began taking vital signs, she did not comprehend the numbers in the blood pressure readings. "I would see it go up, but I didn't know what it meant." Once, James removed a catheter and became frightened when blood rushed out of the patient, and with the blood some little "shells."

The aides also had difficulty feeding Edna Mae Witt. When her daughters were not at the nursing home, Edna Mae would refuse to open her mouth, Pamela James recalls. The busy aides had little time or patience for such crankiness on their shifts. If the old woman didn't want to eat, it was her problem, not theirs. The constant shortage of help at Autumn Hills produced attitude problems for James and the other aides. "When we didn't have enough help, I said, 'If they didn't care, why do I?'"

Pamela James became accustomed to the filth of Autumn Hills and the conditions in which the patients lived. "When we came on [shift change], feces was on their hands and under their fingernails, where it had dried, and we knew that it had been there awhile. Patients ate with feces on their hands."

Aide Carol Josey was equally frustrated by the lack of help at Autumn Hills. There were not enough hours in the day to finish all the work expected from the aides. Even though there were doctors' orders to turn bedfast patients every two hours, there simply were never enough people to accomplish even that simple task. Josey even saw ambulatory patients with feces on their hands.

Josey, unlike Pamela James, had experience working in hospitals, and that fueled her frustration. She saw patients without even minimal care for long periods of time. She also saw many patients who were wet, and left to stay that way. She was appalled to see catheter bags left on the floor, increasing the likelihood of contamination. During laundry time, as she passed the nurse's station, she would notice the call-light board lit up like a Christmas tree as patients called for help that never came.

Carol Josey complained to the director of nursing for Autumn Hills, Sandy Canlas. Canlas, equally frustrated, said she was trying to hire more aides and that "as soon as they give me the okay, I will." Josey also complained to the administrator of the home, Virginia Wilson, about the personnel shortages and about shortages of dressings, linens, soap, and Ensure food supplement, which for many patients was the only source of nourishment. Wilson listened, smiled, and nodded in agreement. But few changes were made.

Josey also knew that the Autumn Hills ice machine was filthy. So did Sandy Canlas, who thought the ice machine might be contaminated, and a culture was taken to determine what was growing in it.

Josey had noticed that several patients had leaky catheters and were constantly wet. Dutifully, she told the nurses of the problem. She also told the nurses of another aide who was particularly bad, worse than the others in not performing her duties. The aide did not know how to take vital signs, and even when Canlas taught her to do simple tasks, she still refused to perform them; she was often more interested in taking a nap.

Josey also knew that the nursing home did not have enough thermometers and that the aides who did take vital signs often used the same thermometer on several patients without sterilizing it. She observed that when an aide finished taking a temperature, she simply put a paper around the thermometer and moved on to the next patient with the same instrument.

Josey complained about one nurse in particular, whom she had seen falsifying reports. Josey knew that was not standard nursing practice, and it disturbed her profoundly.

One day Josey found a patient whose dressing had fallen off her bedsore, a large, running, foul-smelling wound. With the personnel shortage, it was not unusual for loose dressings to go unchanged. But on closer examination, Josey discovered something she had not seen before. In the large hole in the center of the ulcer, maggots were eating the rotting flesh. She complained to her nurse, who said she would check on it.

Josey also noticed that the supply of lotions for skin care was almost nonexistent at Autumn Hills and that the only time such lotions were available was when a patient's family brought them in. She also saw that the only time Autumn Hills patients had toothpaste was when the family supplied it.

The work of a nurse's aide in a nursing home is not a pleasant task. Even the routine duties would appall most people. But to Carol Josey, Autumn Hills was worse than that. She quit the facility to return to hospital work. In the nursing home, her patients didn't get better; they usually got worse. And so it was with Edna Mae Witt, whom Josey tried to help by cleaning feces out of her bedsore with peroxide.

The bedsores of Edna Mae Witt became more numerous, and the large one on her lower back grew. Agnes Buxton described it. "It was red, with yellow, and with a hole in the center. It had yellow pus like fester stuff around it." Still, every time the daughter went to Autumn Hills she found the bed wet, with fresh circles of dried urine on the sheets. None of the staff came into the room and offered to help.

Maxine Anonsen gave up trying the bed buzzer. No one ever responded to help her care for her mother. The bed buzzer finally disappeared from the room. And by that time, Edna Mae had lost all of her own clothes. She was wearing clothes provided by the nursing home—strange clothes. The cabinet was bare of her own clothing, food, and toilet articles that her daughters had brought from her home in Galveston. Maxine searched for the clothes, but "I never could find them. She had on their clothes."

Edna Mae Witt often complained that the large bedsore hurt her. Every time her daughters visited her at Autumn Hills, they found the sore in contact with urine and often with feces. Other, smaller sores were developing on Edna Mae's body. One, on her foot, turned black. When Maxine lifted the sheet to examine it, the sore stuck to the linen.

Maxine Anonsen started making telephone calls. She called the doctor, Merrill Stiles, who was now in charge of her mother's case. Stiles was her brother Charles's physician and had taken over Edna Mae's case from the doctor who had cared for Edna Mae Witt for many years in Galveston. "You never got a chance to talk to them doctors. You never could get them," Maxine remembers. She called her brother, wanting to take her mother back into her home. Finally, in desperation, she called Paulette Miller, a state health department worker she knew from chance meetings at the beauty salon. She was afraid that she was making a pest of herself, but Maxine kept calling Paulette Miller every night.

Miller tried to help, yet even she was blocked. The State of Texas and Autumn Hills interpreted the law in such a way that Charles Witt, who had placed his mother in Autumn Hills, had custody, even though Edna Mae had lived with him only a few days after living with Maxine for the preceding ten years. Neither Agnes nor Maxine could remove Mrs. Witt from the nursing home, without going to court.

Edna Mae Witt was getting weaker. Her body was under attack from its own excrement. By now, the sore on her back was a gaping, putrescent cavern that reached to her backbone, the white of her spine showing through. Huge quantities of body fluids were draining from the sore and onto its dressing and the sheets. The doctors continued to fail to return her daughters' calls, although in later testimony Dr. Stiles stated that he always tried to return a family's calls at the end of the day. Persistently, the women continued in their efforts to have their mother released from the nursing home.

Edna Mae was deteriorating rapidly. New bedsores appeared on her already frail body. She was helpless to do anything about it, and the reality—and the finality—of her condition became less and less apparent to her. As she slipped into her final coma, a total of 22 bedsores ravaged what little strength she had left. Into those sores poured contamination that caused septicemia, a massive infection of her entire body.

On October 11, 1978, state nursing home inspector Betty Korndorffer saw Edna Mae Witt. Autumn Hills nursing director Sandy Canlas had summoned her to a consultation at the home. When Korndorffer arrived, she found the office closed. She continued down the hallway of the skilled wing of the nursing home to room 22, where she saw Edna Mae Witt on her side with her knees exposed and with no urine in the bag into which her catheter tube drained. The tube was clamped between Edna Mae's knees. Korndorffer continued down the hall, looking for a nurse or aide to correct the situation, but found no one. She then returned to Edna

Mae's room, where she lifted the knees of the elderly woman and found two identical sores on her inner thighs. It appeared that something had been left between the woman's legs for a long time, creating the pressure that had formed the sores.

Angrily, Korndorffer went looking for Sandy Canlas. She found the director and told her of the problem. Canlas was not aware of the two sores. The two women returned to the room and pulled down the sheet. "We looked at her whole body," Korndorffer remembers.

Korndorffer asked Canlas to roll Edna Mae on her back, which the large nurse did with ease. They found another bedsore on her heel, which Korndorffer described as a "foul, smelly decubitus with rotting tissue." Korndorffer also found other sores on Edna Mae's legs.

Korndorffer and Canlas then rolled Edna Mae onto her side and exposed the huge bedsore on her back. Korndorffer described it as "foul, very smelly, and large enough that you could put your fist in it. I looked across the bed at Mrs. Canlas, and I mouthed the words, 'Mrs. Witt is going to die.'" The two women looked at each other across the bed and began to cry.

On October 14, 1978, Agnes Buxton and Maxine Anonsen finally got their wish. Their mother was transferred from Autumn Hills to nearby Galveston County Memorial Hospital. Maxine, whose own bout with the flu had kept her away from the nursing home for fear of contaminating her mother, was shocked at Edna Mae's condition. A nasal gastric tube extended from her mother's nose as she struggled silently against death.

At the county hospital Maxine and Agnes met other families who had followed their kin from Autumn Hills to the hospital to watch them die. On October 16, 1978, Edna Mae Witt, who loved to eat, loved her grandchildren, and loved life in the sunshine of Galveston Island, died. For the first time in 47 days she was clean.

Nell Reams was not one of the new pioneers who came to Galveston County. On the contrary, she had lived most of her life in Florida and Georgia. As age began to take its toll, she and her family decided it would be better for Nell if she spent her remaining years in Texas. At age 68, she came to live with her daughter in League City, a growing bedroom community that had grown up around Houston's giant Johnson Space Center. Five years later, she found her way to Autumn Hills.

On July 6, 1978, Nell Reams suffered a fall and was taken to the hospital. Now 73, she was in discomfort but was able, with help, to get around the hospital. Her problems were complicated by her Parkinson's disease. While in the hospital, she complained about her heel.

Two of her daughters made the decision that it would be better if their mother went to live in a nursing home. Mary Vaughn, a daughter who also lived in League City, says, "She had checked on nursing homes. Autumn Hills was the only one available." On July 17, 1978, Nell Reams entered Autumn Hills, where she also came under the care of a new physician, Merrill Stiles.

When the daughters visited their mother at Autumn Hills, they often could not find staff members in attendance. They also found their mother's room dirty. In particular, they found the water pitcher dirty and empty next to their mother's bed. They also noticed that their mother's condition worsened as the summer passed.

Brenda DiCristina visited her grandmother at Autumn Hills in September 1978. She and her grandmother were very close. Her parents had divorced when she was younger, and Brenda had lived with her grandmother off and on. When she arrived in Texas City from her home in Atlanta, Georgia, the entire family went to the nursing home. When Brenda entered Autumn Hills, she noticed a strong, nauseating urine odor. The family walked down the corridor to Nell Reams's room, two doors past the nurse's station on the left side of the corridor.

There Brenda DiCristina hugged her grandmother. She missed the woman who had partially raised her. After small talk, Brenda asked her grandmother if she could assist her to the bathroom. When she raised Nell Reams from the bed, she found pills under her. She scolded her grandmother for not taking her medication, but Nell responded that the pills doped her up, and "she didn't want to take a chance on that."

The nursing home had found that Nell Reams was a problem. On several occasions, she had become combative, and the doctor had prescribed Valium to quiet her.

Brenda was shocked by the physical condition of her grandmother. "Her hair was greasy, and her eyes had matter in them. She had body odor, and she also smelled like urine." She was also shocked to see a large "oozing, pussing, black sore on her heel." Brenda called her aunt to the bedside to examine the sore, then called for someone to come and clean the sore. No one responded.

Each day for a week, Brenda came to her grandmother's bedside. "I always found her lying flat on her back. Her hair was dirty and she was dirty." The young mother of two boys cleaned her grandmother and powdered her, as she had done with her own children when they were babies. She also clipped her grandmother's toenails. "They were long and square and curling around her toes."

Brenda never saw the nursing home staff give her grandmother a bath, mouth care, or skin care. She never saw anyone get her grandmother up and out of the bed. In fact, each time she came to the nursing home, she found Nell lying flat on her back in the bed. Nor did she ever see a doctor. Her mother had tried to call Dr. Stiles, but Stiles did not return the call.

Day after day, Brenda watched as the sore on her grandmother's heel remained unbandaged and oozed pus onto the sheets. On each of the final three days of her visit, Brenda DiCristina found her grandmother unconscious.

Rydel Braunsdorf lived in nearby Dickinson, seven miles across the coastal prairie from Autumn Hills. She was a friend of Mary Vaughn, Nell Reams's daughter. They had originally met in a department store where they both worked. The two friends often visited Mary's mother in the nursing home after work. Rydel also noticed the pungent odor of urine as she entered the nursing home.

She also thought Nell Reams was not getting the care that is normally expected in a residential health care facility. "Nothing was ever right about her. She smelled bad. Her hair wasn't clean. Her room wasn't clean." Rydel Braunsdorf looked beneath the sheets of Nell's bed. "She had had a bowel movement, and she was lying in it." Rydel went to the nurse's station to summon help. On her way, she noticed others calling out "Help" and "Nurse." She found someone at the station. "I asked a black aide to help me. She was rolling her hair with pink hair rollers. She kept rolling her hair. Call buttons were going off in front of her. She never came."

Rydel Braunsdorf returned to Autumn Hills four more times. Nell "was always unkempt and the odor was always there. I never saw water in the room. I never saw the nursing staff assist the woman in eating or in any other manner when I was there." Braunsdorf also saw that Nell Reams had developed a bedsore on her hip. "I could see the bone. It was bad."

Mary Vaughn saw the hip sore too. "I only looked at her hip one time, and it broke my heart." Vaughn did manage to talk to Merrill Stiles, though she never got to see him and to this day doesn't know what the doctor who cared for her mother looks like. Stiles told her, "Your mother is very ill." Mary knew that. As things got worse, she called Stiles again and again. She did not hear back from him. "I don't know if he ever examined her or not," she says. Vaughn says, "I don't recall her ever having been turned."

Mary was frustrated with the care Nell Reams was receiving at Autumn Hills. She saw that her mother's clothes were not being changed, that her bed was wet, that there was no drinking cup next to the bed, and that Nell was not being fed and couldn't feed herself.

She was also disturbed by the nursing aides who were charged with caring for her mother. What care she saw was done in such a perfunctory manner that it might as well have been left off. She quickly learned that some of the aides were very inexperienced. One aide came into the room to take her mother's temperature with a rectal thermometer. Vaughn remembers that "instead of using the thermometer in the place it should be used, it was used in the vagina."

On September 16, 1978, Nell Reams, who had come to Texas to be with her family in her final years, was taken to Galveston County Memorial Hospital, where she stayed three weeks. On October 6 she returned to Autumn Hills, where she stayed another one and a half weeks, only to be taken back to the hospital. On the day after Christmas, Nell Reams died in another nursing home near Autumn Hills. Her family had succeeded in removing her from Autumn Hills, but it was already too late.

Marie Richards, another Autumn Hills patient, could walk, and Carol Josey remembers caring for her. Josey also testified that she often found Richards soiled at the beginning of her shift at the nursing home. "It would be dry," she says, indicating that Richards had been left lying in her own excrement for a long time. "It would be all in her back." Josey says that when she got the woman up to go to the restroom, she would find that Richards had been left to lie in her own feces. Carol Josey also remembers 79-year-old Edith Walmsley of Galveston. She had been in the home off and on since

1971. Josey noticed that Walmsley was always wet from a leaking catheter.

Betty Korndorffer also noticed that on October 31, 1978, Walmsley had not been cared for. The woman had dirty nails and a "cruddy" catheter. She was also suffering from a bad cough. Two months later, she was dead.

Jerry Mutina, 87, had come to Autumn Hills from Seabreeze Care Center, also in Texas City. His family was from nearby Dickinson, a small town situated in a rare coastal pine forest. In August 1978, Betty Korndorffer observed Mutina's condition. He had no clothes on and was restrained to the bed with his leg over the side rail. The urine in his catheter bag "looked very bad." She pointed out the lack of care for the man to Sandy Canlas as they made rounds that day.

Frank Coss, 65, was much younger than many of the other patients in Autumn Hills. He was also one of the few male patients on the skilled side of the nursing home. He was dying from a brain tumor when he was admitted on October 5, 1978. By the time Betty Korndorffer saw him later in the month, his condition had been compromised by the care he was receiving. "He was wet; his bed was wet. I mean old urine. He was unkempt."

Many patients in hospitals and nursing homes must be restrained to prevent harm to themselves or others, and Coss was such a patient. But Korndorffer discovered that something had gone wrong in his case. The man's wrists were attached to the bed rail with a restraint, but the restraint was too tight. The hand was swollen. Korndorffer ordered the restraints untied. She described the swelling in his hand as grotesque and so pronounced that the fingers touched each other.

Coss was also incontinent of urinary function, and the nursing home had applied a Texas catheter. Unlike an internal, or indwelling, catheter, the Texas catheter is attached to the penis externally. It is simple to put in place, although some male patients will attempt to strike the person handling them, thinking that they are being molested. A condom is gently taped around the organ on one end, and around a tube leading into a urine bag attached to the bed on the other. Removal of the tape from the tender skin must also be done very gently to avoid abrasions.

As Korndorffer and Canlas lowered the sheet they were horrified to see what had happened to the man's genitalia. His penis had swollen to four inches in diameter, and his scrotum had engorged to a diameter of ten to twelve inches. Korndorffer found that a physician had not been called about his condition.

Guadalupe Martinez was born August 10, 1889. She was 83 when she entered Autumn Hills. She had, like many of Galveston's poor Hispanics, lived in Magnolia Homes, a low-income public housing project on the city's east end. As with almost all Autumn Hills patients, a funeral home was designated to be called in the event of Guadalupe Martinez's death. In August 1978, Betty Korndorffer, on a state inspection of the home, noted that Guadalupe Martinez had an extremely large bedsore eight inches across and a couple of inches deep. The inspector also saw that a nurse had written on Martinez's chart that the sore was only one inch wide and two inches long. Korndorffer informed Sandy Canlas of the discrepancy and also pointed out that Martinez had been wet for some time. "Urine was on the bedsore, and the dressing was soiled with urine."

Ursela Barrilleaux was a very old woman. She was born during Grover Cleveland's first term as president. Korndorffer was familiar with Barrilleaux, whose son called the nursing home inspector often. Korndorffer noted one day upon entering the nursing home that Barrilleaux was tied in a normal chair, not the geriatric chair normally used for aged people. She "tagged" the elderly woman so she could determine if the staff moved her, since nursing standards dictate that a patient restrained in a chair must be released and repositioned every two hours. On March 10, 1978, Ursela Barrilleaux, Korndorffer noted, "sat tied in that chair all day long." No one did anything to the woman for the entire period that the inspector was in the nursing home.

Christine Tadlock had lived more than eighty years. She suffered from arthritis and had lived in Autumn Hills since April 1975. Tadlock knew Betty Korndorffer by name, so when the nursing home inspector came to Autumn Hills on November 21, 1978, she made a special stop to visit with Tadlock. She found the elderly woman sitting in a geriatric chair, soaked to her shoulders with urine. Korndorffer checked Tadlock's buttocks for bedsores but found none. Later in the day, Korndorffer again checked on the woman, who had been alert enough to remember her name. "She was still sitting in that drenched gown and that little housecoat, all afternoon."

On that same day, Korndorffer found a Mrs. Galmich soiled and wet in her bed. "The nurse just pulled the cover up and left her that way," she said.

Also on November 21, Korndorffer encountered 78-year-old Zachary Taylor. Autumn Hills admitting records indicate that he had lived with his brother one block north of Broadway in Galveston before entering the nursing home two weeks earlier with a bedsore. Taylor was sitting in a wheelchair when Korndorffer bent down to ask him how he was. "Big tears rolled down his cheeks," and Korndorffer soon found out why. "He had a big decubitus ulcer that went from hip bone to hip bone." Taylor died in Autumn Hills in April of the following year.

CHAPTER SIX

In July 1981, David Marks felt the exhilaration that comes with a victory against long odds. He had gotten Autumn Hills Nursing Home in Texas City reindicted by a Galveston County grand jury and the case was beginning to attract national notice. The more Marks worked on the case, the more convinced he was that he was doing the right thing, that there was, in fact, little room for any other course of action.

Marks was frustrated with his boss because Hury had paid so little attention to the case. Marks had subpoenaed almost all of the Autumn Hills records, a voluminous collection of dietary, medical, and financial documentation. He had conducted extensive interviews with witnesses and experts he felt were critical to the prosecution of the case. He had worked into the wee hours of the morning, researching the law as it related to criminal liability of corporations. He remembers that during this time "Hury spent no more than five minutes discussing with me the factual or legal aspects of the case. He reviewed absolutely none of these extensive records or analyses. He had absolutely no knowledge through me or my staff of volunteers of the extensive analyses of those records and the results."

Marks also felt that Hury had not spent enough time with the second grand jury. "From October 16, 1980, through March 31, 1981, Hury spent no more than ten minutes discussing with me the factual or legal aspects of the case. Again, he reviewed absolutely none of these extensive records, analyses, or witness testimony. Again, he had no knowledge through me or my staff of our findings. Although specifically invited to attend important grand jury proceedings involving crucial witnesses, Mr. Hury never attended any of the proceedings."

Marks had been secretive about his investigation of Autumn Hills. Hury had thought that all was going well; he had no reason to believe that Marks was frustrated by his seeming inattention to the case. In fact, Hury had been reassured by Marks that the situation was well in hand and his direct personal attention was not needed.

Hury had his hands full trying some major cases, including one for capital murder. By his own admission, Hury didn't like administrative duties. He had come to the Galveston County district attorney's office in 1972 because he wanted to be a great trial lawyer. Despite the fact that he had moved up in the ranks, finally being elected to the top job, his real love was in the pit, trying cases.

Marks was also financially strapped by the case and Hury's disinterest. He revealed in a 1982 affidavit,

> During the course of this three-year case I have spent approximately $3,000 of my personal funds just so as to keep our head above the water. For over a year we have had a monthly financial crisis which has caused myself and other members of this staff to reach into their own pockets. Although the immenseness of this case is beyond description, we have never been provided a secretary. Indeed, for a better part of the year, members of this staff have had to pool their money to rent a typewriter. Extensive secretarial work such as the lengthy change of venue briefs had to be sent out, with the financial burden shouldered by myself or other members of the staff.
>
> Mr. Hury had been aware of our financial condition for over nine months. As stated above, I have spoken with him, in addition to having submitted a budget and even made short presentations, in an effort to bring his attention to this matter. As a result of his inactivity I have done everything but conduct bake sales in an effort to raise funding necessary for the basic logistical support of this case. For over two years, private funding has been provided by private foundations, church organizations and concerned citizens. Mr. Hury has been aware of the receipt of such funds.

Not all of Marks's funds came from bake sales and donations. Hury had secured a grant from the Texas Prosecutor's Council in the amount of $30,000 to help defray the cost of the investigation. The funds largely helped pay expenses of paid professionals along the way. Hury had secured, as well, $25,000 from the local commissioner's court to pay for an investigator. Hury was also directly responsible for Marks's salary as well as help from the Texas attorney general's office.

At the same time, in offices on the courthouse's upper floors, James Hury was discussing lawsuits and thinking about his political future. The legal philosophies and ambitions of Marks and Hury were now on a collision course. In his isolation, Marks maintained enough contact with reality to know that he had to pay careful attention to what Hury was doing with the case. Technically, the district attorney still called the shots.

The high-powered legal talent that Marks knew he would face in prosecuting the case was being rapidly assembled by Autumn Hills. On April 4, 1981, the Austin firm of Minton, Burton, Foster, and Collins was hired to conduct the defense, after the defendants fired former Houston district attorney Carol Vance. Minton and associates were developing a powerful reputation in Texas legal circles after their defense of Texas House Speaker Billy Clayton and their involvement in Brilab, the FBI labor sting case. In addition, former Travis County prosecutors Minton and Burton had well-oiled connections in Austin. Minton is fond of saying, "We don't have any political power, don't want any. We just go down there [to the capitol building] when they're trying to pass some damn god-awful criminal law, or when somebody gets in trouble." But both men are deceptively modest about their reputations at the end of Congress Avenue, where the statehouse stands.

Minton and Burton are two of a handful of blue-chip criminal defense attorneys in Texas. Of the legitimately famous members of the criminal bar, only a few have national reputations on a par with the legendary but aging Percy Foreman, Foreman protégé Dick De-Guerin, Odessa's Warren Burnett, Houston's Richard "Racehorse" Haynes, and Haynes protégé Mike Ramsey. Interestingly, Minton and Burton still do not limit the practice of their ten-man firm on Austin's Guadalupe Street to criminal matters. Half their business comes from the practice of civil law.

Minton and Burton are inseparable friends, maintaining close

ties both in and out of the courtroom. Theirs is the kind of relationship that comes from shared experiences, triumphs and losses.
Where Charles Burton is quiet and cerebral, Minton is an outgoing
man whose foibles make him almost comical. Observers say that
Burton is the brains behind the firm. Minton is quick to perpetuate
that myth. In truth, they are intellectual equals, possessed of razor-
sharp minds and an almost uncanny sense of timing. In Minton's
case, his ample intellectual talent is compounded by a highly developed propensity for theater. To Roy Minton, the world is a stage,
and the courtroom is simply a place to practice that craft. While
Burton is at home playing Hamlet, Minton is equally pleased por-
traying Falstaff.

Roy Qullin Minton was born in Dallas on November 9, 1931, but
grew up in nearby Denton. Both his parents worked for newspapers, as had his grandfather. Minton's father worked for both the
Hearst chain and Scripps-Howard before his career was cut short
when he drowned on an outing to Galveston. Minton's mother
worked for the *Denton Record-Chronicle* from the time she was seventeen until her early twenties. Later she wrote a syndicated column of poetry and features from New York and Europe.

Minton's parents knew each other in Denton, and when his
mother ran out of money while traveling in Kentucky and Ten-
nessee, Minton says, she wired his father that "I owe $400 plus my
bills. Here is the price of my train ticket. You send me the money
and we'll get married." The two were wed shortly thereafter at the
Little Church Around the Corner in New York.

Minton's mother had a profound effect on his life. She had traveled to the beat of a different drummer for a woman in the late
twenties. According to her son, she had a realistic and worldly attitude toward life. Perhaps it was the natural cynicism of a journalist,
but it rubbed off. Today, little is sacred to Minton, who produces a
steady stream of one-liners directed at anyone who will listen. He
is a complex study in contrasts. He, like many of his generation, is
worldly wise yet somehow innocent of the morality of the eighties.
Perhaps that is the influence of his mother and his North Texas up-
bringing. Perhaps, under the worldly facade, Roy Minton is a prude.

After high school, Minton joined the military and he served as a
fighter pilot. He stayed in uniform from age 19 to 25. The glib-
tongued Minton even managed to pass his physical for flight training, although the examining doctor knew he had less-than-perfect

vision. After his stint in the service, he attended North Texas State University in Denton, graduated with honors, then went on to the University of Texas Law School in Austin, where he was a member of Phi Delta Phi, the law honor society. After law school Minton went to work for the Travis County district attorney's office, where he first collaborated with Charles Burton. The two left the D.A.'s office and went to work for Austin attorney Perry Jones. After Jones's death, they changed the name of his law firm to Minton and Burton.

Burton also spent time in the military, joining the Navy two months out of high school. He served as an interior electrician on the aircraft carrier *Valley Forge*, but never saw combat. After the service he attended college, then the University of Texas Law School.

Both Minton and Burton are ardent Travis County liberal Democrats. Travis County liberals are distinct from other Democrats, more liberal, more outspoken, more knowledgeable of state government—thanks to their proximity to the capitol—and sometimes less practical than other left-leaning Democrats in traditionally conservative Texas.

The two built their law practice on Austin's Guadalupe Street slowly. When they came into the business, it was hard for a young lawyer to make a living. It was particularly hard for a young criminal lawyer to get by. Perhaps it is the fear of hard times as much as anything else that keeps Minton and Burton, two of the best criminal lawyers in the state, involved in the civil-practice game. Some recent cases have propelled them to the top of their profession.

Roy Minton and Charles Burton always come as a team when a major case comes to trial. Together, they represented former Texas House Speaker Clayton in the FBI Brilab case, as well as cowboy clothing millionaire Rex Cauble in a major narcotics case. They have earned sizable fees in those cases and in less celebrated legal jousts. In true Texas fashion, they sometimes fly to court in their own plane. And although Minton says the tariff for the Autumn Hills defense sometimes ran to as much as $70,000 a week, the two lawyers assert that the lengthy case was so time-consuming that it cost them money in fees from other clients.

When the price of legal poker skyrocketed with the hiring of Minton and Burton in April 1981, David Marks began to feel the heat. Most Galveston district judges had distanced themselves from the Autumn Hills case. As practical men, the judges knew the case would require months to try because of the massive collection of evidence and the large number of witnesses that had been called. Additionally, the case was politically volatile. George Mitchell, part owner of Autumn Hills, was the wealthiest man in Galveston County. Both Hury and Minton scouted around for a visiting judge to hear the case. Both men would find a soulmate in Beaumont, state judge Larry Gist. Hury describes him as some men would their fathers. Minton, more practical, simply talks of Gist's judicial abilities.

One of the first things the new attorneys for Autumn Hills did was ask for a change of venue, Minton charging that a fair and impartial jury could not be found in Galveston County. The case had indeed generated a huge amount of publicity in the *Houston Post* and the *Houston Chronicle*, as well as on Houston television stations. The usually sedate *Galveston Daily News* had even given the case greater than normal coverage. Galveston bureau chief Steve Olafson of the *Post* had taken a personal interest in the case, and Marks credits him and others with keeping the case alive at times when public interest seemed to wane. Because of the heavy schedule of the lawyers, the motion to move the trial was not heard for another ten months.

To counter Minton's motion for a change of venue, the state presented the results of a poll conducted by Rice University sociologist Dr. Chad Gordon, which showed that respondents thought coverage of the case in the local and area media was balanced and that few people even had Autumn Hills on their minds. Hury presented several members of the Galveston community who stated that the nursing home chain could receive a fair trial. The Beaumont judge ruled in favor of the state. The trial was to be held in Galveston County.

After the venue hearing, Gist, Hury, and Minton met in the visiting judge's chambers. Gist suggested a plea bargain. At the time, neither the state nor the defense had discussed such a deal.

On May 20, 1982, Hury and Minton agreed in principle that a plea bargain could be struck. Hury wanted the corporation to plead guilty to at least one felony count; further, he wanted settlements in all the civil suits filed by families of Autumn Hills patients, with a suitable fine to be paid by the corporation. Minton, in turn, wanted charges against all the indicted officers of Autumn Hills

Convalescent Centers dismissed without guilty pleas. He was willing to settle for a fine in the neighborhood of $50,000. Seven months later, Marks learned that Hury and Minton had struck a deal when he read about it in the *Dallas Times Herald*. Marks had attended a meeting in the district attorney's law library earlier where Hury had made it clear to his staff that a plea bargain was a likely route for the case to follow. In fact, Marks believes that Hury kept him on the case only to blunt the criticism that the Autumn Hills grand jury had leveled at the district attorney and to provide leverage with Minton to strike a plea bargain.

The case was now three years old and needed resolution. Two grand juries had spent long hours hearing testimony, and David Marks had worked on nothing else during those years. He was determined that the trial that could propel nursing home reform into the history books not be plea-bargained away. In the case's early going, Marks was just another hungry young lawyer seeking cases that would accelerate his career. But by May 1982, his personal involvement had become so deeply entrenched that what had begun as a complex and important case was now a compelling mission, a calling. Marks was by now a zealot.

Hury didn't believe that the Autumn Hills case belonged in the criminal justice system. He thought that the families of the Autumn Hills patients deserved something for the pain and suffering their loved ones had endured, yet he didn't believe the criminal laws on the books fit the crime with which the defendants were charged. It was much simpler, much cleaner and more precise, Hury thought, to settle the matter in the civil courts.

Marks continued to work obsessively on the case, begging and borrowing resources from any source he could find. Volunteers came and went from the first-floor office suite. Some stayed permanently. Nursing students, a sociologist from Rice University in Houston, a former legislative aide, all worked without pay to help the young prosecutor with his mission. In the meantime, communication between Hury and Marks became more and more strained.

Negotiations continued as Autumn Hills' civil attorneys from the celebrated Houston firm of Fulbright and Jaworski settled civil suits in amounts finally totaling in excess of $300,000. The settlement amounts were substantial, considering that no one argued that the patients of Autumn Hills were at the end of their productive lives. Betty Kyle, whose 86-year-old mother, Rosa Whited, had allegedly been brutally beaten by an Autumn Hills nursing aide, settled out of court, believing Marks when he told her that Hury would take the case to trial. She said she was given assurances that the case would be prosecuted.

Galveston Island is a hotbed of rumor, gossip, and innuendo. The closed, island mentality produces a rumor mill, which in turn multiplies in the city's coffee shops, bars, and bistros. Outsiders are often the hapless victims of the gossip, which makes its rounds as often with foundation as without. Islanders naturally distrust newcomers, who require acclimatizing to become a part of the Island's process, though eventually newcomers are embraced with the natural warmth of Galveston's citizens. David Marks, who was stirring up trouble for powerful friends of the Island, people who were listened to and respected, received the full measure of the rumor system. The young attorney was branded "crazy," and the rumor mill made no distinction between an obsessive but well-intentioned crusade and psychosis. Furthermore, only bits and pieces of the horror story unfolding in Marks's files had come out. When Islanders were told by people they respected, people who had done so much for the Island, that the nursing home had run a good shop and that an insane attorney was ruining some mighty fine people, their natural inclination was to believe that such was the case. Marks had stirred up a hornet's nest, and now he was fighting part of the power structure alone.

At the same time, James Hury got tired of being district attorney. He had been in battle after battle in the courthouse and had powerful enemies of his own.

Hury was also disgusted with the criminal justice system itself. No matter how hard his office tried, felons were beating the system. Hury had his eyes on more-fulfilling work in a higher office, such as the U.S. House of Representatives seat held by Congressman Jack Brooks, whose district encompassed Galveston County. The aging Brooks was mistakenly seen by some as vulnerable. Like many in Congress, Brooks had become more or less a permanent resident of Washington. He seldom came home to his district to cultivate the voters who had returned him to office again and again for more than thirty years. Despite Brooks's congressional seniority, some felt he had not let the folks at home know enough about his importance in Washington.

Hury coveted the seat, but he was a realist. He was also prudent in consulting savvy local politicians and his supporters to see if he should make the race. But an Island-born politician, state representative E. Douglas McLeod, took the bait to run against Brooks. Hury quickly announced his candidacy for McLeod's seat in the Texas Legislature and soon left his problems in the courthouse behind. Austin politics was more to his liking, and lawyers who also serve in the Texas Legislature often develop lucrative law practices. To Hury, it was coincidental that Roy Minton was a powerful lawyer from Austin. And besides, Minton was infinitely more enjoyable social company than David Marks.

As July came, Hury became more convinced that the case should be plea-bargained. His position was reinforced by two rulings of Judge Gist. Minton had questioned some legal technicalities in the indictments in an inch-thick set of motions. Marks received the document on a Thursday. He called his boss, James Hury, to tell him that he couldn't possibly answer Minton's motions for a hearing the following Monday. Hury told him to do the best he could. Marks called his friend Jim Vollers in Austin and pleaded with the veteran attorney to help. The two worked all weekend, and Monday Vollers appeared in Galveston with Marks. Marks believed that Hury was furious with him for calling in Vollers. Hury was, in fact, glad to see the Austin lawyer, despite his surprise appearance in Galveston. Minton's motions to quash the indictments asked a multitude of legal questions. Did the failure of Autumn Hills to provide contracted-for services to its patients constitute an act, as required by the law involving the acts of a corporation, or an omission? Minton questioned whether fraud is an act dangerous to the health of the patients. He questioned whether the omitted duties were required by the law. He wanted to know if the deaths occurred during the furtherance of the alleged felonies. The Austin attorney also questioned a provision of the state penal code.

There were no legal precedents to guide Gist in answering those technical questions. Gist would be creating legal precedent if he ruled in favor of the state. Hury believed that law should be made in the legislature, not in the courthouse, and that alone was a persuasive reason to plea-bargain the case. Marks believed just as strongly that the case should be tried in order to set a precedent for future cases similar to Autumn Hills. Marks argued that omissions in the care of patients were acts.

On July 9, 1982, Gist ruled against the state, in effect quashing the second grand jury's indictments. He reasoned that "by writing two specific statutes, one defining the term act, and the other defining the term omission, the legislature clearly meant for the two to be considered separately." Marks and his volunteers were back to square one on portions of the indictments. The indictments would have to be rewritten and submitted to a third grand jury. Gist did, however, give the state thirty days to get a ruling from the court of appeals on the validity of his decision. Hury chose not to take the case to the court of appeals, although Marks and Vollers made strong arguments to the contrary.

Gist also surprised everyone by exercising a rare judicial prerogative on the state district court level. He ruled that the state law governing acts by a corporation was unconstitutional. Gist thought the law was vague and did not specify which employees should be held responsible for performing or omitting particular duties. He thought the law gave too much freedom to the prosecution in determining which employees should or should not be prosecuted.

Hury believed that the case was over. He did not call for a third grand jury or appeal the Beaumont judge's ruling. Hury finally had the pesky Autumn Hills case out of his hair. he could finish his term as district attorney without leaving office in the midst of a complicated and controversial piece of litigation.

Hury had handily won the Democratic primary for state representative, and he was unopposed in the November general election. During the spring campaign, it had appeared to voters that Hury was actively prosecuting the Autumn Hills case. Critics charge that after he found himself unopposed in the general election, Hury let the case die a graceful death.

During the campaign, the nursing home industry's political action committee made a clumsy move. While Hury was still sitting as D.A. and prosecuting Autumn Hills Convalescent Centers, the PAC tried to give him a campaign contribution. To his credit, Hury never received the money, and he was furious when news reports later said that he had.

Marks continued to prepare for trial. He was running the Autumn Hills case as an ongoing investigation without funds. Hury had told him, Marks says, that funds would be sought, but Marks later found that the district attorney had requested no further funding. Marks also found that as summer dragged on, rumors of a plea bargain continued.

During the discovery process of the trial, in which the lawyers reveal the elements of their cases, Marks fought hard for his position. Minton later called the young attorney's behavior during the meetings "petulant and angry." Marks was indeed angry. He was also far outgunned by the older and more experienced lawyers who had now come into the case. Marks suffered from a short temper that often boiled just beneath his surface demeanor. He grew angrier at Hury, whom he saw throwing away years of his work. Why, he asked himself, couldn't he make Hury see the importance of the case? He saw his conflict with Hury as a mental chess game, a joust, with his superior.

Tom Sartwelle was an insurance defense lawyer and medical expert with Fulbright and Jaworski, hired by the nursing home's insurance company to handle some of the civil suits stemming from the case. Minton thought that his own knowledge of the medical field was inadequate to mount a convincing defense, and Sartwelle was known in the profession as a tenacious adversary. His knowledge of medicolegal practice was widely respected. A loner in the large Houston law firm built by former Watergate special prosecutor Leon Jaworski, Tommy Sartwelle was an opponent most lawyers dreaded going up against in the courtroom. As his assistant, Sartwelle brought with him Gail Friend, a former nurse who had taught her trade at a state university in North Texas. The nursing aspects of the case would perhaps be the most important factor for the defense. Friend, a petite woman in her early forties, was just what the doctor ordered. Not only did she help Minton, Burton, and Sartwelle by doing research at the firm but she also attended law school at night.

Minton called on the Fulbright and Jaworski team for help because Sartwelle and Friend had already been through most of the medical records in the case. Sartwelle had told Minton that the case was not winnable by the state, and Minton passed that opinion on to Hury. A meeting was set up in local counsel John McEldowney's office in Galveston, where the district attorney would get to hear the Fulbright and Jaworski attorney's opinion of the case as a lawyer. As always, Sartwelle was prepared. As Hury listened to Sartwelle, his faith in the ability of David Marks was seriously shaken.

Bob Gay, the president of Autumn Hills, was sparing no expense in the defense of his corporation and its employees. When Minton decided that he had a problem representing Cassandra "Sandy" Canlas, he called an old friend from Brilab days, Mike Ramsey, a youthful Houston criminal defense lawyer who had once practiced with the legendary Richard "Racehorse" Haynes. Ramsey would represent only Canlas, while Minton and Burton represented the rest of the individual defendants. Sartwelle and Friend would eventually join the two Austin lawyers on the criminal side of the case because Minton and Burton were so impressed with their work. Sartwelle would eventually represent the corporation itself. Gay was footing a bill that would run to half a million dollars before pretrial activity was finished, with Sartwelle and Friend working full time on the case from the day they were hired.

In Hury's opinion, Tom Sartwelle's assertions of what could be proved were "devastating." But Marks had spent a great deal of time on the medical evidence of the case and didn't have a high opinion of Sartwelle's boasting, which Hury found so impressive. Marks was impressed with Sartwelle's credentials, but he thought that the Houston lawyer's medical opinions of the Autumn Hills case were unsound. Marks thought Hury had ignored too much of the case, and he had little respect for Hury's medical opinions. Yet the D.A. was prepared to accept a guilty plea to a lesser charge than murder.

Marks invited the district attorney to watch a videotape of his expert witnesses. Hury watched the tape with Marks present. He would later say that Hury spent more time with the defense lawyers during the discovery meeting than he had previously spent on the entire prosecution case, much less meeting with his own prosecutor, Marks. And Marks believed that Hury knew too little about the case to make any crucial decisions. Hury rejoined that he had read reams of documents and looked at tapes of expert witnesses. Hury knew that a good lawyer can usually produce expert witnesses to counter his opponent's experts. It is also likely that the district attorney believed in the defense attorneys and their million dollars worth of briefings and information more than he did in young David Marks.

Marks's hopes rose and fell like the tide in the summer and fall of 1982. After Hury's election to the legislature in November, the district attorney told Marks that the possibility of a plea bargain was fading. Hury said the same to the local newspaper. But Judge Gist had Hury's ear and clearly did not want a drawn-out trial. Marks was relieved when he read the newspaper account of Hury's statement. His case, no matter how convoluted, still had a chance of going to trial. It was only a waiting game, until James Hury left office, Marks thought.

On December 14, 1982, Hury and Minton made the plea bargain public in a story in the *Dallas Times Herald*. The plea bargain would take place on December 17, in the final days of Hury's term. When Marks read the story, he was devastated. He engaged Houston attorneys Joe Archer and Paul Waldner to file a petition for a restraining order, on grounds that the plea bargain was not in the best interests of Galveston County. The lawyers charged that Hury lacked sufficient knowledge of the case and further that the district attorney had accepted campaign contributions from the nursing home political action committee and a defense lawyer PAC. Marks and his attorneys charged that Hury had violated professional ethics by not avoiding the appearance of impropriety.

Marks brought the petition to the court of Judge Ed J. Harris, who had presided over the original Autumn Hills grand jury. Harris at that time was the presiding civil judge in the Galveston County courthouse, and Marks figured that since his injunction request was a civil matter, Harris rather than Gist should hear the petition. Two members of the grand juries and Betty Kyle, the daughter of the woman beaten at Autumn Hills, quickly joined Marks in his petition. Harris heard the petition on an emergency basis on December 16, 1982.

Marks filed the petition hoping to delay the plea bargain until Hury left office in fifteen days. Mike Guarino, Hury's first assistant, had been elected D.A. in the November balloting, and Marks was willing to take his chances with the young district attorney with whom he got along well. If Harris would grant a temporary restraining order for just long enough, until Hury was in the Texas Legislature and out of the courthouse, the case might still be saved and perhaps go to trial.

In a bizarre hearing in Harris's court, Marks and his attorneys made their initial presentation. The judge then turned to James Hury, who asked permission to introduce into the courtroom John McEldowney, the local counsel who was helping Minton in the defense of Autumn Hills. McEldowney, who worked for one of Galveston's three blue-chip law firms, requested that Harris require Marks to go before Judge Gist with the petition. McEldowney, representing the nursing home Hury had supposedly been prosecuting for years, then sat down next to the district attorney. Both men shot cold stares across the room at Hury's employee and fellow prosecutor, David Marks.

All of this was not lost on the press. Something extraordinary was happening that day in the usually quiet courthouse. Hury was barely in control as he stood before Harris after Marks's charges had been presented. He told Harris, "This whole process is so bizarre as to render me almost speechless on the subject." The district attorney offered to meet privately with the citizens suing to stop the plea bargain and hear their "hopes and dreams." He said, "I cannot adequately inform the court of my anger at the insinuation that, as elected district attorney, there is some impropriety in this operation." He told the judge, "You will save me the most difficult decision I have ever had to make. . . . To be relieved of this burden is something I welcome."

Hury also informed Harris that no plea bargain had actually been accepted. Certainly, in light of Marks's petition, the papers had not been signed. But a deal had in fact been struck between Minton and Hury. The judge ruled that Marks's petition had no standing in his court. After the session, Hury called Marks into his office and summarily fired him. Afterward, Marks was surrounded by reporters outside, where he confirmed that he had been fired.

But he was not about to give up, and he immediately asked the Texas Court of Civil Appeals for a ten-day delay to the plea bargain. Marks was firing his last shots at the Autumn Hills defendants, and he knew it.

Hury had always maintained decent though reserved relations with the press. After firing Marks, he thought he could cut his losses by holding a news conference in his office. In front of the assembled media representatives he denied receiving any campaign contributions from the Texas Nursing Home Association Political Action Committee. Interestingly, at his side, just minutes after Marks had said in court that Hury had received such contributions, stood Cecil Barslowe, chairman of the nursing home association. Barslowe said that no such check was ever given to Hury. Hury did, however, state that he had accepted campaign donations from two PACs made up of lawyers who counted in their membership attorneys from both sides of the Autumn Hills case.

Hury also confirmed to the media that he had fired Marks. "I don't think it is proper for any employee to file a lawsuit in the manner he filed this, . . . to swear to somebody that I have done an illegal act, which is a cold-blooded lie."

Marks had a few salvos of his own left. Charles Wiley had been undersheriff of Galveston County, and since an ill-conceived FBI sting operation, members of the local sheriff's department had done their best to make Hury's life miserable. Always ready to hear anything damaging about the district attorney, Wiley had met Minton for the first time at a Galveston yacht club. Most of the yacht club clientele couldn't care less about boating. It is a place they go to see and be seen, a place for social contacts in a posh atmosphere. The undersheriff was greatly impressed with the Austin lawyer, whom he knew by reputation. The men had drinks.

Wiley said in a later affidavit that Minton told him the plea bargain was a backroom deal.

On or about 16 June, this year, at about 8:00 PM I had occasion to visit the Bob Smith Yacht Club, whereupon I met John McEldowney, a local attorney, who introduced me to Mr. Roy Minton, an attorney from Austin, Texas (whom I had not met previously). Mr. Minton appeared to have had a few drinks. Mr. Minton took me aside to another table, whereupon he advised me that he would be interested in hearing about the "sting" operation, an attempt by the FBI to offer and confer a bribe to Sheriff Joe Max Taylor. In that attempt an undercover FBI agent was arrested. Mr. Minton seemed pleased that someone had embarrassed the FBI, and wanted to know how we did it. Mr. Minton ordered both of us a drink and we talked about the sting for a few minutes. Then Mr. Minton asked me about Mr. James Hury, the Galveston County Criminal District Attorney, and said that he understood that Mr. Hury and I did not see eye to eye. Mr. Minton said that he was one of the attorneys defending the Autumn Hills Nursing Home. He further stated that he had defended many public officials, including Billy Clayton (former Speaker of the Texas House) and that he was in town for a meeting regarding disposition of the Autumn Hills case. It was my understanding that Mr. Minton was to meet with Mr. Hury. It was obvious that Mr. Minton intended to remind Mr. Hury again at this meeting of Minton's importance in Texas and what he could do either for or against Mr. Hury at the State Capital.

Mr. Minton stated that James Hury had made commitments regarding the Autumn Hills case, and that he (Minton) would see to it that Hury lived up to those commitments. Specifically, he said, "When I make a deal with somebody, I intend for them to live up to their end of the bargain, and he will!"

He went on to say that he was a man of his word and that he expected James Hury to be also.

Mr. Minton reiterated the idea that he was a person with a great deal of stroke in Austin and that Hury would need him when he got there because Hury had little or no influence in the Capital.

Minton then said, "If he turns me around on this deal, I'll pull the rug out from under him. I have already told him to fire Marks. I can render Hury ineffective in Austin."

It was clear to me that a backroom deal had been reached with respect to the disposition of the Autumn Hills cases and that the fix was on. From the conversation I had no doubt that this deal involved more than an ordinary plea bargain.

There is little doubt that everyone involved in the defense of the Autumn Hills case exerted every effort, pulled every string, applied whatever pressure could be applied to end the nightmare for Bob Gay, his family, his company, and his employees. But why would Minton bare his soul to an obscure deputy sheriff in a posh bar? Minton stoutly denies that he used political influence to pressure Hury into agreement. Hury also denies that the deal was anything other than what it appeared on the surface, a compromise between a tough district attorney and an equally tough criminal defense lawyer.

When Wiley's affidavit was released to the press, Hury's life became even more miserable. Marks had his former boss on the run. The press was determined that the Autumn Hills plea bargain would not stand. Hury was frustrated in particular by the *Houston Post*. The newspaper had run a front-page story about the Autumn Hills case. Hury says he was never interviewed for the story. He was, after all, the district attorney and was in reality in charge of trying the case. At the time, Steve Olafson, the *Post* reporter assigned to the case was on vacation.

Most of the civil suits brought by Autumn Hills patient families had been settled. Sartwelle had, in fact, paid victims' families $300,000. Hury was comfortable that all that he could do had been done. The civil law had redressed the grievances for the pain and suffering of the nursing home's residents far better than the criminal law ever would. Hury had been told by civil attorneys that it was unlikely that the nursing home's insurance company would go higher. In his own mind James Hury had fought for the families. Hury saw Marks as a stumbling block in recovering anything for those who had sued Autumn Hills.

At two in the afternoon on December 27, 1982, a scant four days before Hury's term was to end, the agreement was signed. A civil attorney told Gist that his requirement that the suits be settled had been met. Autumn Hills Convalescent Centers would plead no contest to involuntary manslaughter in the death of one victim. The corporation would be fined $100,000 for the expenses of the investigation. The court would not find the defendants guilty but would, instead, defer adjudication for ten years. If all the defendants kept their noses clean, the Autumn Hills case would be over at the end of the period.

Hury was already firing shots at his former employee. He told the *Houston Chronicle,* "The arrogance of Mr. Marks is beyond my comprehension. Mr. Marks knows 100 percent of 50 percent of the lawsuit." He said he had "spent more than enough time in discussions with my staff and defense lawyers" to conclude that a plea bargain was the best way to resolve the case. He also attacked Wiley, the undersheriff. "He hates my guts," Hury told the *Galveston Daily News.*

Hury also used the press as a forum to present his views on the statutes involved in the case. In a story in the *Houston Chronicle,* Hury asked, "How are we going to prove that administrators and nurses were deciding to not turn or bathe patients, not feed them, not give medicine, all because they wanted to cut costs? I never heard Marks or anyone say we could suggest they intended to bring about these deaths."

The following day, Hury told the *Galveston Daily News,* "The law of this case has never been undertaken. Here is a judge that said those indictments are no good. There is nothing that showed we could charge them as we charged them. The problems of going back to square one and the chance we had of succeeding did not justify the burden on the taxpayers. I am convinced beyond any doubt that we would never ever be able to sustain an indictment (for murder)." Hury concluded, "If we had brought all of those people in here, convicted them and sentenced them to death, . . . there would be no reform. We could not have brought about any meaningful change."

The district attorney told Steve Olafson, then Island bureau chief for the *Houston Post,* that Judge Gist could bankrupt the corporation "with the stroke of a pen" if they were found guilty of any wrongdoing during the ten-year period. Hury also said, "I know what went on at the nursing home, and I hate them for it."

A few days later, Hury told Tom Curtis of the *Dallas Times Herald,* "I think this is a great victory." He added, "As a result of some hard work, the county has been spared a great deal of effort, because we've been able to have a corporation come in and admit that they killed someone recklessly."

A week later, Hury lambasted Marks to reporter Joel Kirkpatrick of the *Galveston Daily News.* The new state representative said that Marks had misled the grand jury by "telling them he could do something he couldn't do." Hury said that the indictments were "the most unprofessional and incompetent indictments I have seen." Hury also accused Marks of using the families of the patients and of costing them potential civil damage awards by getting them involved in the criminal case without advising them as to their rights to damages in a civil suit. Hury said, "The statute of limitations ran out during the three years Marks investigated the case."

Hury also told Kirkpatrick, "Marks was a man who had tried only seven felony cases during all his tenure with the district attorney's office." Marks says he tried 27 felony jury trials during his first thirteen months in the felony division. Hury went on to say that he had lost the media war waged by "Marks and Company." Hury said, "The press covered him while he's sitting there waving the bloody bedsheet and screaming murder and I'm sitting somewhere else saying, of course, it is spectacular, but it is not murder. There is no wonder they went to his press conferences."

Kirkpatrick also quoted Hury as saying that Marks's "fantasy world, his ego trip of being the first lawyer to try a corporation for murder, fell apart when it came up against the cold, hard facts in a courtroom." Even though Jim Vollers, a former appeals court judge, had redrawn the indictments, Gist threw them out, Hury told Kirkpatrick.

Also in the local newspaper, Hury appealed to the taxpayers, showing them how much money he had saved them and saying, in effect, that Autumn Hills had more money than the state was willing to spend. "What we were facing was a minimum of four months for the state to put on its case, at least that for the defense, two years for appeals, then another possible 35 indictments." He told Kirkpatrick that the estimated cost to the taxpayers was at least $500,000 and "two expert witnesses from the other side for every one that Marks could produce. The compromise settlement of the case was the only thing we could do and salvage something for the families." As a practical man, Hury realized that the cost of justice could be high. As an idealist, Marks decided that nursing home reform and what he saw as justice were worth the cost.

In April 1983, Hury was still blasting Marks, but his comments to Wayne King of the *New York Times* are more revealing about the district attorney's thoughts when the case first came to his attention. "In the early days of this thing, not only myself but others in the office were swept up in the horror of it, and we set about to try to see if we could prove that these people knowingly and intentionally brought about these people's deaths. In other words, before I got involved in the law of it, I got involved in the horror of it." Finally, Hury told the *Times,* "Marks basically was not capable of undertaking that kind of investigation."

But Hury's successor had plenty of faith in Marks's abilities. And new Galveston D.A. Mike Guarino had a strong ally in recently elected Texas attorney general Jim Mattox. The former Dallas congressman had run a populist campaign on, among other issues, nursing home reform. Marks didn't know it in the closing days of 1982, as he was being lambasted in the press by Hury, but he had "the people's lawyer," as Mattox liked to call himself, on his side.

CHAPTER SEVEN

David Marks had given up as he boarded the flight to Washington at Houston Intercontinental Airport. He had spent almost all of his considerable energy and had probably destroyed his career in the process. He now lived alone, separated from his wife, and worse, he didn't even have a job or an income that would pay the rent on his apartment. Marks had found comfort in moving into the apartment, putting behind him the life he had led for such a short while as a married man. Almost every day, he worked out his frustrations by jogging along Galveston's famed Seawall Boulevard, that ten-mile stretch of concrete that protects the city from the ravages of the Gulf of Mexico.

It wasn't so much that finding a job would be difficult. After all, he was by now a somewhat experienced trial lawyer, yet he had spent more than three years on the same case and had lost. He had not only lost but had also not even been able to get the case into court. That was the devastating thing. Marks knew that if a jury heard the horrible eyewitness testimony of the atrocities at Autumn Hills, a history-making conviction was possible. James Hury, Larry Gist, and Roy Minton had changed all of that. Marks respected the legal sophistry that had been employed against him. It was over, and Marks was prepared to put the case behind him, but he continued to think about what had gone wrong.

It was flattering to receive the invitation from John Heinz. Marks had known that the case was attracting national attention. Speaking to the Senate Special Committee on Aging would be his final shot at the case. It was the end of Autumn Hills for him. Perhaps he could in his small way draw attention to the problem of what was happening to old people in nursing homes. He was prepared to try.

Marks's load that day, on board the airplane, was bulky. With him he carried the array of charts he had developed over the course of the case. Those charts, he found, showed the facts to anyone who chose to look at them, in graphic detail. The charts buttressed his arguments. If he could not convict Autumn Hills in the courts, perhaps he could convict the corporation before a Senate committee and, with a little luck, in the national press.

As he sat in the committee room waiting for testimony to begin, he saw familiar faces in the crowd: Roy Minton, attorney for Autumn Hills; Bob Gay, president and founder of the chain; Ron Pohlmeyer, vice president and general manager of the corporation; and Mattie Locke, nursing consultant, a title that belied her real duties as director of nursing for the seventeen homes. Gay had received permission to speak to the committee. Even Marks's final shot would not be left unanswered.

Marks spoke to the committee with quiet passion. The three members present, Senator John Heinz, Senator John Melcher, and Senator Bill Bradley, listened with interest as the young attorney started from the beginning, telling of the Autumn Hills case and how it had grown. As Senate committee members do, they interrupted the testimony from time to time with probing questions about the case. Marks answered as he painted a horrible picture of what had happened in the nursing home. At the end, the senators gave him a heartfelt thanks for his testimony. Later, they barely gave Bob Gay the time of day. It was over for David Marks as he boarded the plane for Texas. He had fired his shot. The Autumn Hills case was history.

Unknown to him, things had been happening in Texas while he was in the nation's capital. Mike Guarino had received word from the state attorney general's office that the plea bargain could not stand. The experts in Austin believed that the unadjudicated ten-year probation for the corporation was impossible to enforce. In conferences with the new district attorney in Galveston, the state's attorneys were encouraging Guarino to reopen the case and present the evidence to yet another grand jury.

On the day he took office, Mike Guarino was picketed by opponents of the plea bargain. The protesters, carrying signs outside the Galveston County Courthouse, consisted of church groups and

Dr. Richard Campbell's nursing home reform group. Guarino had been saved by Hury's eleventh-hour decision to close the Autumn Hills case. Guarino, however, knew that his predecessor's decision had not been a popular one.

The attorney general's opinion had also come to him in written form. The opinion said that deferred adjudication is a form of probation and a corporation cannot be given probation. Marks's position, unknown to him, had been upheld. Guarino, in light of the opinion, asked Judge Gist to find the corporation guilty.

Bob Gay and the others who had been indicted had not felt good about things since the plea bargain. None of them genuinely felt that they were guilty of anything, and the plea bargain had cast a shadow on their corporation, their individual lives, and their careers. Gay, Gay's wife, Pohlmeyer, Mattie Locke, and Virginia Wilson asked Minton what could be done.

Mattox had offered the opinion that a guilty plea by the corporation could mean a loss of medicaid funds. Such a plea might also mean a forfeiture of the corporation's charter. Gay instructed Minton to withdraw the plea bargain. Gay knew that by doing so, his corporate officers could be reindicted for murder. Gay told Minton, "If they are going to indict these people, I want them to indict me too." In the previous indictments, the president of Autumn Hills had escaped facing trial.

When Marks returned from Washington, his phone was ringing. It was Guarino calling to tell him that the attorney general's office wanted to talk to him. Marks had by now resolved to put Autumn Hills behind him. He had to think of his future. His family had been worried that the case was occupying too much of his career. Out of courtesy as much as anything else, he called the attorney general's office. He was told to be on the next plane to Austin.

In the state capital, Marks met with Mattox and his men. He was told that the new attorney general wanted to reopen the Autumn Hills case and furthermore that Mattox was convinced that the case could be won. Marks was not absolutely sold on what the men in Austin were telling him. He had been burned by Autumn Hills, burned badly, and he was reluctant to face again the team that he knew would be assembled against him. Furthermore, Marks didn't want to play second fiddle to any other lawyer if he came back. Jim Mattox was an ambitious, headline-grabbing politician. If Marks was to come back, he alone would call the shots. Mattox agreed that

Marks would be in charge of the case.

On February 11, 1983, Mattox issued a press release and announced that he had appointed Marks as an assistant attorney general. Marks had been hired to concentrate on the Autumn Hills case. The attorney general's office would assist Guarino in bringing the nursing home chain to trial. Mattox met with reporters and told them, "I am going into the investigation with the intention of convicting the corporation of murder and perhaps some of the officers and employees for murder." Mattox also committed $250,000 in state funds to the case. Two attorneys were hired to help Marks prepare to take Autumn Hills to court. The attorney general estimated that it would take an additional six months to bring fresh indictments.

Marks plunged into his work again, barely breaking stride to reorganize his office. He mobilized his team of volunteers and added to the team. Finally he had the support to really prosecute the case. A key ingredient added to the new team by Mattox was Jim Vollers, a career state's attorney brought into the case as special prosecutor. Vollers was now in private practice.

Vollers was new to private practice. He had spent most of his career working for the state. For nine years the balding lawyer had worked as state's attorney, a unique office in the Texas legal system. His job had been to handle appeals to the Texas Court of Criminal Appeals. He was appointed judge of the court of criminal appeals by a law-enforcement-minded Republican governor. Unfortunately for Vollers, he served only one year. He was soon defeated by Democrat Sam Houston Clinton. The Autumn Hills case was a windfall for his law practice. The case was bound to take months, if not years. Vollers clocked his legal fees to the state by the hour.

Marks and Vollers worked well together. Marks was comfortable having the more experienced lawyer at his side as the case was prepared for presentation to yet another grand jury. Vollers was thorough and meticulous. His years of appellate work had shown him that a good case can fall through the cracks because of sloppy pretrial work. He was determined that no such thing would happen in this landmark case. Vollers was also astonished by the massive amount of work Marks had put in on the case and the massive amount of evidence the young prosecutor had gathered against the nursing home chain and the individuals the team hoped to indict.

The older man had helped Marks earlier in the case, so he was not totally unfamiliar with what had to be done as he mounted his attack on the pages of records that had to be checked and re-checked if the case was to go anywhere. Marks in turn worked even harder on his projects, studying how and when the Autumn Hills patients were fed, developing the theory that the nursing home had actually caused an epidemic of bedsores. The two men hovered over experts who themselves hovered over volunteers tabulating data. In a very real sense, the computer became a prosecutorial tool for the men.

Guarino also worked closely with Marks and Vollers. The new district attorney took a much more active role in the case than did his predecessor. Guarino was a born prosecutor. Growing up in an affluent family as the son of a Houston state district court judge, he was a natural trial lawyer. As district attorney of Galveston County, he had ample opportunity to try as many cases as he liked, and he liked to try a lot of them.

Minton also regrouped his forces. This time, he and his clients were not facing a local district attorney who held a natural warmth for him and believed that law should not be made in the courtroom. Instead, Minton faced the worst possible combination: an ambitious state attorney general; a former appeals court judge and long-time friend, Jim Vollers; and the obsession of David Marks. The chance of getting indictments thrown out this time was remote. Minton would be lucky if he could get his clients off with their skins intact.

Minton wasted little time after Mattox's announcement that the case would be reopened and that Marks would go to work full time on Autumn Hills. If Bob Gay and his people wanted to clear their names in court, and it looked as if they would have ample opportunity to do so, Minton would have to assemble the best team money could buy. He called Tom Sartwelle to come to work as co-council on the case. The insurance defense lawyer had tried only one criminal case before in his entire career. Sartwelle had defended a rapist early in his career. He is proud to tell how he, as a blue-chip lawyer, made the system work for his impoverished client. The idea of working on a criminal case again was novel.

Leon Jaworski had a strong influence on Sartwelle's career. Sartwelle had enjoyed practicing law in the firm built by the former

Watergate special prosecutor. Jaworski had written in *Confession and Avoidance*, "Every young lawyer interested in trial work should start out with two or three years' experience in the practice of criminal law. Whether you prosecute or defend, you get a faster understanding of human nature and psychology in a courtroom." Few lawyers at Fulbright and Jaworski had followed the advice of the legendary lawyer who led them, Sartwelle included, but the advice was still there and it was never too late to learn.

Sartwelle did pattern himself after Jaworski in another way though. In speaking of his career, Jaworski wrote, "My clothes were conservative, never flashy." Sartwelle wore only business suits in the courtroom, surrounded by colleagues in sport coats and blazers.

Sartwelle was tough before ever entering the Autumn Hills case. A former federal prosecutor who knew Sartwelle told a reporter friend whose notes Sartwelle had subpoenaed, "For God's sake, get a lawyer and get that subpoena quashed. Don't let Tommy Sartwelle get you in a courtroom." The reporter took the lawyer's advice.

Sartwelle was tough, but was he tough enough to meet Jaworski's standards? The old man had written, "Most criminal lawyers either develop a protectively thick skin or doom themselves to a lifetime of sleeping potions and stomach remedies. No matter how the case ends, although the client may be going to prison or beyond, a lawyer is only going back to his office." Sartwelle was more inclined toward sleeping potions, stomach remedies, and a good bottle of booze now and then. He took his clients' problems to heart, and he took those problems home with him at the end of the day. Sartwelle was the kind of lawyer anybody in trouble would like to have on his side. The man worked all the time. The blue-chip lawyer knew another Jaworski maxim, "The vulnerable, not the strong, knock on an attorney's door."

Sartwelle had always been on the up side of Houston society. In Houston there is an old and cherished saying. The Houstonians say that there are two country clubs at each end of River Oaks Boulevard. At one end is the River Oaks Country Club, where the scions of Houston's petro nobility play; at the other is Lamar High School, where their children learn from each other and share what they have learned at home. Sartwelle was a product of Lamar, but he, unlike most of the others who attended school there, had another, more agrarian side to him.

His family owned the Port City Stockyards, Houston's answer to its rival to the north, the cow town of Fort Worth. His roots were on the flat prairies of Matagorda County, just north of the Coastal Bend of Texas. His family started in the cattle business there in the 1830s. One of his forebears was the first justice of the peace in that county, and his grandfather was mayor of the small coastal community of Palacios. Sartwelle himself worked on a maize farm west of the town as a boy.

After high school, Sartwelle did something unusual for a graduate of Lamar. He got married at the age of 18. He also entered the University of Texas and finished in record time. From there he went to the University of Texas Law School. Again, he was out before most of the rest of his class. He was a lawyer at the age of 23.

Sartwelle worked his way through the law firm, as most young lawyers do in large firms such as Fulbright and Jaworski, taking the menial tasks at first, then slowly moving on to cases of more importance, finally to cases where he was in charge. Yet there was something about Sartwelle that was different from his patrician colleagues. He was a loner. When the firm got together for social functions, Sartwelle was reluctant to attend. Also in trial and in the office, he didn't spend a lot of time going to lunch with other lawyers, instead staying behind to eat a small sandwich with the clerks and secretaries.

Others found him hard to get to know, hard to get along with. Another lawyer had called Sartwelle "a prick by reputation," and not without cause. He was not by any stretch of the imagination a Texas good ol' boy. He was, instead, a legal technician fanatically devoted to his work. There was little room for familiarity. Sartwelle was not without humor though. He possessed biting sarcasm and was capable of a hayseed jocularity that sometimes bordered on the grotesque. Although he spent much of his life at the other country club at the end of River Oaks Boulevard, his rural roots showed most in his humor. He was also more sheltered than most of his associates. He admits that he didn't board a commercial jet until he was in his late twenties.

The man had endearing qualities also. At 41, he was idolized by his clients. His knowledge of legal-medical information was so complete, so thorough, that he engendered faith built on his unquestionable competence. Remarkably, he says he once failed biology in school. Like most lawyers in his specialty, Sartwelle is largely self-taught.

When Sartwelle came to work on the criminal side of the Autumn Hills case, he was joined by Gail Friend, who had already been working with him on the civil suits. Friend's nursing training served her well in the law. She was the ideal assistant. Like Sartwelle, the woman lived for work. As a nurse, she had been taught to care for her patients, to bring them things when they needed them, to be fast, to work her way through life running. That prior training translated itself to Sartwelle's advantage. No matter what document the senior member of the team needed, he soon had it at his fingertips. The two worked together so closely that Friend anticipated Sartwelle's needs.

Sartwelle was cool and often aloof; Friend was warm, always smiling, eager to please. Sometimes playing second fiddle to Sartwelle aroused a fierce sense of feminine frustration in Friend. She still found herself trying to compete in a man's world. Women lawyers have made great strides toward closing the gap between their colleagues of the opposite gender. Most of those who have done so have not had to work behind such a man as Tom Sartwelle. Sartwelle believes that women often don't measure up to his standards. Friend, besides the court reporter, was the lone female in the company of ten other lawyers trying the case. Her treatment in this male-dominated group was sometimes humiliating.

The two Fulbright and Jaworski lawyers plunged into the criminal case with the characteristic thoroughness that was their trademark. They had already interviewed many of the employees of Autumn Hills in Texas City. Now they interviewed more of them. Sartwelle wired himself to record those interviews on tape. He went to the homes of black nurse's aides and sat in their living rooms with small children playing around him as their mother cooked dinner. He also stalked them to their jobs, where some of them found his presence embarrassing and a threat to their work.

Friend also left the downtown Houston office of Fulbright and Jaworski to track down anyone at all who might know anything that would help their clients. One such person was Ruth Linscomb, the sister of Elnora Breed. Mrs. Linscomb did not want to talk to the defense lawyers, yet on a cold day in January 1984 she found Gail Friend on her front porch. The elderly woman did not invite Friend into her house, but she came out on the front porch because Friend would not go away. Friend finally found her way into the home.

Linscomb said, "I didn't invite her in; she came in."

Many of the black aides were frightened about their own criminal culpability. Some had been intimidated by the prosecution into believing that they too could face indictment. Sartwelle offered his services, offered to represent them as their lawyer should they have problems with the state. Marks would contemptuously say that Bob Gay was so generous in offering to pay for the legal talent for the aides so that they would not testify against their former employer.

As Sartwelle and Friend worked on the case, their billable hours for the law firm mounted. Fulbright and Jaworski lawyers bill between $70 and $200 an hour, depending on the experience of the lawyer and the complexity of the legal matter they are handling. Sartwelle, a partner in the firm, was racking up significant fees, which Autumn Hills paid to build its defense.

Minton and Burton in Austin were not idle either. The two kept in close contact with Sartwelle and Friend as well as their clients, who took an active role in their own defense. As Sartwelle and Friend were chasing down patients' families, nurse's aides, former nurses at the home, suppliers, and anybody who could shed more light on the case, Minton and Burton had their own way of doing research. They hired a private investigator to follow other trails and to trace the personal lives of Autumn Hills patients.

Marks worked in his office day and night and was accessible to anyone who came by. He had known a Galveston County deputy constable since he had come to the courthouse years before as a misdemeanor prosecutor. It was not terribly unusual when the constable dropped in for a chat one day. The deputy had business on his mind though. He told Marks that he had been stiffed on a time-share deal, and he was wondering if Marks as an assistant attorney general could help him do anything about the problem. Marks, to be kind to an old though not close friend, told the lawman that though such consumer problems were not in his area of the attorney general's office, he would be happy to find out who handled such things and speak to the person on the man's behalf.

The deputy constable dropped in from time to time to see if Marks had found out anything from Austin, to see if there was anything that could be done to help him. Marks's entire being was occupied with the Autumn Hills case, but he promised to continue trying to help. Marks honestly did want to give what help he could to his friend in law enforcement, and he did make some calls on the deputy's behalf.

Marks continued to jog frequently on Seawall Boulevard. He found the running to be a release from the pressures that the case and his personal problems had built up inside him over the years. When he returned from his jog one day, he ran into the parking area of the apartment complex where he lived and was surprised to find the deputy parked near his car. Marks walked over to the man, thinking that his friend was waiting for someone who lived in the apartments. The lawman was shaken to see Marks. The deputy blurted out, "There are some people who want to know what you are doing." He then told Marks that he had been tailing him and had been hired to do so by a Houston private investigator. As he confessed, the deputy told him that he was the second person to follow Marks and that the first had said he received a $5000 fee to do so. The constable also told Marks that he had gone through his garbage, and he showed him a report that said he had gained entry to Marks's office by coming up with the time-share scam story.

Marks was furious, though for a change he held his anger in check. The young attorney simply thanked the man for telling him of his activities, then said, "I'm going to make you a lot of money and save you some work. I'm going to keep a log of where I'm going and give it to you." The deptuty told Marks, "I know where you were last night. You spent the night at Betty Korndorffer's house." Marks had indeed spent the previous night at the home of Betty Korndorffer and her husband, the Galveston County medical examiner. He had been drinking and felt that it was unsafe for him to drive.

The deputy constable's fear was well founded. Marks drafted a letter to the attorney general and to Mike Guarino detailing the matter. Marks now realized just how much money the defense lawyers were willing to spend on behalf of their clients. They were not playing a gentlemanly game and were willing to spend substantial sums to increase the odds in their favor.

In the course of redefining the parameters of the case, Marks and Vollers decided that the new indictments should be drawn charging the corporation and the individual defendants with only two murders instead of the multiple deaths as Marks had done in the previous instruments. As they began to close the gaps, tightening their case, they narrowed the field to two women who had been patients at the nursing home at roughly the same time, Edna Mae Witt and Elnora Breed.

The two prosecutors had decided that although Autumn Hills would stand trial only for the murders of the two women, 59 other patients would be mentioned in the indictments. Both prosecutors were convinced that the nursing home did contribute to the deaths of almost all of those patients; however, it would be far simpler for the jury to grasp the minute details of the deaths of just two patients than to grasp the horror of a large number of deaths. The 59 other cases would be used to buttress their findings on Witt and Breed. As the summer of 1983 wore on into fall, Marks and Vollers expanded their team of volunteers to tighten the noose around the corporate neck of Autumn Hills. When they finally took their case to the grand jury, this time there would be no room for a plea bargain, and the indictments would be letter-perfect.

Roy Minton didn't need any more complications in his life. He, with his partner Burton, was handling a host of complex cases, not the least of which was the job of keeping the people of Autumn Hills out of jail. His platter was full when Jim Mattox, attorney general of Texas, came into his office asking him to be his lawyer. Mattox had been making appearances before the Travis County grand jury because an ambitious local district attorney was trying to get him indicted. Ronnie Earle had built his reputation on the carcasses of elected public officials who, in his opinion at least, had run afoul of the law. The grand jury had indicted Mattox for commercial bribery.

Minton was reluctant to represent Mattox because of the involvement of the attorney general's office in the Autumn Hills case. Mattox was also fighting Tom Sartwelle's law firm, and that in itself could conceivably cause complications for the clients Minton was already representing.

The attorney general prevailed. Minton became Mattox's lawyer and took the case to trial. Earle, who had little courtroom experience, tried the case personally. Mattox walked, and his political clout was seemingly enhanced rather than diminished by the episode. Minton's reputation grew considerably as the Texas news media grew increasingly aware that there was another Texas trial lawyer who could conceivably develop a national reputation.

The financial drain on Bob Gay and his corporation had been great. Roy Minton and Charles Burton did not come cheaply to those desperate enough to need their services. Neither did a firm like Fulbright and Jaworski with lawyers like Tom Sartwelle and Gail Friend. Mike Ramsey was still representing Sandy Canlas, who was being friendly with the state, but Gay continued to foot the bill. Something had to give.

Gay explored his options. The president of Autumn Hills was nothing if not realistic when it came to money. Gay had to do something to preserve what he had spent years building. He would either have to sell some of his properties or at the least lease some of them.

On January 22, 1983, Autumn Hills Convalescent Centers leased the Texas City facility to the giant Beverly Enterprises. Beverly immediately changed the name of the home to College Park Care Center.

Autumn Hills had caused David Marks anger and fear, but now he felt only hatred, a loathing for Sartwelle and what and whom he represented. Besides, Marks believed that Sartwelle had meddled in his personal life. Marks thought that the Houston attorney wanted to represent Marks's estranged wife in their upcoming divorce. Sartwelle stoutly denies that he ever wanted to represent her. He says that he spoke with her hoping only to find "a woman scorned." Sartwelle too had come to despise Marks. The upstart prosecutor had caused some good people a lot of trouble they didn't need. In his quest for a defense of Autumn Hills he convinced himself that the facility was a good nursing home. Sartwelle accepted at face value the brutal reality of nursing home care in America.

Sartwelle also continued to stalk potential witnesses who might be friendly to his clients. Again and again he went to their homes, to their jobs, always taping his conversations for later use. In his office he was amassing a storehouse of information as he called and wrote letters to experts on care for the elderly. In the hope of disproving Marks's theory that bedsores had killed many of the patients in Autumn Hills, he contacted every recognized medical expert doing research on decubitus ulcers in the country. The researchers told him that there was really no evidence to support the theory. Sartwelle had something he could hang his hat on. He thought he could pattern a defense based upon the findings of the researchers. He was striking pay dirt. Minton had made a wise choice in bringing Sartwelle into the criminal case.

Sartwelle also honed in on Edna Mae Witt and Elnora Breed. He thought it would be easy to prove that Breed had died of cancer, not bedsores, because she had a long history of the disease. He studied Witt's records carefully, hoping to find a way to disprove the prosecution's contention that the woman had died from a massive infection brought about by the open sores on her body and their seemingly constant exposure to her own excrement. Sartwelle took the medical records of all of the Autumn Hills patients and compiled detailed notes for his own use, showing both medical events that would be helpful as well as medical events that would be damaging to the case. The notes on each patient were massive and extraordinarily complicated, but they told the lawyer what he needed to know.

By late summer the prosecutors were ready to present their findings to a third grand jury. That jury had been impaneled by Judge I. Allen "Babe" Lerner. The panel began hearing from witnesses in the fall of 1984. One of them was Cassandra Canlas, the director of nursing at Autumn Hills in Texas City during a four-month period in 1978.

Cassandra Sue Canlas was a product of Alabama. She grew up in Eight Mile, a small town in Mobile County, and graduated from high school in Prechard. The young woman was a product of the blue-collar South. She came from a hardworking family, a union family. She was proud that her father was a pipefitter with Local 119. A single mother of two children, Sandy was making her way through life the best she could when she went to work at Autumn Hills. Youth was her only obstacle.

Her record at Autumn Hills was good, very good compared with others at the home. She had tried with the limited resources at her disposal to clean up the home. She had helped establish an inventory system in the medication room; she had started to document bedsores on patients by taking photographs. She had sent off cultures from the contaminated ice machine on the skilled wing of the facility.

Sandy Canlas also had displayed the good sense to work with the state during the investigation. She felt that she had clearly done nothing wrong, and after all, Betty Korndorffer was her friend. Yet Sandy Canlas had been indicted by the first two grand juries. Something was wrong. When the third grand jury got under way, the woman, who had become by now accustomed to the proceedings, again came to the Galveston County Courthouse to testify.

Sandy made a terrible witness before a grand jury. She sat in front of the panel smoking, throwing her head back and blowing out long streams of smoke as she answered questions. The grand jury again indicted her. The prosecutors believed that the jurors just didn't like her looks and demeanor, not to mention the inconsistencies between her testimony and that of some of the other witnesses.

The grand jury also indicted four others. Bob Gay got his wish: he would stand trial for murder along with his people. Ron Pohlmeyer, the nervous general manager of the corporation, would also face a jury of his peers. The corporation's director of nursing Mattie Locke, also nervous, was indicted. Mild Virginia Wilson, the wife of a Baptist minister and for a short while the administrator of the Texas City home, would be tried for knowingly killing the people under her care. The corporation itself would be a defendant, the first nursing home corporation to stand trial for murder in the nation. All would be tried for knowingly killing Edna Mae Witt and Elnora Breed as well as contributing to the death of 59 others. Not one Texas City nurse, not one Autumn Hills nurse's aide, would face the jury. David Marks was putting the executives on trial. It had taken him six years of working on nothing else, but Autumn Hills was finally going to trial.

CHAPTER EIGHT

On November 28, 1984, just nineteen days after new indictments were returned against Autumn Hills, David Marks presented Mike Guarino and the state attorney general's office with a 27-page, single-spaced budget memorandum that would become the prosecution's Blueprint for the Trial of *The State of Texas* v. *Autumn Hills Convalescent Centers, Inc.*, et al. In the memo Marks detailed how the massive quantity of evidence his office had collected; the numerous studies conducted by medical, nursing, and nutrition experts; and the witnesses would be used when the case finally came to trial. He also anticipated how the Autumn Hills defense would respond to each of the allegations. Marks also proposed counter-arguments to those responses in an impressive demonstration of how well he understood the case that had become his personal passion.

In the same memorandum, Marks noted that the prosecution's thinking now centered on Elnora Breed as the victim whose life—and death—would come under a legal microscope in the courtroom. Marks and his staff had become uncomfortable with two of the witnesses they hoped to produce, the daughters of Edna Mae Witt, Agnes Buxton and Maxine Anonsen. The two women were simply too emotional about their mother's death. They cried often, and at the slightest provocation. And though Marks had developed an affection for the sisters during the years he had known them, he and other members of the prosecution team were not comfortable with them as key witnesses. He would prove himself wrong when he placed the two sisters on the witness stand.

The November 28 memo detailed the findings of three major

projects developed during the years of the case, projects Marks believed proved his case beyond a reasonable doubt. Under the general heading "The Data Project," the prosecutor had compiled seven major subprojects:

1. The Staffing Project—"This project analyzes all staffing evidence for the purpose of identifying violations in minimum staffing requirements, and identifies contradictions between staffing documents, allowing us to establish falsification of an official record and giving us actual numbers of staff on duty on any given day to meet patient needs and allowing us to identify exactly when a given employee worked, with whom, and how often."

2. The Decubitus Project—"This project stores all data relating to decubitus (bedsores) at the Autumn Hills Texas City facility between Jan. 1, 1978, and August 31, 1979. This allows us to determine the number of sores in the facility on any day (which impacts on the amount of work a nurse could perform); and the number of sores which became infected and the number of sores that deteriorated and the number that improved and the time from date of admission it took a sore to form and the time after formation that it took a sore to deteriorate or become infected."

3. The Physician Project—"This project includes the number of visits made to the facility by each physician and the dates of visits, the number and identity of patients attended by each physician. Also on computer are all instances found in which the medical record fails to confirm notification of physician of changes in patient condition. Physicians' response or lack of response to notification is also being documented."

4. The Nurse Failure Project—"This project identifies in all patient records all evidence of omitted care and failures in nursing care, including failures in observation, intervention and/or documentation; failure to follow up on noted patient problems; and failures to follow physicians' orders; and false documentation."

5. Patient Assessment Project—"This project enables us to identify all patients at risk, i.e., bedfast, immobile, incontinent, etc. (This is valuable in light of Locke's testimony that she reviewed all bedfast patients.)"

6. Nurses' Notes Project—"This project analyzes patterns in nurses' notes, and allows us to determine if a particular nurse, over a long period of time, was writing repetitious and meaningless notes."

7. Texas Department of Health (TDH) Project—"This project analyzes patterns of problems occurring over a period of time, as noted in TDH reports."

Under the heading "The Red Cross Project," Marks outlined five major studies his office had compiled over the years:

1. "The review of all documentation on our targeted victim (in the past, Edna Witt; now it appears it will be Breed) for the purpose of testifying to the nursing needs of such victim as of time of admission and as condition changed while in the facility."

2. "The review of all writings by Mattie Locke, as well as all references listed in Locke's writings, for the purpose of establishing Locke's criteria for judging patient care."

3. "The review of all TDH reports for the purpose of testifying as to the meaning of such reports and for the purpose of offering a summary of patterns of poor care evidenced by such reports."

4. "The review of Mattie Locke's work notes written in response to TDH findings."

5. "Co-involvement in the Nurse Failure project so as to be in a position to corroborate, through chart audits, the findings of TDH."

Finally Marks demonstrated the importance to the case of his nurse failure project:

1. "Reviews charts to identify violations of nursing standards."

2. "Reviews charts to capture all problems and complications arising in regard to patients."

Marks was determined not to be caught again by Minton and the other lawyers of the defense team. He had by now seen what he was up against. He knew the lengths to which Sartwelle and the

Austin lawyers would go for their clients, and he didn't care if the trial took six months to complete; he would get in all of the evidence, all of the studies, all of the data he was sure any reasonable person would find convincing, convincing enough to put the Autumn Hills defendants in the penitentiary. Marks had becme thorough, as thorough as Sartwelle. He had become a seasoned lawyer in the seven years he had spent on the case. He had also learned to control his feelings and had developed inner strength. He would not be surprised again.

Marks anticipated how the defense would attack key prosecution witnesses in an attempt to destroy their credibility. He first outlined for his colleagues how the opposing lawyers would handle testimony by the state health inspectors.

1. "Why was not more strenuous action taken? If people were being killed, why didn't you close the place down?"

2. "You are not an impartial witness and objective witness. Your observations and opinions are tainted by your involvement in the prosecution of this case. In assisting the State in this case, was not your goal to help the State obtain a conviction? You are a part of the prosecution." Marks listed three health inspectors who had worked closely with him on the case, including Betty Korndorffer.

3. "You have an axe to grind; are you not a disgruntled former employee of Autumn Hills?" Again Marks singled out Korndorffer, who had worked at the corporation's Friendswood facility before becoming a state inspector.

4. "How can you comment on the care that was or was not provided on days when you were not present in the facility? You were in the facility no more than six hours, for one to three days, during the 46-day residency of Mrs. Breed/Witt, isn't that correct? Are you in a position to contradict the testimony of professionals who were there around the clock during the other 43 days and were documenting their observations and services 24 hours a day? Further, can you contradict the evidence of professionals whose qualifications and credentials are equal to. if not superior to, your own? (i.e., credentials of attending physicians and professional consultants for Autumn Hills.)"

Marks was also convinced that Minton and the rest of the Autumn Hills defense team would mount a vigorous attack on the former Autumn Hills employees who had agreed to testify for the state. The defense had previously attacked the state for trying to turn the aides and nurses into prosecution witnesses. Marks was proud of most of the women; they had steadfastly refused to cooperate with Sartwelle, Friend, Minton, and Burton. He was painfully aware of the tenacious efforts of Sartwelle to talk to them, to catch them in inconsistencies. He also expected that the defense would attack them on moral grounds:

1. "Why didn't you take action if people were being neglected? Why didn't you report abuse and neglect to the authorities? (This is your signature on this document obligating you to report abuse and neglect, isn't it?) Why did you continue to work there; why didn't you quit?"
2. "You are not an impartial witness. You have an axe to grind. You were fired. You had a personality conflict. You are a disgruntled ex-employee. These 'defects' have tainted your recollection and testimony."
3. "You are saying these things to save your own skin. You are guilty if anybody is; you made a deal with the State and that's why you are [not] named in these indictments as a murderer.
4. "You are relying on your memory seven years later against your own documentation at the time."
5. "By your own testimony you claim you falsified records, but you ask to be heard now as a credible and truthful witness."

Finally, Marks thought the defense would attack family members who had placed their loved ones in Autumn Hills. He predicted—correctly—that the most natural question in the minds of the jurors would be "Why didn't you get your family member out?" Marks also anticipated that jurors would be asking themselves:

1. "Why didn't you take further action? Why did you abandon your relative to what you call neglect and abuse? Why didn't you remove your relative from this facility?"
2. "How often were you in the facility and how long did you stay? How knowledgeable an observer are you? Do you understand what is valid and reasonable health care criticism and

what is unreasonable and invalid? What are your health care credentials?"

3. "You are relying on memories of events seven years ago. You are setting that memory against records of these events made at the time."

4. "You are testifying as to complaints voiced to you by your relative. Was your relative alert and clear-headed? Did he or she fully understand what the staff was trying to do for them? Did they understand what was possible for the staff and what was not possible? Would they not have complained about some things even if they had been at home under your care?"

Marks concluded, "In light of such cross-examination, I believe that if our case were to rest solely on the shoulders of the witnesses, Autumn Hills would have a strong 'reasonable doubt' argument. Therefore, to counter such arguments by successfully attacking Autumn Hills' assumption-of-care argument, as well as meet our burden of proof, we must depend on the expert projects mentioned above. These projects derive from a source which Autumn Hills cannot afford to impeach, their own records." Marks ended his memorandum with a detailed destruction of the defense case. At the end were the charts he had come to rely on over the long years of his work.

Among the witnesses Marks planned to call to the stand were the relatives of Mary and Amelia Sarich, a mother and daughter who entered Autumn Hills on the same day, March 30, 1978. The two had lived together on a quiet street in Galveston where Amelia cared for her aging, blind, and diabetic mother until she herself contracted cancer. When the older woman broke her wrist, both were placed in Autumn Hills. The physician for the two women was Dr. Merrill Stiles.

Amelia Sarich's cancer had taken its toll on the 64-year-old woman. Yet when she entered Autumn Hills, she could still walk, although, like many cancer patients found in nursing homes, she was already in her final decline. She lived only a little more than a month after entering Autumn Hills. Family members say that her last days waiting for the inevitable end were spent not quietly but in an environment of horror.

Mary Utley had placed her mother and sister in Autumn Hills so they would be near her home in LaMarque, where Mary and her teenage daughter, Lorrie, lived. Lorrie, a pretty, frail girl with a fair complexion, had her own health problems and had been forced to miss a year of high school, convalescing at home. She visited her grandmother and aunt in the nursing home twice a day.

When she visited her aunt, the teenager saw at firsthand the nightmare of dying of cancer. She also saw that there seemed to be no one at the nursing home who would help Amelia through the pain and suffering of her last days. "At times you could hear her yelling for help, you could hear her as you came through the door," Lorrie remembered.

Lorrie knew there was something wrong at Autumn Hills. "When you first came in the door there was a very acidy smell. It was very strong; sometimes it was nauseating." She often found that there was no ice in her aunt's room, and her aunt was always thirsty. Amelia Sarich was often found bound in a vest with a sheet tied around her.

When Mary Utley visited the nursing home she found many of the same things wrong that her daughter had reported. She also found that at night the nursing staff took the buzzer away from Amelia, who, as her cancer worsened, screamed of pain and thirst. Mary asked the staff at the nurse's station to put back the buzzer, but they refused. She was told that she would have to talk to the administrator if she wanted the buzzer reinstalled. When Mary complained to the administrator, the buzzer was replaced.

Mary Utley usually visited Autumn Hills in the morning. She often found Amelia wet from the night before. She also noticed that the room never had washcloths or towels and was dirty. She would later say that she found those conditions six days a week. And she remembered that her sister smelled "real bad."

Amelia Sarich had a roommate. Mary was shocked that her sister in her dying days was exposed to the nightmare of her neighbor's misery. In the bed next to her, Amelia could see a young woman who had been shot in the head by her deranged husband, leaving her a mental cripple. As the girl lay there, her urine bag overflowed onto the floor and the filth from her own body covered her. She often disrobed herself, and the staff could not keep clothes on her. The door from Amelia Sarich's room opened onto the hallway, exposing her death agony and the private hell of her roommate. Lying naked in her bed, the young woman frequently masturbated, unconscious of anyone else in the room.

Mary Utley was horrified at what was going on in her sister's room. She complained to the administrator about the problems, but nothing changed. She talked to Dr. Stiles about the condition of her sister, and he told her that the cancer had metastasized, "had gone all over her body." Amelia died at Autumn Hills on May 6, 1978, at the beginning of the month of glorious flowers on the coastal prairie.

Mary Utley and her daughter also faced problems with her mother, Mary Sarich. At 85, Mary was blind and diabetic, with poor circulation, and she had entered Autumn Hills with a fractured right wrist. Despite the infirmities of old age, she maintained a cheerful disposition. She talked to anyone who would talk to her. Unfortunately, it was difficult to carry on a conversation with Mary Sarich. She was Austrian by birth and had never mastered the English language. She too was under the care of Merrill Stiles.

The frustrations that Mary Utley felt in dealing with the nursing home on behalf of her dying sister were compounded by the care her mother was receiving. One of the things that disturbed Mary Utley most was the staff's practice of tying her mother in a chair for hours at a time. "They would put mother's housecoat on her backwards. It choked her." As the elderly woman slipped down in the chair, sliding on her urine and the slime of a bowel movement she had not been able to control, the coat choked her more. Under her chair Mrs. Sarich's urine collected in puddles.

Lorrie was concerned about the cleanliness of her grandmother. When Mary Sarich had a bowel movement, she was allowed to lie in her waste. When her granddaughter came to visit, she found that "Grandmother had gotten her hands into it. It had dried under her fingernails. We found it that way more often than we didn't."

Mary was also disturbed that her mother's clothes had disappeared. She complained to the staff but to no avail. It was impossible to keep clothes from disappearing.

Mary Sarich maintained her appetite despite her other problems. Yet Mary Utley found that Autumn Hills patients had no opportunity to get enough to eat. On the subject of diet in institutions, the daughter was an expert. She was manager of the school cafeteria at nearby Inner City School. Part of the problem was that her mother was blind, and when the nurse's aides brought in her tray of food, they placed it on the bedside table and left without calling it to her attention. She often didn't even know the food was there. When Mary Utley visited the home, she fed her mother herself. "Part of the time the tray was sitting there, and if I didn't feed her, she wouldn't get fed."

Quantity and quality were also problems with the food at Autumn Hills. Repeatedly, Mary Utley arrived at the nursing home to find that lunch consisted of a single peanut butter sandwich, often served on stale bread. One evening her mother was served bean soup, and Mary Utley counted just twelve beans.

Mary Sarich also developed a bedsore in the nursing home, but that was not the biggest problem her daughter encountered. On August 19, 1978, Mary Sarich fell and broke her hip. Her daughter was visiting San Antonio when Autumn Hills notified the family of her mother's injury. Lorrie rushed over to comfort her grandmother, only to find her in great pain. When Mary Utley returned from San Antonio, Lorrie told her what had happened, and she hastened over to find her mother in bed, awake, crying, and wet. Her leg was crossed in an awkward position. Also, "the whole bed was completely wet. She must have wet several times." Mary Sarich complained to her daughter that her leg hurt.

Angry that her mother had been allowed to lie in that condition since the accident, Mary Utley asked a nurse why an ambulance had not been called to transport her mother to the hospital. The nurse replied that she could not call an ambulance without the doctor's permission. Furious, Utley complained until her mother was removed from Autumn Hills to the nearby county hospital. She later learned that her mother's broken hip was separated.

When Mary Sarich was released from the hospital on October 17, 1978, she went to Manor Care, another nursing home in LaMarque. She died there on December 18, 1981.

There would be no family members to testify about the condition of another woman whose life became entwined with the story of Autumn Hills, yet Marks planned to get before the jury how that life ended anyway. He would do it through medical records. The records were extensive and sad.

Pearl Creighton checked into the University of Texas Medical Branch (UTMB), the giant teaching complex on the Island's east end, on June 7, 1959. She was frightened. At the age of 55, she had noticed a sudden weight loss that she couldn't explain. All everyone had talked about at work lately was cancer, and Pearl knew that sometimes people wasted away from the disease. She was not old, but she wasn't young either. Her mother had died at an early age of a throat ailment, and Pearl was afraid she might soon follow her mother to the grave.

Pearl was a small woman, just five foot one and slight of build. At best her normal weight hovered around 115 pounds. Yet in five weeks her weight had plummeted to only 100 pounds, and she was deeply troubled about it. The discussions at work about cancer had preyed on her mind until now it was all she thought about. The doctors at the medical branch's John Sealy Hospital noticed Pearl's nervousness. She was given a battery of tests, plenty of bed rest, and finally released. The tests showed no cancer, so Pearl could rest easy about that. But the doctors did find that she suffered from hypertension and heart disease. They also noted that she suffered from acute anxiety. The doctors chalked the weight loss up as psychosomatic. She could go home, take her phenobarbital, and check by the doctor's office from time to time.

But Pearl didn't relax about her condition. She continued to worry about herself over the next six years; when she checked herself into the UTMB emergency room at 9:45 p.m. on February 9, 1965, she had worried most of the previous night. During the preceding week she had suffered from a bad cold, which was becoming worse. When she heard that her neighbor had died, she could not sleep for worrying. By midnight, she had begun coughing and her nose was bleeding. Sleepless, she did not improve throughout the night or the next day. When she checked herself into the emergency room, the doctors on duty there immediately noted her nervousness.

Her nose bled all night in the ER. Doctors worked steadily with her and finally stopped the bleeding, then admitted her to the hospital and ordered her to lie flat in the bed to stem the nosebleed. Again a battery of tests were run, which showed nothing different from the 1959 tests, except that Pearl now suffered from spontaneous nose bleeds. She was again given sedatives and released to leave the hospital under her own power.

Pearl made it through the next ten years without medical incidents. But she was certainly anxiety-ridden, and when she was admitted to the emergency room again on August 17, 1975, the only medication she reported taking was a white nerve pill. On that day the seventy-year-old woman had been knocked unconscious in an automobile accident. But after five hours in the emergency room, she was released to go home.

Pearl Creighton didn't want to come to the hospital on August 4, 1977. When she got there, she said that a friend had tricked her and brought her in; she denied that anything was wrong. She did say that she had recently been working very hard at the Silk Purse, a church charity shop, but she insisted she had no need of a doctor. She also denied that she was taking any medication but said she occasionally had a beer and smoked one pack of cigarettes a day.

The ER nurses and doctors noted that Pearl wore dentures that needed extensive repair and was an odoriferous, dirty, slight woman with thin hair. She often smiled and appeared in no distress, yet something was clearly wrong with Pearl. On the left foot she wore a sneaker, and on the right, a sandal. Her feet were also dirty, and on her left knee was a large scab. Her ears were blocked with residue. Pearl also had a heart murmur.

Pearl Creighton had gotten old. She now suffered from organic brain syndrome, a malady that often affects the elderly. The doctors at UTMB noticed that she laughed at inappropriate times and that her intelligence was hard to assess. Her mind also wandered, though not badly, but her memory was "recent and poor." Shortly after the hospital exam the woman was found wandering the hallways, saying she had to go home to care for her dogs. She was admitted for nervousness, though her admitting note stated that she had acute brain syndrome and possible metastatic disease.

Pearl had not told the physicians the whole truth. When the hospital checked with her private physician, it came to light that the woman had been drinking heavily of late. Perhaps the alcohol helped her chronic nervousness, but her doctor told the hospital to be prepared for delirium tremens, the observable symptoms of brain damage resulting from chronic consumption of alcohol. In all of her previous hospital admissions, Pearl had had high blood pressure. Could her high blood pressure come from years of heavy drinking?

The following day, Pearl was again wandering the hospital corridors, protesting that she had to go home to take care of her three dogs. The nurses noted that she was confused and that she went in and out of other patients' rooms. The hospital physicians ordered a psychiatric consultation and learned that her friend had brought Pearl to the hospital because of forgetfulness. The doctors also learned that she had been drinking heavily for years, but during the past half year her memory had gotten much worse.

The doctors also noted that Pearl's intellectual functioning was poor and that she was oriented only to herself. They determined that she had poor insight and judgment, and they suggested an uncertain course for the medical management of the woman. The doctors recommended that if she did not improve, steps should be taken to protect her in a proper environment.

Pearl stood by her bedside, continuously smoking cigarettes. She didn't like where she was. She was worried about her three dogs at home. She didn't like being old, and she was angry about it as she rocked from leg to leg and smoked one cigarette after another.

Four days into her stay at John Sealy Hospital the doctors noted that Pearl had a healthy appetite and voiced no complaints, but she was still not oriented to time or place and had no observable change in condition. The following day, the hospital organized a social service consultation. The social workers found that Pearl's sister was arranging for guardianship but had asked for help in securing temporary nursing home placement for her sibling. Pearl's house and bills needed to be put in order, and that would take some time.

On the same day, Pearl wandered the hallways of the hospital again, and her physicians ordered a restraining device known as a Posey belt installed to keep her stationary.

On August 17 Pearl told the staff that she went home every day and that she had drunk a large glass of orange juice at home that very morning. She then tried to leave the unit several times and was again restrained. The following day, her doctor recorded that Pearl was aware of recent activities but continued to wander every day.

On August 19 the doctor stated in his progress notes that Pearl Creighton's family refused to take her home. He also urged that observation be continued to prevent her from wandering. Another physician said that UTMB could not justify keeping the woman hospitalized any longer. She was essentially a nursing home problem now. Later in the day, Pearl told a nurse, "I don't think I'll go to church today." She was cheerful but nervous, smoking and walking around the unit.

The Galveston County Probate Court handles the affairs of the county's residents after they die. It also handles commitments to institutions. A letter from Dr. B. W. Henry to the judge stated that in Dr. Henry's opinion, Pearl Creighton suffered from a moderately severe impairment of her mental processes and judgment caused by an organic brain syndrome that appeared to be chronic. The physician further stated that Pearl could not function adequately in her own best interest and hadn't done so in several months. He believed that her condition was declining rapidly, and because of her condition, she would be unable to secure her basic needs unassisted. He noted that Pearl did not possess sufficient insight to know that such a problem existed. Dr. Henry recommended that the next of kin or a friend be named Pearl's guardian. On August 22, 1977, Pearl Creighton checked in to Autumn Hills in Texas City. Two weeks later, she was seen for the first time by Dr. Merrill Stiles.

On her admission to Autumn Hills, nurses noted that Pearl's physical appearance was fair and the condition of her skin was good. The staff also noted that she was able to walk and dress herself and that she was continent. The Autumn Hills nurses added, however, that she was confused. She was restrained as needed "for her own personal safety," and reality orientation was given.

Records indicate that by early November Pearl's chief problem was that she often wandered away from the nursing home, but the staff was able to catch her before she got far. But later that month the woman developed an infected toe on her right foot, and the injury began to drain. Dr. Stiles ordered the foot cared for, but Pearl's toes swelled to a size that disturbed the Autumn Hills nurses. On December 16, Pearl complained to the nurses about pain in her left foot. By December 20, the leg was badly swollen at the ankle and clearly larger than the right leg. On January 5, 1978, Dr. Stiles examined Pearl Creighton at the request of the nursing home. She was asked to stay off her foot.

Pearl disregarded the instructions of the physician and the nurses and was described as constantly wandering, although her foot was painfully swollen. Again, she was restrained in her bed. When she was allowed to get up, she fell in the dining room, apparently without injury. Stiles directed the nursing home that she was not to walk without assistance and was to use a wheelchair.

Pearl Creighton was frightened. She was in a strange place, a place where she decidedly did not want to be. A nurse noted that Pearl was hostile and argumentative and that she cursed and was arrogant. Physically, she could not urinate on her own. Pearl clearly was in declining health. By March, she was refusing to assist in washing or dressing herself or even pushing herself in the wheel-chair. Despite her problems as a sick and cranky septuagenarian, her appetite remained good.

But Pearl's decline continued, and on May 5 she choked on a piece of meat in the dining room while laughing. Fortunately, she coughed the meat up. But eight days later, while walking into the dining room, she fell, badly bruising her right knee. She had to be tied in the wheelchair to prevent her slipping out. In June she did slip out of the chair. This time Pearl wasn't as lucky; her upper right thigh began to swell. The physicians were called, and the family was notified. Pearl complained to her family that the left side of her face was hurting, and they asked that she be transferred to St. Mary's Hospital. Pearl had broken her hip. The doctor did what he could for her, implanting a compression screw in her hip and noting that she was confused and suffering from organic brain syndrome. By July 7, Pearl was back in Autumn Hills.

After her return to the nursing home, Pearl Creighton's decline accelerated. Betty Korndorffer noted the woman on her inspection rounds for the state. By September 12, Korndorffer had noticed that Pearl was developing bedsores the size of a quarter on her feet. She also noted the woman's general condition. The Autumn Hills nurses also recorded Pearl's bedsores in her chart. Eleven days later, Pearl developed a bedsore on her hip, which soon evolved into a large, open, draining wound. The nurses noted that "the ulcer looks gross." A few days later they also noted that a foul odor was coming from the sore.

Other sores began to develop on the small, nervous woman from Galveston. She would eventually have fourteen of them. On an in-spection tour on October 31, Betty Korndorffer noted that Pearl Creighton was lying in her own excrement. "She had a BM. She had feces all over her, even in her hair. It was dried, indicating that the woman had not been recently cleaned and had been allowed to lie in her own waste for hours. The feces was in the sores, and the woman was burning up with fever."

Korndorffer also noticed that Mrs. Creighton had bright red spots on her cheeks. On rounds with Korndorffer, nursing director Cas-sandra Canlas also saw that the woman was very ill. She told her immediate supervisor, administrator Virginia Wilson, "This woman is critical. Y'all need to call a doctor."

As Korndorffer left Autumn Hills that day, she again looked in on Pearl Creighton. The woman was being taken to the shower in a shower chair. Korndorffer scolded the staff, telling them that they should have taken the woman's temperature before exposing her to a shower. On November 4, Pearl Creighton's temperature was taken rectally. It was 104 degrees. She was admitted to the hospital the following day.

At the hospital emergency room, the examining physician included the possibility of sepsis in his initial diagnosis. Pearl's fever was still high, and the sepsis diagnosis was correct. On her death certificate 84 days later, Dr. Stiles listed as the cause of death arteriosclerotic heart disease and septicemia. Pearl Creighton would have no more fears.

At 83, Carrie McMullin had been in Autumn Hills for more than a year. When she was admitted, she was recovering from a broken hip and cataract surgery. On July 31, 1978, Carrie McMullin went to the bathroom. There were three aides in the room, but only one of them allegedly slapped the blind woman. She couldn't identify who had abused her, so all three aides were suspended by Virginia Wilson, administrator of the home. A daughter later said that another patient might have slapped her mother. The issue of who had committed the act was cloudy. Later, all three aides were reinstated.

Mamie Phillips had also been in and out of Autumn Hills. In fact, she had been a resident of the nursing home for more than four years during her first stay. By 1978, the 71-year-old woman, who suffered from chronic urinary retention, ulcers, and a reactive depression, had become a wanderer. Mamie fell in the front yard of Autumn Hills on May 26, 1978. She complained that she hurt, but the nursing home staff encouraged her to get up and walk around. The woman even went out on a pass. She was finally taken to a physician 25 days after the incident; the doctor did not discover that Mamie had a fractured pelvis. Instead, he ordered medication for arthritis.

When Elnora Breed came to Autumn Hills, she was already frail and emaciated. But when she entered the county hospital on Halloween night of 1958, she was a robust, though ailing, 67-year-old woman of 130 pounds. Before 1958, Elnora had suffered from nothing more serious than a tooth extraction and a wasp sting, which she probably sustained pursuing her avid hobby, gardening. Yet she had complained for nearly three weeks of a dull abdominal pain on her left side, nausea, and vomiting. She also complained of dizziness and tarry stools. Despite those symptoms, Elnora maintained a good appetite.

During her examination, physicians found that she had some heart irregularities, but she was treated for a duodenal ulcer and placed on a bland diet and a drug that decreased the secretion of stomach and intestinal acid. She was released from the hospital, and during the next year she visited her physician 23 times for vitamin injections.

Two years later Elnora was again in the county hospital. This time her weight had dropped to 117 pounds. Again she complained of a stomach pain that increased after she ate and of bright red, bloody stools and occasional bloating. She also told the doctor of a foul-tasting, bitter material in her mouth and frequent nausea and vomiting. She complained, "My urine comes down real slow." The examining physician found that Elnora had occasional extra heartbeats; he also found a small palpable mass in her abdomen. Surgery was scheduled, and a malignant mass was removed.

Despite their advancing age, Elnora and her husband continued their daily lives of work, family, and church. Elnora continued to work in her yard, play dominoes, and go to circle meetings at the Baptist church. At seventy, she had some health problems, to be sure, but continued to be an active resident of Bell Drive.

Even when she returned to the hospital almost a year after her surgery, Elnora was not complaining of serious illness. The junior medical student who examined her noted that she sat there "quietly reading the Bible." She was admitted for rectal bleeding and dizziness and was diagnosed as having rectal bleeding, hemorrhoidal tags, and proctitis. She returned one month later with vaginal bleeding, for which she was treated. Her only further treatment during the following four years was for a bee sting on the jaw. Elnora loved to work in the yard, and bees are abundant on the Texas coastal prairie.

At 75, Elnora was again operated on for cancer. Her recovery was uneventful, and she continued to go about her daily life—albeit more slowly—in the way that had been her custom since she was a child. Every Monday she went to the big, black iron pot behind the house and washed her clothes. She refused to use the modern conveniences of the twentieth century; she was a child of the nineteenth century, and she did not believe that any newfangled machine could get her clothes as clean as she could herself. She had learned well as a girl.

The family doted on their beloved aunt who refused to give in to old age. She tended her flower beds, took care of her shrubs, and played dominoes in the evening with anyone who had the courage to compete with her.

After the death of her husband, Elnora and her sister Ruth became increasingly close. The two depended upon each other to share the old age both were experiencing. Elnora, ever practical, arranged for Ruth to take over her financial affairs. Her younger sister would handle things should Elnora be incapacitated. Her future assured, Elnora could rest easy, knowing that she would be cared for in her final days.

On December 7, 1975, as America prepared to celebrate its bicentennial, Elnora Breed was admitted to the county hospital complaining of constipation and diarrhea, which had bothered her in recent months. She had lost a little weight, but she had a good appetite, as usual, and was oriented and alert. There was no sign of the cancer that had plagued her in the past, and the doctors discharged her on a bland diet. The following February, she was treated for a urinary tract infection.

On July 21, 1976, Elnora suffered a mild stroke that left her with a weakness in her right arm and leg for several days. A little more than a week later, doctors detected a possible recurrence of her tumor, and on August 2, they operated. The cancer was removed, but this time Elnora remained weak and leaned to her right when she walked. She also refused to eat. Her progress was slow, but she was finally released to nearby Hill Haven (now Seabreeze) Nursing Home.

Elnora remained in the nursing home for only a little more than two months. During that time her decline continued. She sometimes had to be restrained in a wheelchair, but she fell out of the wheelchair while restrained and fractured her hip. In great pain, she was again taken to the county hospital. There, physicians determined that Elnora was suffering from organic brain syndrome and had almost no contact with reality. Her sister Ruth helped provide her medical history.

Elnora remained hospitalized until December. Nurses' notes indicate that she was cooperative but periodically confused. She was finally returned to the nursing home.

By May 1978, Elnora, now 86, had recorded a severe weight loss. She was also in severe abdominal pain from impacted bowels, possibly caused by a drug prescribed earlier. By July the pain was so severe that she was using her finger to dig into her rectum in a desperate attempt to move the feces. Elnora cried out in pain again and again. The nursing home called her physician, who transferred her to the hospital. She now weighed 81 pounds. She was treated with an enema and the pain was relieved, yet there was blood in the fluid she ejected.

Elnora was uncommunicative with the physicians in the hospital, but she still responded to verbal communication. After a week in the hospital, she was once more returned to the nursing home, this time with a catheter attached. Significantly, she was still given the same drug that had caused the impaction in the first place. And despite the hospital's report of no new cancer, Elnora's personal physician readmitted her to the nursing home with the diagnosis of carcinoma of the colon.

Ruth visited her sister daily at the nursing home. Despite doctors' observations that Elnora was uncommunicative, she and her sister talked. Other members of her family also conversed with her. The nursing home described her at times as alert, friendly, hostile, withdrawn and unresponsive, forgetful, confused, depressed, and nervous. They noted that occasionally she initiated contact with other residents and the staff and was always able to socialize with her family. On August 24, the nursing home's activities director set a short-term goal for Elnora of participation in exercise classes and a long-term goal of attendance at music programs, birthday parties, and religious services.

Elnora once again began having black, tarry diarrhea, although she could still feed herself and occasionally ate all of her food. But on September 4, 1978, her extremities were swollen, and she began to cry out in pain. By September 27, she had been again transferred to the hospital because she was incontinent, refusing to eat, and very weak. The admitting physician, J. A. Konikowski, described her as a senile *white* female, as he had done in several previous notations.

Elnora was gravely ill, yet she was not tender to the touch of her doctor as he examined her. She had had severe diarrhea before entering the hospital. Elnora Breed was clearly in her final days. On September 29, 1978, she became a tube feeder. A nasal gastric tube was placed in her nose, then into her stomach. She took her meals through it for the rest of her life.

She was released from the hospital and placed in Autumn Hills on October 4, 1978. She came into the home with a bedsore on her right ankle and an abrasion on her right forearm.

Ruth came to Elnora's bedside at Autumn Hills daily, as she had done at the other facility. She knew that something was wrong with Autumn Hills when she first entered the facility. She didn't know that Elnora had received no food or water for the first day and a half she was there. She did notice that there was a strong, noxious odor in the home, and she saw that there was urine on Elnora's bed and soil lines on the sheets.

As Ruth visited her sister, she never saw nurses coming to Elnora's room, never saw her sister turned or given medication. She never saw the staff treat her sister's bedsore and never saw her sister given water. Furthermore, she didn't know that Elnora was on a starvation diet of only six hundred calories per day.

Aides Pamela James and Carol Josey remembered Elnora Breed as she developed the bedsores that Marks believed killed her. James said, "They just ate into her body." James also remembered that Elnora was allowed to lie in her own excrement, a foul running diarrhea that the young aide described as "real smelly." She said, "When she had it we knew because we could smell it."

Another also saw Elnora lying on her back, never turned, soiled and wet. She also saw Elnora's bedsores grow until the bone was showing at the bottom of one of them and there was rotting tissue around the edges. She told her superiors that there were maggots in the sore, as did others of the Autumn Hills staff.

Eventually, Elnora Breed came to the attention of the state nursing home inspectors. Betty Korndorffer saw Elnora on her inspection on Halloween, 1978. Korndorffer entered Elnora's room and found an aide preparing to clean the woman up. The aide wore rubber gloves as she lifted the sheet. Elnora had recently defecated, and the feces got on the glove. The aide started to the bedside of Elnora's roommate without changing the gloves, and Korndorffer immediately scolded her, pointing out that by not removing the gloves, she could cause cross-contamination of the patients. The aide replied, "I didn't know."

Korndorffer had known Elnora Breed a long time. She had talked to her at the other nursing home. "Most of the time she was in a chair, and she was always thin. But usually you could have a conversation with her." But on October 31, at Autumn Hills, Betty Korndorffer was shocked at Elnora Breed's condition. "She had been thin, but she was a skeleton, she was so emaciated."

The inspection team found that Elnora was receiving a starvation diet. In their exit conference that day, they told the staff of their findings. Betty Korndorffer exclaimed, "My God, y'all are starving this woman to death." The nursing home did not notify the physician of the dietary deficiency for another two weeks.

On November 17, Elnora was given a strong narcotic because she was crying in pain as her bodily wastes entered her bedsores, by now oozing her body fluids. Her feet and left hand were swollen. A culture was done on the bedsore on Elnora's right hip. The report later stated that *E. coli* and a *Proteus* species common to feces grew in the culture.

The following day, the sores and the swelling had grown worse, and a nurse noted, "Both feet very edematous, to the point of almost seeping."

Despite the painkillers she was being given, Elnora continued "moaning and groaning" as her agony proceeded. At 3 a.m. on November 20, another nurse noted that the frail woman groaned for only brief periods. At 5:30 a.m., Elnora Breed made a gasping sound, then was still forever. Through thoughtful financial planning, she had tried to make her final days go easily. She hadn't counted on Autumn Hills.

CHAPTER NINE

David Marks's case no longer consisted of the fragile indictments of previous years. With the help of powerful friends in the state attorney general's office and staff members of John Heinz's United States Senate committee, Marks now had the financial resources to pursue Autumn Hills. The studies were refined, more experts were called, and the issue of corporate criminal liability was gone over again and again.

The case was back in the Galveston County courts too. With the new indictments, Judge Larry Gist was back in Beaumont, and it was likely a local judge would have to try the case after all. James Hury was busy preparing for his first legislative session and would not be able to intervene with another plea bargain.

The defense was not idle either. Sartwelle and Friend pressed their relentless pursuit of anyone who could help the medical or legal cause of their clients. Minton and Burton worried that the case might actually go to trial, despite their best efforts. Mike Ramsey refused to believe that Sandy Canlas would ever see the inside of a courtroom. In particular, he was banking on Betty Korndorffer and the warmth that he thought the two women had for each other. Ramsey would later say, "I think she likes my lady."

Mike Guarino had another concern. The Galveston County district attorney needed a judge to try the case. But there was little indication that any of the four state district judges in the county would be inclined to take on a case that they privately confided to friends and lunch acquaintances was an albatross. Ed J. Harris, the most defense-minded judge in the courthouse, had already indicated that he believed he had done what he could for the state by accepting the plea bargain for a $100,000 fine. Harris told friends, "I did my best for the state. I got them a hundred thousand."

Harris was considered excess baggage on the bench by members of Guarino's staff. Hury had indulged in an open quarrel with Harris because of the judge's lenient treatment of criminals that Hury believed should have been behind the walls of Huntsville prison. For practical purposes, Harris was out of the question as a trial judge.

Two of the other three district judges, I. Allen Lerner and Henry Delehite, had recently sat on a complex trial. So Guarino went to the most controversial man in the Galveston County Courthouse and asked him to hear *State* v. *Autumn Hills*. Don B. Morgan, the son of an Austin telephone company chief test board man, agreed to hear the case and promptly set pretrial hearings in six weeks. Morgan was known around the courthouse as a bombastic, opinionated, proprosecution jurist who wore his politics on his shirtsleeve. Morgan was a liberal Democrat who, despite rules against judges' getting involved with politics, would speak at the drop of a hat at a local county Democratic convention. Morgan was regarded as combative, sometimes caustic, and always ready for a verbal tug-of-war.

In the courtroom he was a martinet, some said. Off the bench he was a happy fun lover who took great pleasure in discussing books, wine, classical or country music, the weather, or the latest pecan crop on a patch of land he owned with another man near the small Central Texas town of Luling.

Morgan was also a man of deep convictions. He felt that the Autumn Hills case needed to be heard. He would not openly criticize his friend James Hury, but he still agreed to hear the case when it was not likely another Galveston County judge would touch it with a courtroom pointer.

Morgan had seen his share of elderly people in institutional settings. Shortly after leaving the Army, he returned to Austin and found a job at the Austin State Hospital. There he worked with elderly men and the criminally insane. The state hospital could always use a short, strong orderly, and Morgan was just that after his military service. Morgan remembered how he once helped a friend force-feed pills to an elderly patient. Morgan held the man's nose while the other orderly straddled the patient's chest and forced the pills into the man's mouth.

On another occasion, Morgan accompanied his supervisor on an orientation tour of the ward for the criminally insane. During the tour, the supervisor told Morgan to shake hands with one of the patients. Morgan, ever friendly, stuck out his hand. The patient clasped it in a viselike grip and twisted Morgan to his knees. It was an object lesson from the supervisor, who told Morgan, "Now you see why you have to watch those people every minute. Don't get too close to them."

The hospital job was not Morgan's first by any means. Always energetic as a child, he had spent his free hours working in a butcher shop and a grocery store. In high school, he spent a summer with his sister in California, where he found a job topping onions alongside migrant workers. And it was there that Morgan's strong empathy for working people began to develop. Although from a comfortable lower-middle-class family that gave him little common ground with laborers, Morgan began in California a lifelong love affair with labor and labor movements.

That relationship was further stimulated at the University of Texas, where Morgan majored in economics. There he took a course on labor relations, and the feelings he developed in the onion fields of California were cemented as he learned the theory of the function of the workingman.

Morgan found romance at UT, where he met and married Mary Johnson. He was so poor in those days that he often took his Mary to Baptist revivals for entertainment. There he would sing the hymns he had known as a child at the top of his voice. A firebrand liberal joined with a fundamentalist congregation singing, "Yes, we'll gather at the river, the beautiful, the beautiful river." As his love affair with Mary grew, Morgan determined to marry her. Ever impatient, he knew he would have to support her and knew that was practically impossible if he remained in school. He went to the Army recruiter in the final months of his senior year, signed up, married Mary, and trudged off to basic training. Later, he took Mary with him for an idyllic three years in Germany.

Morgan finished his tour of duty and returned to Austin to finish his education. More seasoned, he graduated and enrolled in the prestigious University of Texas Law School. The university was a magic place then. Folklorist J. Frank Dobie, naturalist and writer

Roy Bedichek, and historian Walter Prescott Webb were fixtures on the campus. They could often be seen talking together at nearby Barton Springs, an ice-cold swimming hole in the center of town. Morgan often felt the urge to approach these legendary Texans, introduce himself, talk. But he could never bring himself to do so, so intimidating did he find these renowned figures.

Law school came easily to Morgan. He remains to this day a man of words, and in the law school he learned to use words to his advantage. In the Travis County Courthouse he watched real trials and found them the greatest spectacle he had ever witnessed. In the first trial he ever saw, a murder case, the state painted a picture of horror to the jury, and Morgan found himself ready to hang the defendant. Then the defense lawyer presented the defendant as an unwitting victim, in the wrong place at the wrong time. Morgan's natural liberalism surfaced, and he was ready to hang the state's attorney instead. When he reflected on the case, Morgan realized that it was the defense attorney who had turned the jury in favor of the defendant. Morgan immediately knew that he would be a Texas trial lawyer.

After graduation Morgan took the bar exam. Then, as today, a grade of 75 was passing. Morgan made a 75. Today he tells friends and colleagues, "I didn't give them a damn thing. I made a 75, not one point more than was necessary and not one point less. That is the sign of a good lawyer!"

Morgan spent the ten months after his graduation working in the Legislative Reference Service Library in Austin, learning his way around the capital and state government. He then got his big break. Morgan landed a job with legendary North Texas lawyer Kearby Peery of the Red River town of Wichita Falls.

Wichita Falls is colder in the winter and hotter in the summer than almost any place in Texas. Morgan didn't mind the inclement weather. He had Peery to watch and learn from. Eventually, Morgan came to idolize his mentor. Peery had a mind that Morgan admired almost as much as he admired Peery's skills in the courtroom. It was thrilling for Morgan to be able to work with the man.

More than the florid language of courtroom orators influenced Morgan. He is to this day equally impressed by the phraseology of fundamentalist evangelists; he believes that television preacher Jimmy Swaggart would have made a great trial lawyer. Morgan has preserved choice lines from Swaggart sermons for future use in his jury arguments.

Morgan practiced for six years with Peery in Wichita Falls and left only when he realized it was unlikely that he would make much money in the foreseeable future in North Texas. In Texas City, on the Gulf Coast, was a lawyer who needed a young associate with spark to join his practice and try lawsuits. Jim Simpson, another legendary attorney, needed a litigator. In Wichita Falls, Morgan had learned his trade. On the coast of Texas he would now practice it.

Simpson had made a name for himself as a young Texas assistant attorney general by almost single-handedly closing down the gambling casinos that had flourished on Galveston Island since the Roaring Twenties. Run by brothers Sam and Rosario Maceo, the gambling houses openly—and profitably—flaunted their illegal activities before a succession of governors, attorneys general, and county sheriffs. Often public officials were their patrons, and Galveston County sheriff Frank Biagine once testified before a legislative committee that he hadn't raided the famed Balinese Room because he "wasn't a member." Simpson, a former FBI agent, was appalled by the gamblers' open contempt for the law, which he thought was corrupting the very fiber of government.

Simpson's brand of idealism was appealing to Morgan. Even in high school he had held deep though not well-defined convictions. Politically active, respected, and enjoying a reasonably successful law practice, Jim Simpson was just what the doctor ordered for the ambitious young lawyer.

In the law office of Simpson, Morgan, and Burwell, politics became an everyday thing, a responsibility that educated men owed to their less fortunate fellows. That feeling was magnified because of the relationship of the Texas City lawyers to one of the state's most unusual political figures. A. R. "Babe" Schwartz too hung his shingle on the small brick building on shabby Eighth Avenue North in the smokestack town. The feisty Jewish politician was first elected to the Texas Senate in 1962. There, he spent lonely years as an unapologetic liberal in a overwhelmingly conservative debating society. Over the years, Schwartz learned to work the Senate, learned the art of compromise, the art of the possible, as Lyndon Johnson used to call it.

As Schwartz grew in stature in the Senate, he would come back to the law office in Texas City and tell his colleagues of the fights he was waging in Austin. Sometimes, the lawyers would join in those fights, calling lawmakers and lobbying for their favored legislation, usually a bill relating to organized labor or the needs of the workingman.

Eventually, Schwartz got Morgan appointed to the state district court bench. Morgan quickly established his turf, imposed rules in his court that to some were arbitrary and dictatorial. He had specific ideas about how a courtroom should be run, and he left little doubt in the minds of everyone there that he was the law. There would be no smoking (although he continued to smoke on the bench), no electronic pagers going off, no tape recording equipment, and absolutely no television cameras shooting a trial or even shooting through the windows of the courtroom. Around the courthouse, behind his back, some called him Little Caesar.

From the bench he chided lawyers who did not follow the rules, harshly reminding them of proper conduct. To critics of his practices, he would remind them of the majesty of the law. He surprised his liberal friends by being a state's judge. Prosecutors soon learned that they had a friend in the courthouse. Although he had a grudging respect for lawyers from the big Houston firms, he distrusted them. He had a natural affinity for the underdog in his courtroom. He had spent his career as a plaintiff's lawyer. To them, he leaned as much as possible from the neutrality of the bench. Don Morgan liked to right wrongs.

Off the bench, Morgan remained the same. He wanted to be liked. It was almost as if his friends saw a different person in the courtroom. At parties he had fun and would as likely as not encourage friends to join him in song, often the old Baptist hymns he had learned as a boy.

From Simpson, Morgan learned eloquence and the ability to use Southern charm to disarm a jury. Sincerity drips from the mouth of James P. Simpson as he questions witnesses. "Are you blessed with children?" he says, lulling the jury into trusting him as he quietly bludgeons his opponent in the courtroom.

For Morgan, speaking is not nearly so smooth. He is, in fact, almost country-sounding in his speech patterns. Maple syrup doesn't drip from his lips. Instead, a high grade of molasses, mixed with a healthy dose of working-class biblical rhetoric, gushes forth in a steady stream until he has made his point. Morgan learned to plead with his juries, to plead the way Darrow and Bryan must have after the turn of the century.

The accent is peculiar, even for Texas. It is not a North Texas accent, certainly not that of his birthplace, Austin. Neither is it Western or the thick and cumbersome accent of East Texas. It is just different, not contrived, although that is the suspicion of many listeners upon spending any length of time with him. Perhaps it is the accent of the Baptist evangelists that he came to love as a boy, for he puts emphasis in strange places, on wrong syllables. Nonetheless, the accent is effective.

In law school, argument is taught almost as a way of life. Morgan learned his lessons well. Today he still has a quick mind and an insatiable curiosity, and he will argue a point just for the fun of it, just for the sake of a robust exchange. Sometimes the points he makes are outrageous, deliberately provocative. Former law partner Jim Simpson jokes, "Morgan may not always be right, but he is never in doubt!"

There are few men in Texas as convinced of the overwhelming rightness of the Democratic party as Morgan. On matters of Democratic politics, the presidency of Ronald Reagan, and the inherent wrongness of almost any Republican, the judge is practically inflexible. For example, he is fond of shocking strangers by saying of Midwestern farmers, and even Texas farmers, and their economic plight, "I hope that they lose everything they got. They voted for Ronald Reagan, didn't they?" Such an outrageous statement would be unbelievable to most, but to Morgan it is political gospel. A New Deal Democrat, Morgan is unforgiving. The farmers were ungrateful to the Democratic party and deserve their sad plight for it.

He also has little regard for two other professions. As a personal injury lawyer, he learned that physicians can often be pompous and ill informed. That observation developed into a considered dislike. It isn't that he dislikes all doctors. To the contrary. He can come to like almost any physician on an individual basis. He simply has a negative reflex reaction to them as a class. Of bankers, Morgan has one simple, straightforward observation. As a whole, he looks upon them as being "dumb." It is unlikely that his feelings stem from any problems of his own with bankers; he is after all, very good with the management of money and has probably never had a serious banking problem in his life. As a whole, bankers simply don't measure up to what he believes the complete man should be.

Who does Morgan like? For the most part, almost everyone. Morgan is as much at home in a Texas bar shooting pool with refinery workers as he is sitting with another lawyer arguing constitutional law. He has a love-hate relationship with journalists and at one time even wanted to be a writer himself. He is impressed with intellectuals and likes to be in their company. He likes Mexicans, Germans, and blacks. Veterans who come into his court can expect a break from the bench. But his favorite person, his favorite class of human being, his dinner companion of choice, is another lawyer. There may be no lawyer in the bar today who relishes the telling of legal war stories and legal anecdotes as much as Don B. Morgan does.

As a former trial lawyer, Morgan loves the drama of a good courtroom performance. He loves the pull and tug, the chess game between attorneys before the jury. It is a deep appreciation of the skills he developed long ago "in the pit." He says that there is no exhilaration to match looking "into those twelve steely eyes."

Morgan longed to look into those twelve steely eyes again. He longed to be in the pit again. After almost ten years on the bench, he missed the glory of the fight. The Autumn Hills trial would be his final major act as a judge. Morgan had determined that he would not run for reelection in Galveston County. Still ambitious, he had considered a run for the Texas Supreme Court but could not get enough support for the race. In rural Texas, there is another kind of pit, a pit where well-bred fighting roosters wage war to the death with steel spurs attached to their legs. Morgan knew that in the courtroom, he was such a rooster. He would sharpen his unused spurs after Autumn Hills.

Another set of people made ready for the pretrial hearings scheduled for late spring. Bob Gay, Ron Pohlmeyer, Mattie Locke, Virginia Wilson, and Cassandra Canlas were coming to the realization that they would stand trial for murder. All had been through the ordeal of being in the public eye, being in the news, for years. All had faced their neighbors, their coworkers, their friends, and their families. They had tried as best they could to explain that this was an aberration for them.

Of the defendants, some had seen their children grow into their teenage and young adult years with the cloud of their parents' murder charge hanging over their heads. It was not as if the parent had been charged with some petty white-collar crime; this was the big one. Murder. Not a murder in the heat of passion. Their parents were charged with the unthinkable crime of killing scores of defenseless old people.

Television, the constant friend of most young people, had become a nightmare as the years passed. Each time something new developed in the case, each time a new indictment was returned, the wounds would be reopened. The television reporters haunted them, tracking them in the hallways of the Galveston County Courthouse. At night, the humiliation of seeing themselves on the news brought the pain close to the surface again.

Some of the defendants were almost stoic. Bob Gay, ever the man of logic and the cool, collected businessman, maintained his social contacts and maintained his contact with George Mitchell, his wealthy stockholder. Mitchell was supportive of his friend and business associate. He was also angry that such a thing was being done to "these good people," as he called the defendants. His friend Bob Gay had not killed anyone. Gay had not even seen the person he was accused of murdering. He was a victim of the obsession of a crazy man, David Marks.

Ron Pohlmeyer, vice president of Autumn Hills, continued to run the company, keeping the nuts and bolts tight, the wheels turning in the by now reduced number of nursing homes. Pohlmeyer had presided over a chain of seventeen homes for Gay at the height of their association. Now, because of the case, there were only six. Ron worked just as hard as ever to help Bob Gay and Mitchell hold on to what remained.

Mattie Locke and her husband, Virgil, had always had dreams together. When they were young, they had dreamed of the butcher shop she and Virgil had long ago opened. Now, Virgil needed an eighteen wheeler, a big rig on which to run the roads of America. Sometimes, in the past, Mattie would go with him. The big rig helped relieve the constant stress. Mattie wanted to write another book, this one on the trial. Her first, a book of lists for nurses, had met with some modest success. Religion had also bolstered Mattie. Born the daughter of a Pentecostal preacher with 21 other siblings, Mattie still felt the warmth of religion wrapped around her.

Virginia Wilson also felt the warmth of religion, but in another way. Lynn, her husband, was a Baptist minister. Together they had gone from church to church as Lynn had received the call. Lynn worked during the week at the giant University of Texas Medical Branch in Galveston. He was so supportive of Virginia. He knew that his gentle wife hadn't killed anyone.

Sandy Canlas felt the frustration of being called a murderer when she knew that she hadn't killed anyone. She also felt the strain of having to be close to Virginia Wilson throughout the ordeal. She hadn't liked the woman who had hired her at Autumn Hills. On leaving, she had even written a critical letter to Bob Gay about "our dear Mrs. Wilson." Now she would have to sit next to our dear Mrs. Wilson in the courtroom day after day. Eventually, they would become good friends, despite their differences in the past. They would shop together, spend weekends together. They got along.

Yet there was confidence in the defendants too. Hadn't Mr. Gay spent almost a million dollars so far on the case? Roy Minton and Charlie Burton were so warm, so assuring. Tom Sartwelle and Gail Friend knew that they hadn't killed anyone, didn't they? They all worked together, the lawyers and the defendants. They were now a team.

CHAPTER TEN

Tom Sartwelle was morally and professionally offended by David Marks. Sartwelle was convinced that Marks, now an assistant attorney general for Texas, was attempting to build a career on the backs of the Autumn Hills defendants, in the process putting them through an ordeal that no one in the nursing home industry had ever undergone. Always an advocate, Sartwelle was determined to stop that ordeal at the pretrial hearings Judge Don Morgan had scheduled six weeks from the time he agreed to hear the case.

Sartwelle's anger at Marks stemmed from what he considered serious abuses of Marks's position as a prosecutor during the course of the six-year-old case. He felt that Marks had violated the Canons of Ethics, the code by which all lawyers practice their craft in both civil and criminal law.

Roy Minton and Charles Burton were aware of the actions Marks had taken that so disturbed Sartwelle, but the Austin lawyers declined to do anything about them. So Sartwelle decided that Marks would at least have to suffer through a public airing of his behavior at the pretrial hearings, due to begin in Galveston in June 1985. Sartwelle began cataloging the tactics that had so bothered him over the years, actions he believed had been orchestrated by Marks. Some of the items were real, some existed only in the vivid imagination of Tom Sartwelle. All, however, he dictated, sometimes long into the night, into briefs to be filed with the court.

Minton was not as disturbed by Marks's tactics because he had been a prosecutor. He had made just one disparaging remark to Marks, telling him that if he, Minton, had been James Hury, he would have summarily fired Marks. Minton attributed Marks's zealous pursuit of the case to youth and inexperience. In fact, Minton said, "I think of David as I do my sons," and "I'm not mad at David. He's just young."

Galveston's beaches were full the last weekend of June 1985, as the lawyers prepared to try the Autumn Hills murder case. The out-of-town attorneys checked into hotels on the beachfront. Jim Vollers, special prosecuor in the case, stayed at Gaido's Motor Inn, next door to the city's best-known seafood restaurant. Sartwelle, Friend, Minton, and Burton stayed in the Victorian Tremont House, owned by George Mitchell, Bob Gay's close associate and stockholder in the nursing home chain.

The halls of the Galveston County Courthouse are usually crowded on Mondays, and Monday, June 24, was no exception, except that this Monday the air was heavy with the sense of something significant about to happen. The long-awaited Autumn Hills case was finally going to trial, and courthouse watchers knew that sparks were certain to fly, given the number of attorneys and the size of the egos involved. The press was also aware that front-page news could come from the case. Some, such as the *Houston Post*'s Steve Olafson, the *Houston Chronicle*'s Kevin Moran, and the *Galveston Daily News*'s Teri Crook, had followed the on-again, off-again case for years. They would be ready when Morgan convened the hearings.

Bob Gay, Ron Pohlmeyer, Mattie Locke, Virginia Wilson, and Cassandra Canlas, the defendants the state alleged had conspired to murder the Autumn Hills patients out of greed, sat in the back row of Morgan's 212th District courtroom. Outside waited the television cameras that surveyed their every movement, the scrutiny so intense that even these veteran defendants were uncomfortable.

As court convened, the attorneys began filing 38 pretrial motions, including one for a change of venue. Morgan addressed the venue request immediately. He told the lawyers to start looking for an available Texas courtroom where the trial could be heard. Dallas, San Antonio, Corpus Christi, and the small college town of Huntsville were possibilities. Most courtrooms in Texas' 254 counties are in constant use. To find one available for a trial that most observers agreed would last for months was no easy task. Getting the attorneys to agree on a town where the demographic makeup of a jury would be acceptable to everyone would be a major undertaking in itself.

No one had ever seen a case like Autumn Hills before. Marks had spent years on this one piece of litigation. And though antitrust litigation often ran to such lengths, it was rare in a Texas murder case. Of those involved, even the experienced Minton and Burton, none could predict the course the Autumn Hills case would take. The case was not a classic Texas cut and shoot but rather the trial of a corporation for murder that could set legal precedents in Texas and nationally. Galveston County district attorney Mike Guarino, who would lead the prosecution team, had vast experience in murder, armed robbery, burglary, kidnapping, and the entire spectrum of workaday criminal litigation. The two Austin lawyers, Burton and Minton, had tried some sophisticated cases, yet even they had never defended a case like Autumn Hills. Corporate murder by neglect, not premeditated but through omission, was a new area of the law. Every lawyer in the case knew he could be setting legal precedent on any day of the trial.

In May 1985, Morgan ordered the bodies of Edna Mae Witt and Elnora Breed exhumed. He then clamped a gag order on the proceedings in an attempt to protect the surviving family members from the glare of publicity that the order was bound to attract. On the second day of the pretrial hearings, publicity was unavoidable when he granted a further defense motion to exhume 58 more of the Autumn Hills dead.

Sartwelle proposed the mass exhumations and suggested that the bodies be transferred to refrigerated vaults in the Galveston County coroner's office. Sartwelle was driving home the point that if the Autumn Hills case was murder, why weren't autopsies performed at the time of death? Sartwelle firmly believed that answers were not found in a court, with lawyers eloquently arguing with each other. "You find out what happened under a microscope," he told anybody who would listen.

Sartwelle's first task was to clean off the dusty file that Marks had discovered when he moved to his new desk by a window in the Galveston County Courthouse. The file contained findings of a medicaid fraud investigation by Julius Bridges, which had produced a misdemeanor indictment against Marie Ritchie, administrator of Autumn Hills' Texas City facility for much of 1978 and for several years before. Sartwelle now wanted to show that throughout most of the Autumn Hills investigation, Marks had told subpoenaed witnesses that the ex parte investigation he was conducting related to the ongoing fraud investigation. Sartwelle wanted it known that murder, and the unusual notion of corporate murder, had never been mentioned to potential defendants, their lawyers, or anyone else.

Early in the pretrial, James Hury, the former district attorney and now state representative, took the witness stand. Hury told of the genesis of the case, how it had come to his attention as a simple abuse case that was no-billed by a long-ago grand jury. He even described the first set of indictments Marks had managed to secure, calling them a "legal disaster" and an "embarrassment to the district attorney's office and to any person who follows the law as a profession."

Hury continued, relating a conversation with Carol Vance, Autumn Hills' attorney at the time. Hury said that he and Marks assured the defense attorney that the grand jury testimony sought by the district attorney's office was not for the purpose of indicting any of his clients but was needed for a fraud investigation.

Furthermore, Sartwelle charged that Marks's ex parte use of grand jury subpoenas was illegal, since much of the time a grand jury had not been meeting during Marks's personal investigation. Sartwelle said, "Marks and his investigators advised the various witnesses that they were legally obligated to appear at the courthouse for interviews with Marks and his investigators and would be arrested and jailed, or generally be in trouble with the law, if they did not comply with these subpoenas."

Sartwelle added,

Some of the subpoenaed witnesses were forced to comply with the subpoena by being taken to the courthouse in government vehicles under the jurisdiction of District Attorney investigators or uniformed peace officers. Once at the courthouse the various individuals were taken not before a grand jury but to the District Attorney's investigative office where they were told they were obligated to give statements to Marks or his investigators. These subpoenaed individuals were told in some instances, and surmised in others, that they were not free to leave but were required to remain, some against their will, until they were released from the power of the subpoena.

Sartwelle charged that the witnesses, many of whom were nurses and nurse's aides, were unsophisticated in their knowledge of the law. Privately, he believed that since many of the witnesses were black, they told "the man" anything he wanted to hear, hoping only to be left alone.

Sartwelle said that during interviews conducted by Marks, uncooperative witnesses were threatened with perjury charges. He added that Marks and his investigators told Autumn Hills employees that Marks was considering charging them with various crimes during their employment at Autumn Hills. And he said Marks threatened some with jail because of allegations that fellow employees had made against them.

Witnesses were told that the grand jury secrecy law was in force, Sartwelle contended, even though their statements were given only to an assistant district attorney, not a grand jury. He charged that some of the witnesses did not get themselves a lawyer and would talk to no one.

Sartwelle even asserted that two of the defendants had been victims of Marks's abuse of the system.

Two defendants, Sandy Canlas and Virginia Wilson, were duped into talking to David Marks, Betty Korndorffer, and other investigators on several occasions over a period of time between 1980 and March 1981. During the interviews, Marks or Korndorffer assured Sandy and Virginia that they were not targets of the investigation and should talk freely to them. Around the end of March 1981, Marks requested one more interview with Sandy. At that time he intimated to her that she was not a suspect and had nothing to fear. He then advised her that she should make an appearance before the grand jury and testify in answer to his questions. This unsolicited legal advice was accepted by Sandy, and she did testify before the grand jury. The free legal advice turned out to be incorrect because several days later Sandy was arrested and jailed for murder, having been charged in an indictment prepared by David Marks and returned on March 31, 1981.

Betty Korndorffer took the witness stand and bolstered the defense position that Sandy Canlas had cooperated with the state and had been duped. The nursing home inspector told Morgan that she considered Canlas a friend and that she had worked with the former head of nursing at the Texas City facility on correcting problems. During the investigation by Marks, Korndorffer had participated in interviewing Canlas and had even accompanied her to testify before the grand jury. "I thought Mrs. Canlas was to be a state witness, and it never occurred to me that Sandy was a target." She went on, saying, "I told her to cooperate and tell the truth, and I didn't think she had anything to fear." Korndorffer was shocked and surprised when the nurse was indicted.

Sartwelle also charged Marks with intentionally deceiving Autumn Hills' former attorney Carol Vance about the true nature of his investigation into the nursing home. He said that for almost a year and a half Marks told Vance that the probe was aimed at the medicaid fraud allegations. "On several occasions Marks and District Attorney Hury reassured Vance that Autumn Hills would be given an opportunity to explain if anything serious was developed."

Sartwelle stressed that exhumation autopsies of Edna Mae Witt and Elnora Breed could have been performed.

> In October 1979, the two patients, alleged in these indictments to have been murdered, had been buried for less than one year. Exhumation autopsies would have been effective to prove cause of death. Other patients now alleged to have been victims were still alive! These patients could have talked for themselves about the alleged abuse, patients' relatives could also have been interviewed, as could employees and ex-employees. In April 1981, many patients had moved, become infirm and forgetful, or simply passed away. Relatives had died, moved away, or become patients themselves. Employees had quit and moved away.

Sartwelle was also critical of Marks's use of volunteers in his investigation of Autumn Hills. He challenged the use of members of a nursing home reform group as his helpers and pointed out that a prosecutor is commanded "to seek justice, not merely convict."

Tom Sartwelle was angered that Marks had solicited money to continue his investigation when Hury would not support his efforts. Sartwelle felt that by soliciting and accepting the money, Marks had violated ethical principles, specifically: "A public official should not accept anything of value from any person when the lawyer knows, or it is obvious, that the offer is for the purpose of influencing his action as a public official."

Galveston attorney Robert M. "Bob" Moore, a longtime activist in liberal causes, and two other attorneys had filed a series of civil suits on behalf of families of Autumn Hills patients who had allegedly been abused and neglected. Sartwelle now implied that Marks had released grand jury evidence and testimony to the lawyers. He also said that Marks had helped the civil lawyers take statements from witnesses the prosecutor was questioning in connection with the murder indictment. The implication was clearly that Marks was attempting to bring pressure on Autumn Hills on any front he could find.

Marks had worked with Rice University sociologist Chad Gordon, who had allegedly prepared a 140-page report on the case. Sartwelle said that the report was the basis of a book that would profile the Autumn Hills case. On the stand, Marks denied that he had seen the long manuscript. Later, the manuscript formed the core for an article in *Houston City* magazine by Gordon and Michael Barryhill.

More serious perhaps was Sartwelle's allegation that Marks had encouraged members of the first Autumn Hills grand jury to give interviews to newspaper reporters. Sartwelle tracked down a *Miami Herald* story that had appeared shortly after the indictments. In the story, two former grand jurors were quoted. Marks said that when he learned that grand jurors were talking to the press, he attempted to stop the practice.

Nor did Sartwelle forget the publicity that came about when Marks was fired by Hury. "In December 1983, Marks engaged in a massive, voluntary disclosure of grand jury evidence and testimony solely to promote his private idea of justice and in complete disregard of defendants' due process rights and in disregard of the Code of Professional Responsibility and the laws of Texas." Sartwelle was angered that Marks had filed affidavits about Hury's involvement in the case and had encouraged investigators, expert witnesses, and former grand jurors to also file affidavits. Sartwelle pointed out that Marks had filed his own lawsuit in the matter. And Sartwelle did not hesitate to mention that the press, in picking up the story, had reported only the state's position. Sartwelle ended his arguments by saying, "After all, if the Autumn Hills case ended,

Marks would not be able to sell his book," suggesting that Marks was also a budding author.

The entire defense team had been frustrated by Marks's refusal to supply them with evidence during the discovery phase of the case. Sartwelle pointed that out to the court. He also said that Marks had told defense lawyers that certain physicians were to testify as state's witnesses, when in fact they would not.

Sartwelle was also angered by an incident that he saw as a clear case of prosecutorial misconduct. In his brief he said, "On January 26, 1984, attorney Julianne M. Dunn attended a seminar on decubitus ulcer treatment presented by Richard Meer." Meer was an engineer who had studied the effects of constant pressure, such as that encountered with bedridden patients, on the formation of bedsores. "After the seminar," Sartwelle continued, "Dunn appeared in the cocktail lounge of the hotel where the seminar was given, approaching the table occupied by Mr. Meer and several other persons, including defendants Bob Gay, Ron Pohlmeyer, and Mattie Locke. After seating herself Dunn engaged Pohlmeyer in conversation, inquiring whether Autumn Hills intended to use Richard Meer as an expert witness. Pohlmeyer declined to answer, saying such decisions were up to his criminal attorneys. Dunn replied, warning that it would be unwise for Autumn Hills to use Meer. Pohlmeyer inquired of Dunn's identity and she told him her name. She failed to identify herself as an attorney nor did she state any connection with the Galveston District Attorney. Later Pohlmeyer received information identifying Dunn's true identity—Marks's employee engaged in the investigation of Autumn Hills, Bob Gay, Ron Pohlmeyer, and Mattie Locke. Pohlmeyer confronted Dunn with the fact that she was an attorney. She admitted it and produced a business card."

Sartwelle went on, "Again she failed to identify herself as a member of the prosecution team and an employee of David Marks. Pohlmeyer pointedly asked if it was true if she worked for the District Attorney. Dunn, after trying to avoid the answer, finally admitted that she was on a contract with the Galveston County District Attorney's office and was associated with the Autumn Hills prosecution."

The defense had been stunned by Dunn's revelation. Sartwelle had been deeply involved in only one previous criminal case, in which he got the reversal of the conviction of a man accused of rape.

Certainly, as an experienced insurance defense lawyer, he had undergone his share of harrowing experiences with investigators. Yet he was appalled that the power and might of the State of Texas was being used against his clients in such a clandestine manner. Sartwelle, the true believer, remained convinced of his clients' absolute innocence.

Sartwelle further pointed out to the court that Marks's Senate testimony was a violation of grand jury secrecy. "After describing the evidence in detail and providing his personal opinion as to the defendants' guilt, not for eight but for 56 murders, Marks used charts prepared by a State expert witness, paid for by the State of Texas, and prepared for grand jury use, to support his contentions that defendants were guilty. These charts were introduced as evidence and accepted in the Senate record and have been published in a public document available from the Government Printing Office."

In March 1983, veteran newsman Kent Demaret published an article on Autumn Hills in *People* magazine. Sartwelle said that the story detailed grand jury evidence and profiled Marks's opinions as to the guilt of the defendants. Totally ignorant of how the press works, Sartwelle fired a shot in the dark; he charged that Marks not only cooperated with Demaret but "undoubtedly" received a fee.

Nor did Sartwelle overlook the moment when the Autumn Hills case first attracted the attention of the national media. In June 1983, ABC TV's investigative news program *20-20* aired a segment with Sylvia Chase on the alleged atrocities at the Texas City nursing home. Sartwelle charged that the segment "was produced with Marks's cooperation, as well as six of the former members of the two grand juries that had indicted defendants up to that time. Again, specific portions of the evidence were discussed and opinions voiced as to defendants' overwhelming guilt."

Sartwelle and his clients had been especially angered by the television program. Gay had cooperated with ABC in filming the segment, wanting to tell his side of the story. When the segment ran, the network aired a picture of patient abandonment that put the nursing home in a completely negative light—on national television. Among the photos of Autumn Hills patients shown, John Peter Warren, a young man, was pictured with multiple and massive bedsores. Warren had developed the sores before he was admitted to the Texas City nursing home.

Sartwelle also intimated to anyone who would listen that Marks had engaged in an extraprofessional relationship with the segment's producer, Karen Burns. Sartwelle continually referred to the relationship as "intimate."

Sartwelle did, in an affidavit for the court, say, "The airing of the '20-20' Autumn Hills segment did not end the outside influence focused on Marks. It is apparent that Karen Burns continued contact with Marks long after June 1983. This contact may have been responsible for various items of major publicity in national and statewide magazines and newspapers. Defendants believe Karen Burns can and should be allowed to relate the facts she knows about the publicity and the manner in which it was solicited and generated."

In a brief that Sartwelle filed with the court asking for out-of-state subpoenas, he continued his charges against Marks and ABC. "The '20-20' records custodian has been subpoenaed to produce copies of all grand jury evidence given to ABC. Defendants have also requested records of payments made to Marks, Korndorffer, and others associated with the prosecution. It is believed that payments were made by ABC because publicly filed affidavits by Marks and a number of his volunteers demonstrate that Marks and others solicited money to continue the prosecution against Autumn Hills." Again Sartwelle showed an almost childlike ignorance of how the press functions. He now admits that he was firing shots in the dark on behalf of his clients.

Sartwelle concluded, "There is a strong connection between the prosecutor and the various media events surrounding this case, especially the '20-20' program. Since defendants were not privy to the intimate contact occurring between the prosecutor and the '20-20' producer and reporter, it is difficult to particularize exactly what the testimony will reveal."

Morgan denied Sartwelle's request because he believed that the information Sartwelle wanted was trivial to the overall resolution of the case and because bringing in the *20-20* staff and records would be too expensive.

The right to avoid self-incrimination by taking the Fifth Amendment to the Constitution is basic to the American system. Sartwelle charged that Marks had abused his position before the grand jury by forcing witnesses to exercise that right. Witnesses who were granted immunity and were taken back to the grand jury to testify felt that Marks "compounded the self-incrimination prejudice that had generated by questioning the witnesses as to why they felt it necessary to hire an attorney to represent them, the date they hired the attorney, the content of the conversations they had with the attorney, and the identity of the person or company paying for their legal fees." Sartwelle was the attorney and Autumn Hills was paying his fees.

Sartwelle added, "Moreover, the prosecutors compounded their errors by attempting to interfere with the attorney-client relationship of several witnesses by telling the witnesses that their attorneys had a conflict of interest and should not represent the witness. Such conduct was designed to influence the witness to believe that his/her attorneys were acting unethically or illegally so that the witness would terminate the attorney-client relationship."

Sartwelle had no more than a cursory knowledge of constitutional law. His specialization was insurance defense—and now, suddenly, criminal law. In struggling to get the indictments against Autumn Hills quashed, Sartwelle attacked constitutional issues involving the civil rights of his clients, issues totally alien to his expertise and experience as an attorney. Sartwelle had no great, sudden desire to become a constitutional lawyer. But he saw that he couldn't get Minton and Burton to pursue the civil rights violations he perceived in David Marks's tactics.

At an earlier conference, Scott Young, Minton and Burton's bright young appellate lawyer, had told Sartwelle and Friend that in his opinion, "there just wasn't anything there." Sartwelle filed his briefs anyway, ultimately to no avail.

The press had played a large role in keeping the Autumn Hills case alive, so much so that Marks believed at some points that media attention was all he had going for him. Unquestionably, Marks had been cooperative with the fourth estate. Now, Tom Sartwelle was determined to bring Marks's special relationship with the press to the attention of the court. Sartwelle subpoenaed Steve Olafson of the *Houston Post*, Michael Barryhill (a freelancer with a doctoral degree who had worked for *Houston City*), Teri Crook of the *Galveston Daily News*, and Jonathan Dahl of the *Houston Chronicle*.

Sartwelle wanted to put the reporters on the stand and force them to reveal how they received information on the case, whether from the grand jury or from Marks. He was also interested in how

Barryhill had managed to get documents for the magazine article he had written with Chad Gordon.

Sartwelle's subpoena of the reporters created a minor media event in itself. On that day, television crews and radio reporters huddled in the hallways of the Galveston County Courthouse like vultures watching a limping animal. The electronic news media are ever hungry for the dramatic moment, the fleshy photo, or the prospect of blood being spilled. Little does it matter if that blood is from an erstwhile colleague in the press. The subpoenaed reporters swore that they would not reveal their sources.

There was little doubt that Morgan would hold the reporters in contempt of court if they declined to answer Sartwelle's questions. Morgan held a rigid position on contempt of court. He also, in the opinion of most of the reporters, had a bad track record with the press. As attention to the situation mounted, Morgan would boast to friends, "I'm about to be the most popular person in the country. I'm about to throw some reporters in jail. Everybody hates the press."

Galveston Daily News reporter Teri Crook hid from the process servers. She didn't want to have to appear on the stand because she had done the first grand jury story and she knew what Sartwelle wanted to hear. She wouldn't sleep at home, and on one occasion, when an officer came to the *Galveston Daily News* offices, she hid in an upstairs room while a staffer ran through the halls of the white building just off Interstate Highway 45 shouting, "There is someone here trying to serve Teri with a subpoena. She's not here."

Kevin Moran of the *Houston Chronicle* was disappointed that he had not been subpoenaed. Moran had received his training at the prestigious University of Missouri School of Journalism. His greatest ambition was to be jailed for not revealing his sources. Unfortunately, Moran did not get his wish. He just did not know enough, had not had enough contact with Marks, and had covered the case only on a spot news basis. At night, he joined Sartwelle in the Victorian bar of the Tremont House, pleading to be subpoenaed.

As time and the judge narrowed the boundaries within which Sartwelle could work, only two of the four reporters took the stand, Olafson and Barryhill. *Houston City* refused to provide Barryhill with a lawyer. He had been fired from the magazine's full-time editorial staff and had since been working as a writing consultant with the *Houston Chronicle*. The giant Houston newspaper provided him

Robert E. "Bob" Gay, President of Autumn Hills, had lived the American dream. That dream became a nightmare when his top executives were indicted for murder. Ultimately he would stand trial for that crime himself. (Photo by Ron Wilson)

Ron Pohlmeyer was a former state nursing home inspector. He had served as a nursing home administrator for Bob Gay's chain of homes before becoming Gay's right-hand man. (Photo by Ron Wilson)

Mattie Locke had helped Bob Gay and Ron Pohlmeyer to build Autumn Hills into an efficient operation. As nursing consultant to the corporation she was on the road constantly, but by her own admission seldom lifted a bed sheet. (Photo by Ron Wilson)

Virginia Wilson had served as administrator of Autumn Hills in Texas City for only a short time. She was indicted anyway. (Photo by Ron Wilson)

Judge Don B. Morgan was the most controversial man in the Galveston County Courthouse when he agreed to hear the murder case against Autumn Hills. Morgan himself was once a successful trial lawyer. He decided to leave the bench after the Autumn Hills case. (Photo by Steven Long)

David Marks was a misdemeanor prosecutor when he discovered a medicaid fraud case in a dusty file. That file grew over six years of investigations and ultimately Marks believed that a corporation had conspired to murder scores of people. (Photo by Ron Wilson)

Galveston County District Attorney James Hury came to believe that the Autumn Hills case was a more appropriate matter for civil rather than criminal law. However, he was profoundly shaken by his experience on the case and later introduced nursing home reform legislation as a Texas state representative. (Photo courtesy of *Galveston Daily News*)

Newly elected District Attorney Mike Guarino talks to Dr. Richard Campbell as protestors picket the Galveston County Courthouse during Guarino's first days in office. (Photo courtesy *In Between* Magazine)

Jim Vollers had served as an appeals court judge before he was defeated in a Texas election. Vollers was brought in as special prosecutor to aid the novice David Marks on the most complex criminal case in Texas history. (Photo by Ron Wilson)

Lead defense council Roy Minton was "mass in motion" when he addressed the jury. While the state had to convince all twelve jurors of Autumn Hills' guilt, Minton only had to convince one juror of their innocence. (Photo by Ron Wilson)

Tom Sartwelle became a true believer in his client's innocence. Sartwelle, an insurance defense lawyer, was trying his first major criminal case. (Photo by Ron Wilson)

Roy Barrera, Sr. had served as Texas Secretary of State under John Connally. Minton brought Barrera in to join the defense team. (Photo by Ron Wilson)

Gail Friend was a former nursing instructor turned recent law school graduate, and she was Sartwelle's efficient helpmate. (Photo by Ron Wilson)

Defendants join in celebration after mistrial is declared Tuesday, March 25, 1986, at murder-by-neglect trial of Autumn Convalescent Centers, Inc. *From top left:* Autumn Hills Vice President Ron Pohlmeyer, President Robert Gay, Nursing Consultant Mattie Locke and Defense Attorney Roy Barrera, Sr. *From bottom left:* unidentified woman, former Nursing Home Administrator Virginia Wilson and Wilson's husband, Lynn Wilson. (Photo courtesy *San Antonio Light*, Chuck Beckley)

with counsel. The *Houston Post* lawyers could not represent Olafson. The newspaper was represented by Fulbright and Jaworski, Sartwelle's law firm. Outside counsel was brought in to handle the matter. Later, Olafson says, *Post* publisher Don Hunt complained bitterly to Fulbright and Jaworski about Olafson's being subpoenaed in the first place.

On the stand, both Olafson and Barryhill refused to answer Sartwelle's questions. The lawyers argued that reporters have a limited privilege not to reveal sources under Texas law. The argument didn't wash with Morgan. He called the reporters into chambers, found them in contempt, and had them booked into the Galveston County Jail. While waiting for the bailiff to take Barryhill to jail, Morgan smiled at the reporter and said, "I've never put a Ph.D. in jail before." Dr. Barryhill was booked and released 45 minutes later.

Olafson, an old friend of the judge's and Morgan's favorite reporter, also spent 45 minutes in jail. A sometimes painfully shy man, Olafson was now in the glare of television lights, a press hero. Later, at a "Free at last" party at his home, where he was joined by Moran and other members of the Galveston County press corps, he watched videotapes of himself being interviewed by the television reporters. "I kind of liked it," he said, grinning.

He liked it much less the following day when *Post* editors told him that he was off the story because he had become a part of it. Olafson, who had followed the case more closely than any other reporter and had managed—at times almost alone—to keep the issue before the public, was now history as far as Autumn Hills was concerned.

Nurses, nurse's aides, Autumn Hills staff members, and experts paraded to the stand as the defense attempted to short-circuit the state's case. During the pretrial period, guidelines were laid by which the case would later be tried. Morgan often acted as mediator as much as judge in the case. There were, by now, ten lawyers arguing over points of law that to the layman would appear minor. To the attorneys, they were the legal building blocks of the case.

Mike Ramsey still found it difficult to believe that his client, Sandy Canlas, would have to stand trial. Morgan came to like the tall Houston lawyer. Ramsey had the air of a country preacher about him. Morgan later described Ramsey, often shod in cowboy boots, as "a good ol' rednecked teenage boy away from the courtroom. He'd feel comfortable farting in front of you." Under Ramsey's rough exterior, Morgan also recognized a good legal technician.

Morgan, in fact, found it easy to like almost all the attorneys in the case. Guarino he had known for years. Vollers, the special prosecutor, had sat on an appellate bench. Miguel Martinez, the district attorney's young appellate lawyer, Morgan thought was intelligent. He thought Marks was young and obsessive but showed promise. On the defense side, easygoing Scott Young was engaging and smart. Minton had charmed the judge early on, as had Burton, whom Morgan had come to trust on questions of law during the in camera conferences. Don Morgan just liked nothing better than being around lawyers.

But there was one lawyer the judge had difficulty liking. Tom Sartwelle, in Morgan's view, was typical of the feisty lawyers from the big Houston firms. For years he had watched them come into his court thinking they were just a little better than lawyers who scratched out a living around the Galveston County Courthouse. It may have been envy of their salaries, their lifestyle, their political contacts, maybe even their grades on the bar exam. Whatever it was, Don Morgan distrusted the big-city lawyer corps.

The relationship between Morgan and Sartwelle would prove to be rocky in the coming months. Sartwelle was determined to represent his clients the best way he knew how, and the only tactics he knew were those of a scrappy street fighter who is overprepared when he hits the turf.

After six years, defense attorneys finally got their chance to grill David Marks when he was called to the stand during the pretrial proceedings. Over a day and a half of testimony, the attorneys attacked Marks on his alleged abuse of the grand jury system, his alleged cultivation of the news media, and his relationship with Karen Burns of ABC.

Marks held his own on the stand, taking a noncommittal position as often as possible. Much of his testimony was about his interpretation of the law and how a prosecutor works within the grand jury system.

He was, however, chastened. Thereafter, Marks was far less cooperative with reporters than he had been in the past. Sartwelle made his point. David Marks took the charges of prosecutorial misconduct seriously. But though he was chastened, he was also delighted. Morgan set jury selection to begin September 9, and the judge chose San Antonio as the site of the trial. Judge William S. Sessions, successor to the late Judge John H. "Maximum John" Wood, would allow the state to try *State of Texas* v. *Autumn Hills Convalescent Centers, Inc.*, in a borrowed federal courtroom, the same one Wood had presided over before his assassination.

Minton wasted little time lining up local counsel in San Antonio. There was little question about the composition of the panel that the Autumn Hills jury would be chosen from. It was a safe bet that a sizable portion of that panel would be made up of Hispanics and retired military personnel. What Minton needed was an older, well-known, Hispanic attorney with a military service record who could sit as part of the defense team. He found his man in Roy Barrera, Sr., elder statesman of the San Antonio Mexican American community, political activist, and lifelong Democrat.

After leaving the service in the early fifties, Barrera returned to Bexar County, where San Antonio is the county seat, as an assistant district attorney. At that time there were few Mexican American lawyers, and fewer Hispanic prosecutors. Barrera learned his craft in the red sandstone courthouse built in the late nineteenth century opposite San Fernando Cathedral on the Plaza de las Islas, old San Antonio's main square.

From the bell tower of the cathedral, Mexican general Santa Anna flew the red flag of no quarter in March of 1836. That flag meant that there would be no mercy shown the ragtag defenders of the Alamo half a mile away. As a young prosecutor, Barrera showed no quarter to the rogues' gallery that passed through the courthouse. Seasoned by that environment, Barrera became bulldog tough. Sartwelle would later describe him as "a wildman," a high compliment from the fierce Houston defense lawyer.

Barrera eventually left the district attorney's office and went into private practice. In the turbulent fifties and sixties, as Texas' Mexican Americans began to realize their power at the polls, Barrera became a political activist in local Democratic party circles. As he gained recognition in state politics and popularity in Hispanic San

Antonio, an opportunistic John Connally asked Barrera to serve as Texas secretary of state.

After serving in the Connally administration, Barrera returned to San Antonio and resumed his lucrative law practice. In 1973, he ran for mayor in a bitterly contested fight against Charlie Becker, anointed candidate of San Antonio's Anglo community. Barrera lost the race and is still sensitive about the television spots during the campaign that alleged, "Roy Barrera is getting all of his friends in the West End to vote for him." The spots encouraged voters in the city's north side to vote for Becker. The north side of San Antonio is largely Anglo, and Hispanics dominate the south and west side. Barrera learned that no matter how polished a Mexican American is, in the city of the Alamo racism still sometimes plays a role in politics.

After that defeat, Barrera turned again to his law practice. He was unchastened by what he had endured, and he remained active in Democratic politics and in the business community. Over the years, he matured gracefully into a respected elder statesman with a statewide reputation, highly respected, much beloved, and now an ideal local counsel to sit at the defense table with Minton, Burton, Sartwelle, Friend, and Ramsey.

CHAPTER ELEVEN

The majestic Menger Hotel faces west on San Antonio's Alamo Plaza, adjacent to the Cradle of Texas Liberty. Built in 1859, just 23 years after the fall of the Alamo, the venerable hotel was, for more than a century, a mecca for Texas cattle barons, a place where dusty cowboys could enjoy a respite from their hardscrabble existence in the brutal Texas sun. They rode to the Menger on sorrels, Appaloosas, and quarter horses. The wealthier guests found their way there in private railroad cars and later in private jets.

Other San Antonio hotels may have become more fashionable in the tourist-oriented city, but a lot of people in the know still consider the Menger, with its atmosphere reminiscent of the nineteenth-century West, the only choice for the traveler. Most visitors find something special about the hotel. They may be enchanted by the white fluted columns in the lobby or the western art that adorns the second floor. Perhaps they enjoy the King Ranch suite or the Roy Rogers suite or any of several similar period rooms that have been maintained in their original decor. They find something quaint in the personalized wake-up call from Bridgett: "Good morning, my darling. It is time to wake up, my dear."

Don Morgan was determined that his stay in San Antonio would be as comfortable as he could make it. Certainly, the judge could have chosen the fashionable St. Anthony, the historic Gunter, the Hyatt, the Hilton, or the Marriott for his stay. Galveston County was paying, after all, and a state district court judge is expected to live well. Morgan chose the Menger. He expected the trial to last three months.

Morgan traveled to San Antonio with Don Rooney. At 67, the bailiff of Morgan's 212th District Court was totally devoted to his boss. Rooney had spent a lifetime working for United Fruit Company as a troubleshooter. But after surviving a near-fatal heart attack, he moved to Texas for his health. Active all his life, he eventually became bored with the lethargy of retirement. After learning from a friend in a poker game that there were bailiff positions available in the Galveston County Courthouse, he went back to work and eventually found himself in Morgan's court. The two men became fast friends. In the Menger, they shared a suite of rooms.

Across the street from the Menger, the Crockett Hotel is a masterpiece of restoration. The Crockett was once a railroad hotel, a stopping place for drummers, cattlemen, and anyone who couldn't afford the better hostelries. But the hotel had fallen into disrepute and decay until an imaginative entrepreneur spent millions to turn it into a small jewel. When the Autumn Hills trial came to San Antonio, the hotel did excellent business for several months. On its sixth and seventh floors, the defense team of Tom Sartwelle, Gail Friend, Charles Burton, and Roy Minton occupied it as their home and headquarters. Fellow defense attorney Mike Ramsey rented a condominium near the San Antonio River, a grassy-green stream that snakes its way through downtown San Antonio. Ramsey had been in the city for long trials before. He had enjoyed the solitude of living by himself during those stays. Besides, the Crockett was only a few blocks away.

The Autumn Hills prosecutors did not check into a fancy hotel. Instead, they found a large condominium in the northern part of the city. There Mike Guarino, Vollers, Martinez, and Guarino's chief investigator, Felix Mares, lived during the trial. David Marks could not bring himself to share living space with his colleagues, but he took a condo in the same complex. His parents had followed the case closely and would be coming to San Antonio to see their son climax the obsession that had dominated his life for so long. They would need a place to stay.

And there was Colleen. After his divorce from his first wife, Marks plunged himself into his work more than ever. During a brief respite from his efforts, during Galveston's annual Blessing of the Shrimp Fleet, Marks met Colleen Comstock, a 22-year-old nurse working at the University of Texas Medical Branch. They fell in love and were eventually married. Colleen would be coming to San

Antonio to provide support as Marks proceeded against Autumn Hills.

Colleen provided Marks a measure of peace he had not known in his first marriage. Colleen Comstock understood David Marks. Colleen knew what her dedicated husband-to-be needed, and it wasn't the limelight he had been bathed in for years. In reality, Marks was a homebody, a product of small-town East Texas, who craved the stability of family over the camaraderie of friends and colleagues.

Marks and the other prosecutors also had to contend with moving the massive amount of paperwork that the case had generated to San Antonio. The state attorney general's office, for which Marks now worked, provided the prosecutors an office in a nearby state building. There, Marks again assembled his paid staff and volunteers, who once again organized the case.

At the Crockett, Sartwelle and Friend filled a room with filing cabinets containing the defense material they had accumulated over the years. Paperwork, videotapes, an anatomical model—all the tools of the insurance defense lawyer almost filled the room to capacity. In the center of the room stood a conference table that would serve each night as a workplace for Sartwelle, Friend, and the expert witnesses that the defense team was preparing to bring to San Antonio.

Minton and Burton shared a suite, complete with kitchen and bar. The two men had worked together for so long that they were entirely comfortable living together. In one room, a bed was covered with documents that they had assembled during their almost four years on the case. Barrera worked from his office on East Nueva next to La Villita, the original Spanish village of San Antonio de Bexar. Barrera tried, as best he could, to continue his law practice as he prepared for the trial.

Bob Gay, Ron Pohlmeyer, Mattie Locke, Virginia Wilson, and Cassandra Canlas, the individual defendants in the case, moved into condominiums along the river. Their abodes were a closely guarded secret throughout the case.

Judge Morgan had set jury selection to begin September 9, 1985. He planned to assemble an extraordinarily large panel from which the twelve attorneys would select the final slate of jurors. The old

Bexar County Courthouse was not equipped to handle such a large group, so Morgan moved jury selection across the street to the downtown Travel Lodge Motel. There, he was prepared to spend whatever time it took to find twelve people who would give up their jobs and much of their home life for months.

The jury panel would also include four alternates. The alternates were particularly important in a long trial, because illness and even death could become a factor among the jurors. Morgan was determined to provide the case a hearing and did not want to face a mistrial situation because he didn't have enough jurors to continue the proceedings.

In one of the first of hundreds of motions in the case, Ramsey moved to alter the indictments. Two indictments named 61 patients, including Elnora Breed and Edna Mae Witt, who were allegedly abused or neglected at Autumn Hills' Texas City facility. Almost all the patients named in the indictments had died. Ramsey moved that the names be expunged from the indictments so that the jury would not think it was dealing with a mass murder. He urged that the names be struck so "that a fair trial could be articulated" and also noted that the state was not alleging murder in connection with the names. But Judge Morgan left the names in the indictments after the teams of attorneys argued for a full day over the issue.

Special prosecutor Jim Vollers, who had temporarily left his Austin law practice to work for the state, told the two hundred potential jurors that the Autumn Hills defendants "failed to provide a sufficient number of licensed nurses, a sufficient number of aides and other personnel. They failed to provide sufficient food and medication. They failed to properly supervise the people they were charged with supervising. As a result of these failures and omissions, Mrs. Breed died." Vollers said the state would produce evidence of abuse and neglect and would establish a case of murder by omission. "A nursing home has a legal duty to provide care to its patients. If they didn't give the needed care they were required to under the law, and that resulted in death, they would be guilty of murder."

Vollers explained Marks's theory of corporate criminal liability to the jurors. "This is a new or novel concept to most of you, that a corporation has been charged with a criminal offense, that of committing murder. When these officers and employees act within the scope of their employment, they are acting for the corporation.

That is the only way a corporation can act."

In questioning the potential jurors, the attorneys looked for personality traits and personal qualities that would be supportive of their side. In the background, psychologists were running profiles on the prospective jurors. The state wanted jurors who would relate to the pain and suffering that the Autumn Hills patients had endured. One potential juror, however, went overboard for the state. The woman had to be dismissed when she stated that she couldn't stand to be in the same room with the defendants, because she was familiar with conditions in nursing homes.

Six days later and almost three weeks after the jury selection phase began, seven men and five women were seated. The attorneys chose Pamela Duran, an employee with San Antonio Savings; Frances Arcliff, a utility clerk with San Antonio Savings; Domingo Montez, a postal supervisor; Raymond Rodriguez, a splicer with the telephone company; William Alvarado, unemployed; Janet Barse, a housewife; Tony Coronado, a retired civil servant; Guadalupe Hernandez, also unemployed; Linda Peña, a secretary at Datapoint; Linda Aldridge, a clerk at nearby Kelly Air Force Base; Guadalupe Nuñez, Jr., a medical clerk at the V.A. hospital; and Sherman Miller, a cook at the Lackland Air Force Base officers' club. The average age of the jury was 41, although eight of the jurors were younger than 40. Only two jurors were as old as 60.

Two men and two women were retained as alternates. They were Aurora De Leon, a housewife; Barbara Garcia, a school crossing guard; John Sutherland, a salesman with the William Wrigley, Jr., Company; and Clinton Jenschke, Jr., a civil servant who worked with boiler plant equipment. None of the alternates were told that they were not, in fact, jurors.

Sartwelle was concerned about the jury. In fact, Sartwelle was concerned about the entire jury system, so concerned that he was considering leaving his profession. He planned to present complicated, sophisticated, medical testimony during the trial. Would this jury have the educational level even to understand what he was saying? He wasn't sure. What he was increasingly sure of was that he no longer liked his work. A lot of that dislike stemmed from his increasing belief that the American legal system had somehow failed.

Minton, ever quick with a quip, stood before the jurors and looked them in the eye as he addressed them. The selection process had taken longer than most Texas trials. He could understand that perhaps some of the jurors were already tired. He told them, "We know this has been just about as much fun as a good car wreck," just before Judge Morgan dismissed the panel. They were to return October 4, 1985, for opening arguments.

Judge Morgan walked briskly through the front doors of the Menger Hotel at 9 a.m. on October 4. The trial that would climax his career as a judge was scheduled to begin fifteen minutes later in the courtroom once used by murdered federal judge John H. Wood, Jr. The historical significance of the case he was about to try was not lost on Don Morgan. He had been involved in important cases before, but no judge in Galveston County and few in Texas or the rest of the country had presided over a case with such potential for social change, at least not on the district court level.

Morgan had wanted to be a federal judge. He admired how William Wayne Justice affected social change from his bench in Tyler, Texas. If he ever got the opportunity (and in Reagan's America that was increasingly unlikely for a man like Morgan) he would use the bench to right glaring wrongs.

But Autumn Hills was different for Morgan. His preliminary thoughts had been extremely negative toward the defendants. In fact, when Minton told Morgan that the attorneys would recommend sentencing by the jury rather than the judge, should there be a conviction, Morgan told the Austin lawyer that he had made a wise choice.

Increasingly, Morgan was troubled by the indictments for murder. As he read it, the jury would have to find that the defendants had willfully killed Elnora Breed. Morgan was simply not convinced that anyone had willfully killed anyone else. He already knew that tragic neglect had occurred at Autumn Hills in Texas City, but murder?

Court bailiff Don Rooney, sharing the Menger suite with Morgan, was convinced that murder had not been committed. Rooney had seen Marks in action as a prosecutor early in his career. He had little regard for his talent against the likes of Minton and Sartwelle. Rooney often reminded Judge Morgan of the weakness of the case Marks had built during his six years in pursuit of Autumn Hills.

Morgan walked across Hemisfair Plaza to the building that served as the American pavilion during the world's fair in 1968. The pavilion was now part of the federal complex, another sign of the presence of national government in the Alamo City. White and austere, the John H. Wood Federal Courthouse had in recent years been the site of some of the most right-wing legal decisions in America. Some called the late Judge Wood a maniac on the bench. His successor, Judge William S. Sessions, they said, was almost as conservative as Wood.

But Judge Morgan was grateful to Sessions. The presiding judge of the Western District of Texas had been kind enough to allow Morgan to use the courtroom of his predecessor to try the Autumn Hills case at a time when no state courtrooms were available in San Antonio. Barrera had been instrumental in securing the courtroom for the trial. Barrera had first tried to secure a lecture amphitheater at St. Mary's University School of Law, but to no avail.

As Morgan approached the courthouse he strode through a forest of television cameras. The judge did not speak. He just kept walking. He would sit with print journalists for hours, but Morgan had little time for their colleagues in the electronic media. During the Autumn Hills pretrial, a television news photographer chased an angry Morgan down the hallway of the Galveston County Courthouse. The judge did not look very good that night on the six o'clock news.

Bob Gay, Ron Pohlmeyer, Mattie Locke, Virginia Wilson, and Cassandra Canlas also passed through the horde of newsmen who had staked out the opening day of the trial. Gay, Wilson, Locke, and Canlas had become somewhat accustomed to the constant glare of news media attention. Not so Ron Pohlmeyer. The tall, graying man who had grown up in rural Brenham, Texas, still did not feel comfortable around any kind of camera. Pohlmeyer had first heard of his indictment on television—not from his lawyer, the court, or a peace officer—and he remembered that moment with pain.

Pohlmeyer was angry at being where he was. He was humiliated at being tried for murder, being called a mass murderer. He had worked hard to become Bob Gay's right-hand man. Pohlmeyer made the business tick. While Gay worked with the financial end of the nursing home chain, Pohlmeyer held the day-to-day operations together. A common office joke was that Pohlmeyer had telephone ear. That was close to the truth. In 1978 he was in contact with all seventeen nursing homes on an almost daily basis. Autumn Hills had to be profitable to survive. Pohlmeyer saw that the individual nursing home directors were aware of costs, maintained the exteriors of the facilities in excellent shape, hired personnel who were in the Autumn Hills mold, and kept state inspectors happy, to name only a few of his duties.

The courtroom was filled to capacity, and it was a large courtroom. At the attorneys' tables, the opposing lawyers shuffled papers, greeted onlookers, smiled at the assembled press, and prepared to earn their keep. Each attorney also understood that he must hold his considerable ego in check; there could be only one captain on each team if that team was to avoid total disorganization.

Minton served as lead counsel for the defense team, although as much could be said for Burton. The two worked so closely and thought so much alike that it was often difficult to tell which one called the shots. And the arrangement frustrated Ramsey. He was a top criminal lawyer in his own right and was not accustomed to sitting second chair to anyone. Ramsey was highly paid and well regarded in Houston. Barrera attracted top fees and was something of a legend in San Antonio.

Minton often referred to lawyers like Sartwelle as rug lawyers, a member of a big Houston firm with lots of carpet on the floor. Sartwelle was equally unaccustomed to following another lawyer's lead. As a senior partner in Fulbright and Jaworski, he usually handled his own cases with a young associate assisting him. In San Antonio, he had such an associate, though not a young one. Gail Friend, small, pert, a recent law school graduate, had covered a lot of miles with Tom Sartwelle. Now she sat at his side in the courtroom, her years of work perhaps about to pay big dividends.

For the state, Guarino, the young Galveston County D.A., would call the shots, not Marks. Jim Vollers, the eldest member of the state team and a former appellate court judge, would also play second fiddle to Guarino. Miguel Martinez, born in Nuevo Laredo, Mexico, but educated at Georgetown University and the University of Houston, would serve the team as book lawyer, handling any appeals and scurrying to the law library in search of precedents from which the state could argue.

Although Marks would not make the final decisions for the prosecution team, he did have one responsibility that would be vital to the presentation of *State of Texas* v. *Autumn Hills*. Marks would make the opening argument on behalf of the state. He would describe for the jury the points his colleagues planned to make during the coming months. He would, his team hoped, succinctly set the tone and the keynote for the rest of the trial.

On the night before the trial opened, Marks was too nervous to accomplish anything with his opening remarks. He had rehearsed the speech a thousand times in his head, but now he felt frustrated. There was too much that needed to be said, and he knew too many facts. At 11 p.m., Marks went to Guarino with his problem. Calmly, deliberately, Guarino helped Marks organize the opening remarks. By 1 a.m., Marks was home and writing the final draft of the argument he would deliver before the jury the following morning.

The next morning, Marks paused before the judge and jury as he began the climax of a six-year crusade that had taken him, an obscure Southeast Texas misdemeanor prosecutor, to a borrowed federal courtroom in San Antonio, where he stood before the eyes of the national press. Silently, he thought, "This is it, boy." Nervously, he began.

"The case revolves around two questions of fact. The defendants claim that Elnora Breed was in a terminal state when she entered the nursing home. The claim by the state is that her death was unnatural. Did the doctor no-code her?" ("No code" is medical shorthand for "no heroics.") "Were the obligations of the nursing home in any way limited? Did she have cancer? The evidence will show that she did not have cancer."

He continued, "Five months before she entered the nursing home, four doctors found that she did not have cancer. . . . They performed a battery of tests. . . . They found no cancer." Marks went on to show Breed's medical history. He told of her bouts with cancer—including three operations—beginning in 1961 and continuing on and off the rest of her life. "How did the lady exist with a raging cancer for seventeen years?" he asked.

"Were the bodily systems of Elnora Breed shutting down when she entered Autumn Hills? Her heart was normal, her lungs were normal, her kidneys were normal. Elnora Breed's body was not shutting down; she was improving when she was transferred to Autumn Hills."

Marks's nervousness diminished as he continued to recount the subject he had come to know so well. He told of how Elnora suffered from senility, how she liked to talk about the past, how she was capable of speech, how she was generally cheerful and alert before she was brought to the Texas City nursing home. He also told the jury that on her chart a doctor had noted, "Patient recovering slowly."

Marks outlined a six-point list of duties the law requires a nursing home to perform. Then he outlined the duties each of the individual defendants in the dock was required to perform. He told the jury that in 1978 the defendants sitting before them were "the brains of the company."

Marks said that prospective employees were lured off the street with no training in health care. He told the jury that the Autumn Hills administrators placed these untrained people in the skilled wing of the nursing home, where patients most needed medical care. He said that the corporation was greedy and had cut corners.

Next Marks outlined the witnesses and evidence that the state would present to the jury. In the coming months, the jurors would view documents, hear former Autumn Hills employees, hear relatives of Autumn Hills patients, and listen to testimony from Texas Department of Health inspectors who were on the scene in 1978. He pointed out that for two thirds of the 47 days that Elnora Breed spent in Autumn Hills, the nursing home was on probation.

Marks hammered his points home to the jury, becoming more emotional as he continued. He told the jury how Bob Gay and Ron Pohlmeyer cut back on supplies and equipment in order to maximize profits. He said that Gay was on an expansionist program to buy as many nursing homes as he could. Marks said that Gay and Autumn Hills were $8 million in debt. He described how the company had based its bonus program for nursing home administrators on profits.

Marks concentrated on Elnora Breed. He pressed the point that Breed was given no food, water, or medication for the first day and a half of her stay at Autumn Hills. He pressed the point that she was allowed to lie in her own urine and feces for days, and he told how the nursing home staff did not get her up from her own waste. He said that her bedsores were so deep that the bone was visible when pus was cleaned out of her wound.

He said that on October 31, 1978, Halloween, Elnora Breed's condition came to the attention of Texas Department of Health inspectors, 27 days into her stay. The date was not lost on the audience. The inspectors, he said, learned that the woman's physician had not been informed of her massive sore. Marks pointed out that the nursing charts did not reflect Elnora Breed's true condition. He said that the nursing home staff was falsifying records, covering up, overreporting the care the patient was receiving. Marks described other Autumn Hills patients. "What was happening to Elnora Breed was symptomatic of what was happening to other patients. Autumn Hills was an epidemic of rotting flesh."

Marks outlined the personal spending habits of the president of Autumn Hills. He said that those spending habits were a major diversion of funds that should have been spent on patient care. "In 1978, Bob Gay sucked $600,000 out of that corporation. He spent over $18,000 on trips, dinners, golf club memberships, tennis club memberships, trips to Vail, trips to Europe, all billed to the corporation." Almost crying now, Marks concluded by charging that Bob Gay's policy was to maximize profits with a total disregard for patient care. He then thanked the jury and sat down. Minton rose and declined to make an opening argument. Again, Marks rose, and called his first witness to the stand.

At 83, Ruth Linscomb was a prim and proper light-skinned black woman who entered the courthouse wearing a burgundy-colored suit. She had completed the first airplane ride of her life the day before. David Marks questioned her gently about her life as he laid the foundation for the story she would tell. Ruth was an articulate octogenarian, a beloved aunt to the family that lived on Bell Drive. She had been a devoted sister to Elnora Breed.

Marks had Ruth tell of how she had traveled by taxi from her home to Autumn Hills twice a day to visit her sister in room 12. He also led the woman into relating how she had complained repeatedly to the nurses and administrators about the filth in Elnora's bed. She said that she complained to no avail. She then described how her sister was allowed to lie in her own urine and feces for 47 days.

Marks also turned Elnora into a person, not just a name in an indictment. Ruth Linscomb described her sister as an active person in her later years who mowed her own yard, washed clothes by hand on a scrub board, and boiled those clothes in a big iron pot, though she owned a washer. Marks also allowed Linscomb to tell of Elnora's trips to the grocery store, to her church circle meetings, and to the doctor.

Before he was through, Marks and his witness had painted a vivid picture of the frail but active woman who had become the most important alleged victim in the case. The picture was a sympathetic one, for Ruth Linscomb still exuded caring love for the sister who had been dead nearly seven years. Marks adroitly used Ruth Linscomb's appearance to set a tone with the jury that he would follow throughout the testimony of his witnesses and those of the defense. That tone, that repeated theme, was of unconscionable neglect, and Ruth Linscomb had been an eyewitness to its effect on her sister for 47 days.

When Marks passed the witness to the defense, Tom Sartwelle rose, introduced himself to Ruth Linscomb, and proceeded to question her with a half smile on his face. Sartwelle clearly found it trying to have to deal with Ruth again. He had previously settled a civil suit that she had brought against Autumn Hills when he was representing the nursing home's insurance company.

Sartwelle was still involved in the case for one reason. He was one of the best lawyers with medical expertise in the country. Now, he immediately established that Elnora Breed was being fed through a tube in her nose when she left Galveston County Memorial Hospital for Autumn Hills. He quickly pointed out that as early as 1958 Breed had suffered from stomach problems, blood in her stool, and dizziness. Marks objected to Sartwelle's sidebar remarks, and Judge Morgan sustained his objection. Sartwelle turned back to the witness.

Ruth Linscomb told the court that her sister had suffered a stroke at home, but she also answered Sartwelle that her sister could speak just after the stroke. Sartwelle immediately shifted to another subject, pointing out through Linscomb that Elnora Breed couldn't control her bowels and bladder. He also reminded Linscomb that her sister had suffered a fractured hip while at Seabreeze nursing home. Sartwelle, however, got more than he bargained for when he attempted to establish that Elnora Breed was unable to speak while at Autumn Hills. Linscomb cut him off, saying, "Well, she talked pretty good when I was there."

Sartwelle went on undaunted. "She would slap the food away and throw it on the floor," he said. Pressing, he pointed out that in May 1978 Elnora was having severe diarrhea, that her weight was down to sixty pounds, and that she had been hospitalized for not eating. Ruth Linscomb remembered little of that. Nor did she remember a nasal gastric tube at Galveston County Hospital before the transfer of Elnora to Autumn Hills. She did not remember being told by a nurse at Autumn Hills that her sister would always be fed by a nasal gastric tube "from here on out."

Sartwelle also pointed out that Elnora Breed was catheterized at the hospital before she came to Autumn Hills, and he added that the catheter was in place until the day she died. He asked Ruth Linscomb if she had noticed any problems with the catheter tubing or bag. She had not. Nor had she known that her sister was being treated for diarrhea in the hospital and at the nursing home. In fact, she said Elnora often had solid bowel movements in her final days.

Finally, Sartwelle told Linscomb and the jury that Elnora Breed was on a narcotic for pain, pain he attributed to terminal cancer. Sartwelle finished with Ruth by saying that Elnora "was maintained in comfort until she could peacefully pass from this earth."

Marks on redirect had only one question for Ruth Linscomb. He asked if she knew if a strong narcotic was being given Elnora to stop the pain from the bedsores, which were so deep that the bone was showing through. Despite Minton's sustained objections, Marks had made his point in the face of Sartwelle's medical-legal sophistry.

Though Guarino was leading the prosecution team, there was no question that Autumn Hills was David Marks's case. For years, he had been developing expert witnesses, learning from them, absorbing details of the medical, nursing, and nutritional needs of the elderly patients at Autumn Hills. Just such an expert was Delores Alford, a Dallas-based gerontological nursing consultant who had cared for hundreds of elderly patients. Marks brought the woman to the stand as the first in a parade of expert witnesses.

In three and a half days of testimony, Alford told the jury of the neglect that Autumn Hills was charged with in the case of Elnora Breed. She told first of the bedsores, then slowly educated the jury about such sores and ways to prevent them. She described how, in some of the sores, the tissue died and the ulcer oozed pus. Alford said that Elnora Breed was in pain because of the neglect.

"Did you find in the records that any food, water, or any medication was given during the first one or two days?" Marks asked.

"She could not have received anything because her nasal gastric tube was out. It wasn't replaced until a day and a half later [after her admission]," she answered. Alford had earlier told the jury how such tubes were used to sustain patients who could not feed themselves.

Marks also questioned the nurse on Elnora Breed's medical records. The records "demonstrated after extensive diagnostic studies no evidence of cancer." Alford continued, "No, I wouldn't say she was terminal. She was well on her way to recovery." She explained to the jury that Breed didn't have to develop the bedsores. She said, "Pressure sores are preventable 99.9 percent of the time. Rarely are they not preventable." Alford said that bedridden patients such as Elnora Breed needed to be turned at least every two hours and to receive skin care and hygienic care. Alford added that the sores progress in several stages. If a patient develops one, "it means we have let the patient down."

Delores Alford believed that her profession had failed Elnora Breed. "They abandoned her," she said. Alford also testified that Breed's medical records indicated the woman was being fed a diet of only six hundred calories a day. "Anything under seven hundred calories a day would be starvation." She said she had discovered that a doctor had given a written order that the 87-year-old woman be given six hundred cubic centimeters of liquid nourishment each day. Alford went on to say that there was no designation of what kind of food she was to receive. The state alleged that Breed was given Ensure, the supplement that the Texas City home kept in short supply in 1978.

Alford also testified that a culture from one of Elnora Breed's bedsores turned up bacteria usually found in feces and urine. "It means the patient had to be lying in feces and urine for it to infect the pressure sore," she said.

Alford gave the jury its first glimpse of what a bedsore looks like when she presented a color slide show. Some of the jurors turned their heads as the full horror of rotting flesh was flashed on a five-by-ten-foot screen before them. Alford provided a clinical narration to accompany what the jurors were seeing.

Alford ended her testimony with another shock for the jury as she described the medical record of Elnora Breed. She noted that serious discrepancies in the medical record "make me wonder at the veracity of the record. . . . These were the same nurses who were charting her condition as unchanged and were charting that they gave her medicine after she was dead and gone to the funeral home." The records showed that Breed had received medication at night after she had died early in the morning of the same day.

On cross-examination, Sartwelle tried to shake Alford to get her to admit that some bedsores are simply not treatable, but the Dallas nurse denied that suggestion. She pointed out to Sartwelle that a bedsore on Elnora Breed's foot was healing when she was brought to Autumn Hills from the hospital. Her profession had been insulted by what had happened at Autumn Hills, and Alford refused to be shaken by Sartwelle's inferences. Delores Alford had an unshakable belief that bedsores are preventable through good nursing care. She was convinced that such care was a rare commodity at the Texas City nursing home.

Pauline Goodwin and Mattie Locke had been friends. Goodwin was director of nursing at nearby Manor Care nursing home. The two women's paths crossed as each pursued her career; they had much in common. They also were able to have fun together when they went to dinner. On a social level, Pauline and Mattie had been able to put their work with the near-dead behind them. The inherent sadness of a nursing home was easily forgotten when a friendship was shared.

Now, as Mattie Locke sat in the courtroom on trial for murder, she was hurt that her friend was called as a state witness. After all, hadn't she had such good times with Pauline? Why would she do this? Why was she cooperating with David Marks? There were so many whys and so few answers for Mattie.

Mattie had recommended that Pauline be called to work at Autumn Hills when she became convinced that there were problems in the Texas City home. Pauline had, in fact, visited the home, using her vacation time to look the place over. In the time she was there, she found a multitude of problems, of which she informed the administrator. She said on the witness stand that those problems were only "the tip of the iceberg."

When she came to the home, Pauline Goodwin found the patients' beds filthy and immediately washed them down. She also watched a nurse fill in gaps in a patient treatment chart for days that a nurse was off duty. Goodwin also noticed that it appeared that patients were not being given enough food and water and that some call buttons were out of reach, preventing patients from summoning aid. Another finding was that the water pitchers were dirty in patients' rooms, catheters were leaking, and the home had the persistent odor of urine.

Now on the witness stand, Pauline Goodwin Kaper, married and with a new last name, described how she had found Elnora Breed. During the five November days she spent at Autumn Hills, she said, walking past the room of the frail woman was not an easy or pleasant task, because the odor in the hallway outside Elnora Breed's room was that "of a rotting animal."

Sherel Johnson, a longtime Autumn Hills nurse's aide, now took the stand as a prosecution witness in the murder trial of her former employers. She said she had worked at the nursing home almost five years before she received any training in patient care. But Johnson had a relatively short memory. Roy Minton produced documents on cross-examination showing Johnson's signature on forms that proved she had attended such sessions. Johnson had said that she had never been taught to bathe patients, feed them, or change their linens.

Minton would follow that cross-examination pattern throughout the trial whenever nurse's aides took the stand. He and his colleagues proved that Autumn Hills did provide in-service training for aides. Minton, however, had little luck in proving that the quality of that training was anything but marginal.

What Johnson did accomplish under Marks's direct examination was to establish eyewitness testimony about an incident that sent shudders through the courtroom audience and made headlines in the press. Elnora Breed had reached such a deplorable condition in the final days of her life that one of her untended bedsores developed maggots, even as she lay alive in her own filth.

In previous testimony, Nurse Jurline Boone mentioned that she had found maggots in the foot of another patient, Carrie Bacon. Later testimony by other witnesses would show that Bacon's toes were in such a condition that they were falling off. Through shock, state prosecutors were getting the attention of the jury and the public.

Sartwelle and the defense team were obligated to put the best face possible on the conditions at Autumn Hills in Texas City. Sartwelle truly believed that the nursing home was no better and no worse during 1978 than most other nursing homes. In fact, Sartwelle believed that Autumn Hills had given its patients the best care possible.

Through the eyes of two nurses and two members of the nursing home's staff in 1978, the state had given the jury a look at the horror that it contended was the pattern at Autumn Hills. Three of the witnesses so far had been eyewitnesses. As the trial proceeded, Marks brought on more of the witnesses he and his volunteers had developed over many years. Next up were members of the families of some of the alleged victims of the nursing home.

The first family member the state called was Brenda DiCristina, a 36-year-old mother of two from Atlanta, Georgia. She related to the jury what she found when she visited her grandmother Nell Reams in the nursing home for a week during September 1978. She unveiled a horror story about conditions in her grandmother's room and the condition of the woman she had loved for so long. She told how she had discovered an "oozing, pussing, large black sore on her heel." She related how her aunt called someone to clean the sore out, but no one came.

Tom Sartwelle tried to break Brenda DiCristina's story, as he would with almost every witness who testified against his clients. As he began questioning the woman, he wore a friendly but insincere smile. A master at slipping in testimony of his own that would be negative to his opponents, Sartwelle quickly made sure the jury knew that Nell Reams had Parkinson's disease.

He also mentioned Nell Reams's doctor Merrill Stiles. "I never saw Dr. Stiles," DiCristina responded. "My mother tried previously to call him and never heard back from him." Sartwelle quickly changed the subject from Stiles' failure to return the family's phone calls. "Did you know that your grandmother had become combative on several occasions? That's why the doctor had prescribed Valium."

On redirect, Guarino again pressed DiCristina to relate more of the horror of her grandmother's condition. He skillfully directed attention away from the ailments of Nell Reams and attempted to refocus the jury's attention on the issue of neglect by the nursing home. DiCristina was prepared for him. She related that her grandmother's sore was not bandaged, that there was no dressing, and that pus was oozing onto the sheet of her bed.

Brenda DiCristina was followed in quick succession by other witnesses who were either friends or relatives of Nell Reams. Rydel Braunsdorf was a friend of the woman's daughter Mary Vaughn. Braunsdorf told much the same story of Nell Reams's treatment. "Nothing was ever right about her. She smelled bad, her hair wasn't clean, and her room wasn't clean. . . . I lifted up the sheets to look, and she had had a BM. She was lying in it." Braunsdorf also said that other patients were calling out "Help" and "Nurse." She described a bedsore on one woman's hip. "I could see the bone. It was bad."

Mary Vaughn was the daughter of Nell Reams. With her on the stand, the prosecution continued to hammer home to the jury the horrible condition in which the 73-year-old woman had found herself during the final months of her life. The courtroom audience reacted with shock when Vaughn related how a nurse's aide had come into the room to take her mother's temperature. "Instead of using the thermometer in the place it should be used, it was used in the vagina."

CHAPTER TWELVE

Early on, Judge Morgan laid down the mechanics of putting Autumn Hills on trial. Most observers assumed that the case would last until Christmas. Some of the participants, particularly Sartwelle, believed it would last until the spring of 1986. If it did, the trial would pose a hardship for the attorneys and their clients other than Autumn Hills, unless some arrangement was made to allow time to deal with those cases. Morgan ruled that testimony in the trial would end each Thursday afternoon, allowing the lawyers the following day to work in their offices. The ruling was particularly important to Minton, Burton, Ramsey, and Vollers, all successful criminal defense attorneys. (Vollers had taken leave from his defense work to help the state prosecute the case.)

The ruling also allowed the defendants to go home and continue to run their businesses. Autumn Hills was still operating six nursing homes in and around the Houston area. The staff in the company's home office was handling the day-to-day operations, but Gay and Pohlmeyer needed to exert overall supervision, which they could do on the Fridays they were out of court. A month into the trial Gay would say, "After all this is over I am going to rearrange my life. I have learned that you can run a business working one day a week."

Mattie Locke flew home to Virgil and the children in Houston each weekend. The two had a small publishing business they had to run. A strikingly attractive woman in her early forties, Mattie stood out in a crowd. Her sense of humor was infectious, and she seemed always to have a smile. Courtroom observers believed that her displays of laughter served her poorly, making it appear that she was not taking the charges against her seriously enough. That impression overlooked two things: Mattie Locke had absolute faith in her attorneys, and in the unlikely event that they failed, she had absolute faith in God. She thought she had nothing to fear because she knew she was innocent.

In airports, the tall, blond woman attracted onlookers as she traveled to and from San Antonio. Occasionally, she would attract a lonely man who would strike up a conversation as they awaited departure, including the classic pickup lines heard in every airport in the world.

"Where are you going?" a man would ask.

"To San Antonio," Mattie would reply.

"What are you doing in San Antonio?" came next.

"Oh, I'm on trial for murder," Mattie would respond benignly.

That response invariably short-circuited the conversation as the man beat a hasty retreat. And Mattie would laugh at the humor of the situation.

Sandy Canlas, alone of all the defendants, stayed in San Antonio. Her home, Alabama, was just too far away. She missed her two children and the rest of her family as she whiled away the weekends alone in the condo on the river. From time to time, she got out and saw some of the city, but her situation didn't really lend itself to the life of a tourist. Ordinarily gregarious, Cassandra Canlas made the most of her loneliness; she knitted.

Morgan, Guarino, Martinez, the bailiff, the court reporter, and Guarino's assistant Felix Mares all went home to Galveston County on weekends. Morgan often went to Austin to visit longtime friends and his mother and sister. He was devoted to his family. And Austin exhilarated him, recharged his energies by getting his mind off the case.

Morgan needed that. He had a lot of thinking to do. He was convinced that he again wanted to try lawsuits, this time from the attorney's side of the bench. The Democratic primary would take place in the spring. If he filed again for his position, Morgan was almost certain to win reelection. If he did not file, he could find himself unemployed, a situation unthinkable to Morgan. He and Mary had provided their children the best possible education. Sarah, their youngest child, was attending elite Sarah Lawrence College in New York. Ann, their middle child, was at American University Law School in Washington, D.C. Tom, their eldest, was attending the London School of Economics. Morgan had to produce a substantial income to continue to pay for his children's education.

There were no guarantees that a private firm would hire a former state district court judge at the salary level required by his family's lifestyle. Under ideal circumstances, Morgan would have to bring business to a future employer. As a judge, out of practice for ten years, it would be difficult for him to attract clients immediately. But Morgan and his wife had made up their minds that he would not run again. After Autumn Hills, Don Morgan would have his opportunity to again look into those "twelve steely eyes" of a jury and use the ringing biblical rhetoric that came to him so easily.

It was the task of young Pamela James to describe for the jury the day-to-day activities of an Autumn Hills nurse's aide. An articulate young woman, James had good recall of the period in 1977 and 1978 when she worked at the nursing home. She said she had been hired the same day that she applied for work. Guarino skillfully led James through her average workday.

First, the prosecutor established that James had received no training other than that given by another aide after she was hired by Mattie Locke. She then told the jury about conditions in the home from the point of view of an aide who had been hired at $2.65 an hour.

Guarino and the other prosecutors had earlier pointed out that patients sometimes didn't get fed at Autumn Hills in Texas City. Now James explained why. "The nurses would tell us who we were supposed to feed. . . . We would go back and feed the ones that needed to be fed. They knew a patient needed to be fed but they wouldn't go in there," James said.

"Who?" questioned Guarino.

"Some of the aides," James responded.

Guarino also had James relate how patients whose family members fed them suffered when their relatives could not come to the nursing home.

"Her son came and fed her. When he didn't come, some of the aides would get mad and say he should have come to feed her," James recalled, explaining that the aides thought it was the son's fault if his mother didn't get fed.

James also told the jury that there was a constant laundry problem at the Texas City nursing home. "There was never enough laundry in the building to supply the patients with enough laundry," she said.

Guarino pressed her to describe how the laundry system sometimes worked to the detriment of patients if their particular aides were not in favor with the laundress.

"Sometimes, she would have the laundry scattered out for who she wanted to get it," James said.

"You mean the ones she liked?" Guarino questioned.

"Yes," James answered.

"How often did you have laundry problems?" Guarino continued.

"Every day I was there."

At Autumn Hills, the morning bath was often neglected because aides were busy helping with the laundry, James said. Some patients did manage to pressure the aides simply by raising hell. James testified that the aides bathed patients who were already up because "they would get mad if we didn't bathe them. Most of the time they didn't have soap to bathe the patients with. They didn't have lotion."

Guarino led James through descriptions of laundry, bathing, and feeding to filth. She testified, "You could tell about the urine because they had brown spots on the bed. . . . It was sometimes 1 p.m. before we could change them." James started work each morning at seven. She also remembered that "pitchers were sitting on the table with slime and stuff in them."

As Guarino and James laid out the routine day on the seven-to-three shift, the prosecutor asked, "Did you ever do anything you shouldn't have done?"

"Watched TV," James responded. She testified that she would go into a patient's room and watch her favorite soap operas, *The Young and the Restless*, *Search for Tomorrow*, and *The Guiding Light*, when she should have been taking care of her patients. She testified that nursing director Sandy Canlas had warned her not to let administrator Virginia Wilson catch her watching TV.

Guarino moved on to the issue of state inspections. James told him, "The only time we would have a full staff was when we were informed the state was coming. Mrs. Wilson would have a quick staff meeting. She would tell us that the state was coming and they wanted us to look good. . . . Mrs. Wilson and Mrs. Canlas would actually help us a little when the state was coming. The rest of the time we didn't see them."

She also told the audience, "None of the bedfast patients had call lights. . . . When the state was coming they would put call lights in front of the patients." The young woman said that she had complained to Virginia Wilson about the problems. She said that Mrs. Wilson "looked at me and laughed."

The prosecution team was making an impression with the testimony of Pamela James, and they knew it. The following day, they continued to press their advantage. Guarino opened his questioning by having James testify that there was little hope of financial advancement for an Autumn Hills nurse's aide. The state's attorney established that in her seven years working for Autumn Hills, James received pay raises totaling just 80 cents an hour.

Then Guarino returned to the issue of patient care, asking about charting, the critical records that must be kept on any inpatient situation. James answered, "Half the time we didn't do that because we didn't have any time." She also testified that she paid little attention to the possibility of cross-contamination; she didn't wash her hands between patients when cleaning up, and she sometimes used the same hairbrush on five different patients.

That brought Guarino back to the lack of training that the state charged was evident of the Autumn Hills aides. James testified that when she first came to work at the nursing home she "had never taken a vital sign in my life. . . . I didn't know how to read a thermometer or take blood pressure."

Next, Guarino moved James to the issue of physical abuse of patients. She said she had seen an aide "put the whole bar of soap in Mrs. Walmsley's mouth. I told her you're not supposed to do that. She just laughed." James said several aides were in the room when the incident occurred and added that a washcloth was used in a similar way.

James's testimony clearly damaged Sandy Canlas's case, and Guarino pressed that point just before concluding the state's examination of the witness. James testified that she "would see Mrs. Canlas once a week. She would come to the room."

The damage to Canlas had not been missed by Mike Ramsey, and he quickly tried on cross-examination to salvage something for his client. After Canlas resigned from Autumn Hills, a petition was passed around and signed by many of the nursing home's employees, asking Canlas to stay on and requesting that the home office reinstate her as director. But Pam James did not recall the petition.

On redirect, Guarino pressed his advantage. "Does that petition relate to the same Sandy Canlas who allowed aides to watch TV?" he asked James, then inquiring about her morale and attitude. James responded, "When we didn't have enough help I said, 'If they didn't care, why do I?'" Guarino asked again about Canlas's knowledge that the aides were watching TV. James replied, "On many occasions she would see us."

But Ramsey then tried a long shot that helped Canlas a little. Questioning James in his strong Texas accent, Ramsey established that many of the patients also liked to watch soap operas. He worked to show that the presence of aides in a patient's room was usually coincidental to the patient's watching their favorite soap operas. His progress on the issue was somewhat stunted by an ill-timed sexist remark. "You know," he said to James, "you and the patients were just watching soap operas like women do." The courtroom erupted in laughter for the first time in the trial, and Judge Morgan later said, "Well, he got them to laughing. I don't like that, but the jurors do."

Sartwelle also needed to cut his losses from James's testimony. She had established fairly conclusively that the nursing home was understaffed. Guarino had repeatedly questioned her about the amount of work an aide was expected to do, and James had described a work load that would be difficult under the best of circumstances. Sartwelle managed to establish for the record that Autumn Hills met staffing levels in July 1978. It was a small gain, but crucial; the trial would be long, and Sartwelle would continue to chip away at the state's allegations one witness at a time.

Sartwelle did not, however, do well with Pamela James. He reminded her of his visit to her home around dinnertime, when her children were running rampant through the house as she prepared the meal. But James's memory was good too; she responded to his question by asking, "Is that the time you wanted to represent me?"

In most trials—and all celebrated ones—what happens behind the scenes is as enthralling as what happens in the courtroom. That is especially true in cases that require a change of venue and all the parties involved are from outside the city where the trial is held.

Boredom can become an important factor for jury, attorneys, defendants—and judges. And while a suite at the Menger Hotel is nice by any standard, staring at the four walls of a hotel room for months is not a pleasant experience. Judge Don B. Morgan refused to allow himself to become bored in San Antonio.

As a lawyer, Morgan had traveled throughout Texas to try cases and had often journeyed out-of-state on behalf of his clients. So being on the road in pursuit of justice was certainly nothing new to Morgan. He had learned to find and enjoy good restaurants in any community, regardless of size. Morgan enjoyed the good life and was determined to have as much of it as he felt was his due.

Roy Minton and Charles Burton also enjoyed the good life. The two Austin lawyers relished a good restaurant as much as Morgan. They also reveled in good conversation, longneck beer, and stories about past cases. In Galveston, during the pretrial hearings, Morgan had come to respect the two men and had developed an affection for them, born of common experiences. Besides, Roy Minton made him laugh.

"Roy is the funniest man I have ever met," Morgan told acquaintances. He was right; Minton, whose physical appearance was that of a balding Stan Laurel look-alike, possessed a brutal, rapier wit that the Galveston judge appreciated. But Morgan also respected Minton's abilities as a lawyer. He had watched Minton get away with courtroom tactics few other lawyers would dare try in any court, much less Morgan's. Those stunts often paid off handsomely for Minton's clients, with surprisingly little objection from the prosecution team, a failure Morgan attributed to simple stupidity. He knew that behind Minton's clowning exterior lurked "one of the meanest lawyers I have ever known."

Morgan, Minton, Burton, and Ramsey often went to dinner after court. There, long into the night, the lawyers would swap stories, each funnier than the last, as they whiled away the lonely evening hours. The prosecutors knew that the judge was out dining with the defense; some of Guarino's team were chafed by the suspicion that the defense was scoring points with the judge in the evening hours. But Guarino wasn't worried. He knew his judge, knew that Morgan was considered a state's judge in the Galveston County Courthouse. He also knew Morgan would be just as happy spending the evening with the state as he would the defense. There would be plenty of time in the Autumn Hills case for Guarino and his men to meet socially with the judge. Guarino knew that Morgan was just being Morgan: open, honest in his relationships, and, above all, fun.

Morgan noticed that an ingredient was missing in his evenings with the attorneys. Tom Sartwelle never came. The Fulbright and Jaworski lawyer was, by nature, a loner; he also knew that Morgan didn't care for him. Morgan had publicly humiliated him early in the case and had come close to finding him in contempt over the questioning of a witness. Morgan had shouted, "Don't you ever, ever, in my courtroom suggest to a witness questions that are not true. I will take the most drastic action that I can." Sartwelle tried to argue the point, and Morgan told him, "You do it one more time, Mr. Sartwelle, and I'll give you the opportunity to test me." After that, Sartwelle spent as little time as possible in the judge's chambers, calculating that it would be better for his clients if he didn't risk angering Morgan again. The tension in their relationship was obvious; Sandy Canlas noticed that "the judge doesn't like Tom and Tom doesn't like the judge. And Tom knows the judge doesn't like him."

Carol Josey Oliver, another former Autumn Hills nurse's aide, took the stand to describe the year she worked at the Texas City nursing home. Under questioning by Guarino, she established her credibility well. She testified that she quickly learned that working in a nursing home was a no-win situation. Previously, she had worked in hospitals, where many patients got well. At Autumn Hills, the patients did not recover.

She had married but still worked to help support her four children. Now a nurse's assistant, she had gone back to hospital work at the University of Texas Medical Branch in Galveston.

Carol Josey Oliver told much the same story as Pamela James. She also described how appalled she was by conditions at the nursing home. Oliver had been experienced enough to realize that conditions at Autumn Hills were not as they should have been. She was accustomed to the pristine atmosphere of the teaching hospital. Autumn Hills did not meet her standards.

She did establish one new point in the case the state was attempting to build against Autumn Hills. Central to the state's theory of the cause of death for Edna Mae Witt was that the woman's bedsores had been a direct source of infection. The state hoped to prove that when the patient was lying in her own waste, bacteria entered her bloodstream, creating the massive infection that killed her. Oliver told the jury that she remembered cleaning feces out of Edna Mae's sores with peroxide.

On October 20, 1985, David Marks spent his Sunday afternoon driving from Galveston to San Antonio. The drive was beautiful in the Indian summer the state was experiencing. Marks did not drive alone. In the car with him were Agnes Buxton and Maxine Anonsen, the daughters of Edna Mae Witt. He had come to know the two women over the years, and they in turn had come to trust the young prosecutor who was trying to make some sense of their mother's death.

Both Agnes and Maxine had edured family difficulties as a direct result of their mother's final illness. Going to San Antonio was a trying experience for them both. But Marks had convinced them that their testimony would be useful, perhaps even essential. Neither Maxine nor Agnes had ever been on a witness stand in her life. Both were timid, emotional women frightened of the experience. Marks assured them that everything would be fine.

On October 22, Marks called Agnes Buxton to the witness stand. The large woman was terrified as she entered the sterile courtroom over which Judge Morgan presided in stern, austere dignity. Her emotions caved in to uncontrollable crying. Immediately, Roy Minton was on his feet and objecting to the state's "even bringing a weeping witness into the courtroom. I've heard about this witness throughout the case. This woman even cries at the death of a gerbil." Morgan had the jury removed for a while, and Barrera asked the judge to scold the prosecution for bringing Agnes Buxton before the jury in her condition.

Seated in the witness box, Agnes composed herself enough for Morgan to bring the jury back in. The judge would later say that he was as shocked as anyone else when Agnes entered the courtroom. "I have had witnesses cry on the stand; that's common. I have never had a witness walk into the courtroom crying."

Tentatively, Marks asked his first question of Agnes. He wanted to restore order to the trial and lay the groundwork for his future questions—if she could hold up to them. "Who was Edna Mae

Witt?" he asked.

"My mama," Agnes answered, love in her voice still evident for the woman who had been dead seven years. "I had a unique mother who raised five children through the Depression."

Marks gently led Agnes through the horror of her mother's final months. It was a slow process, for Marks knew he must tread lightly if he was to get into the record the testimony Agnes Buxton could provide. The elderly woman bolstered herself, summoning inner strength that no one in the courtroom suspected she was capable of, as she told the story of her mother's decline.

The dying process had not been easy for Edna Mae Witt. Nor had it been easy for her family as they daily went to the strange place called Autumn Hills, across the causeway from Galveston. Methodically, Marks helped Agnes relive the nightmare all over again in front of the jury. She told a tale of filth, callous disregard for even minor patient care, abandonment.

Minton watched the jury as Agnes Buxton testified. Minton always watched the jury; he prided himself on being able to establish eye contact with the jurors he thought were sympathetic to his clients. As the woman testified, he wondered who those jurors were, if any.

As Marks concluded his questioning, he asked Agnes Buxton about the final days of her mother. The woman's emotions were at the breaking point as she told of the horrid bedsores her mother had developed at Autumn Hills. Finally, she said, her mother was taken to the hospital. There Agnes found her "with tubes sticking out of her." At that point, Agnes's resolve broke, and she began to weep as she agonized over reliving her mother's death.

Marks, as well as the jury, observed the five defendants who sat next to their lawyers. Marks had come to know these people over the years, and nothing in that period had induced him to like them. And now, at the rate of about $2000 an hour, their lawyers were using every legal weapon in their considerable arsenal to extricate them from what Marks saw as justice.

In particular, Marks loathed Bob Gay, the successful president of the chain of seventeen nursing homes. Gay and the corporation were footing the enormous legal bill that came with such talent as Minton, Burton, Sartwelle, Friend, Ramsey, and Barrera. Marks would say, "He's so generous that he's authorized the lawyers to represent any of his former employees so they can't testify against him."

Marks looked across the room at Cassandra Canlas. "I think they bought her new clothes. I'm sure they've done the same for Locke. They kind of are all in this together."

Marks also observed the lawyers who were defending Autumn Hills and the five individual defendants. Of Sartwelle, he said, "He's going to bitch and moan. If he came out looking wonderful, he's going to bitch and moan." Marks told friends, "I've heard good things about him in terms of his knowledge of medicine, . . . but no matter how hard he tries, he can't hide the fact that he is basically a prick. That's my advantage in front of this jury; the more he's talking, that may be one of the best weapons I have. The more he gets angry and throws his books around and misbehaves like he did, the more that jury thinks, 'What an asshole this guy is.'"

Marks, however, knew that without Sartwelle or someone like him, the case was his almost by default. Minton and Burton were not capable of handling the complex medical testimony that formed the foundation of the young prosecutor's case. Grudgingly, Marks gave Sartwelle his due. "All of those lawyers are dependent upon Sartwelle. Without Sartwelle, they would not have much ability to defend the causation aspect."

Jane Churchill, a volunteer who had worked with David Marks to bring Autumn Hills to court, escorted Betty Korndorffer up the steps of the John H. Wood Federal Courthouse at one o'clock on a windy late October day. Korndorffer was concerned that the wind was snarling her hair, and she was reluctant to go inside the courthouse. Inside were the people she had so long ago come to know, people who had let her profession down by failing as nurses to provide care for the elderly patients Korndorffer so cared about.

Betty Korndorffer had not had an easy life since 1978; life is rarely easy for a whistle-blower. The Autumn Hills attorneys had told everyone who would listen that the whole conflict between the state and Autumn Hills came about because Korndorffer had developed a personality conflict with Mattie Locke when both were directors of nursing for the corporation. The attorneys intimated that Korndorffer was out to get the nursing home chain and Locke because Locke had been promoted to the home office and she hadn't.

Betty Korndorffer was well aware of such innuendo. She hadn't wanted to work for Autumn Hills in the first place. And now she wondered how anyone who knew her could say that she was jealous of Mattie Locke, could charge that she was a disgruntled former employee who as a state inspector had filed false reports about the conditions at Autumn Hills in Texas City. That was the charge corporation lawyer Carol Vance had made to the news media shortly after the first indictments were handed down. Betty Korndorffer and her attorneys, Joe Archer and Paul Waldner of Houston, filed a $6 million libel suit against Autumn Hills, Carol Vance, Bob Gay, Ron Pohlmeyer, and Mattie Locke.

The courtroom was almost full when Betty Korndorffer walked to the witness chair. For weeks, reporters had been waiting for the person many felt would be the star attraction in the case. The middle-aged blond woman with a Southern accent was poised as she began her three days of testimony.

As a state inspector, Betty Korndorffer had taken volumes of notes, written volumes of reports on the Texas City nursing home. Now she related what she had seen as a registered nurse who knew the rules. And what she had seen had appalled her, repulsed her, and finally angered her. She recalled how, during her first inspection of Autumn Hills, she discovered that "patients were going blind and deaf. In a couple of months, they would become completely incontinent."

Korndorffer spelled out in minute detail for the jury how Autumn Hills personnel were not charting properly, how they were, in fact, falsifying patient records. She also told the jury how Dr. Merrill Stiles did not sign many of the necessary forms relating to patient care at the nursing home; she said the nursing home personnel used a rubber stamp of the physician's signature. Korndorffer pointed out that she was familiar with the way Stiles normally signed progress notes with a distinctive "S" instead of his full name. Korndorffer testified that the "S" on many of the forms she examined was not the same as the one she knew Stiles used, suggesting the possibility of forgery.

Korndorffer told the jury that during a periodic medical review on February 7, 1978, she tagged bedfast patients and patients restrained in geriatric chairs to see if they had been turned. She determined that the patients were never turned except onto their backs and when they were fed.

She also described how she checked the patients' charts to see if doctors' orders were being followed. Of 99 charts examined, the physician's orders had not been followed in 71 cases, she said. On the skilled wing of the nursing home, where the most dependent patients were kept, she found the doctor's orders followed on only 5 of 49 charts. Medicine for 3 of those patients was unavailable, she told the jury. At the conclusion of that visit, she told the jury, the inspection team recommended that Autumn Hills be placed on vendor hold, meaning that medicaid funds would be withheld until the nursing home passed inspection.

On the follow-up visit, the inspection team was met by personnel from the Autumn Hills home office. The nursing home was considerably cleaner. "Patients looked much better; the facility didn't smell bad. They had really cleaned it up," Korndorffer said. That testimony was central to Marks's contention that the only time Autumn Hills did anything to improve conditions was when its medicaid funding was threatened.

Korndorffer then described subsequent visits to Autumn Hills, including a complaint follow-up and an open hearing for residents, families, and interested citizens.

She talked about a May 4, 1978, visit concerning a complaint that an LVN had instructed a high school student to insert a nasal gastric tube. On that same visit, Korndorffer watched Dr. Stiles make rounds. "He walked into a room, then out of the room very quickly. He was dictating progress notes into a Dictaphone. . . . He had a number of patients there at the time."

As Korndorffer continued to cite instance after instance of improper documentation, Sartwelle repeatedly objected. But Judge Morgan allowed Korndorffer to continue her testimony.

She described a luncheon she attended in December 1977, where she tried to send a message to Gay and Pohlmeyer through an Autumn Hills home office employee. She asked the woman, "Please go back to the central office and tell Mr. Gay and Mr. Pohlmeyer that Autumn Hills is a mess." Korndorffer said that meeting, at a Steak and Ale restaurant on Houston's Gulf Freeway, lasted two hours. She said she told the woman that the nursing care was deteriorating. And she swore she told the woman to tell Gay and Pohlmeyer that "unless Autumn Hills is cleaned up, there will be big problems."

Thus, Betty Korndorffer's first testimony ended with the question that had proved central to the Watergate investigation. Prosecutors had concentrated on the issue of Richard Nixon's knowledge of the events in question; what did he know, and when did he know it? Unless it was disproved, Betty Korndorffer had told Autumn Hills that there were big problems in the Texas City nursing home eleven months before the death of Elnora Breed.

On the second of her three days in the stark San Antonio federal courtroom, Korndorffer pointed out continual documentation errors she had discovered on her visits to Autumn Hills in Texas City. At times Mattie Locke, Korndorffer's erstwhile rival, smiled as the nursing inspector testified. Locke often smiled, both in and out of the courtroom. Some observers thought that Locke was smiling in arrogance.

A characteristic of Korndorffer's testimony, and one reason she was on the witness stand three full days, was the repeated objections from the defense. Korndorffer waited, sometimes impatiently, as the crowd of lawyers approached the bench and conferred with Morgan. Almost as often, the attorneys and the judge would retire to the judge's borrowed chambers, a room that contained a brown leather couch, a few chairs, and little else in the way of adornment. At times during the early weeks of the trial, the only picture the television sketch artists could produce was one of the herd of attorneys hunched over the bench with their backs to the courtroom.

So Korndorffer's testimony reached the jury in bits and pieces. Despite the fragmentary story, she emphasized the details of the inspections and named the other inspectors with whom she had worked, demonstrating that she was not alone in finding major problems at the home. Month by month of 1978 was paraded before the jury as Korndorffer described her visits to the Texas City nursing home. And with each visit, another example of neglect emerged, often more than one.

"I saw Mrs. Walmsley on August seventeenth," Korndorffer said of one inspection visit. "She was eating with her hands. They were covered with dry feces around the cuticles and under the nails." Korndorffer related how Cassandra Canlas, on rounds with her that day, left the room to tell an aide to clean up the elderly woman. Later, Korndorffer told the jury, she returned to see if Mrs. Walmsley had indeed been cared for. She still had feces on her hand.

During that same August inspection, Korndorffer saw patients with no teeth served fried pork chops and fried chicken. She testified that the staff did not cut up the meat for the patients who could not chew.

She also testified about bedsores and said she believed that with proper nursing care, bedsores could be prevented. "I don't believe that any decubitus should ever develop. I certainly don't believe that you get decubitus with good care." But no such care had been documented, she said. "There were no orders; there was no evidence of the physician being called."

Despite Cassandra Canlas's indictment for murder, Korndorffer and the former director of nursing had become friends, had even cried together at the bedside of Edna Mae Witt. Korndorffer still considered herself Canlas's friend. Sandy Canlas still had warm feelings for this woman who was testifying against her. She recalled that they had shared an emotional moment in the nursing home as they checked the condition of Edna Mae Witt. "She had a large decubitus on her buttocks that was foul and very smelly. It was large enough that you could put your fist in it. I looked across the bed at Mrs. Canlas, and I mouthed the words, 'Mrs. Witt is going to die.' I started crying and Mrs. Canlas started crying. She was very distressed."

So Betty Korndorffer did something for her friend. She told the truth about Cassandra Canlas, who had been hired by the nursing home at the relatively young age of 25 to care for patients who, in the opinion of many, should have been in a hospital intensive care unit. By her testimony, Korndorffer showed that the young nurse who was on trial for murder was a sensitive, caring human being. For practical purposes, although she was not dismissed, Cassandra Canlas was out of the case. Though she was to sit in the courtroom with the rest of the defendants for two more months, the state would not produce any substantive testimony or evidence against her.

Like so many witnesses in the Autumn Hills case, Betty Korndorffer ended her testimony in tears. The woman who, more than any other person, helped bring Autumn Hills to trial had finally told the story that had troubled her for six years. It was over. Roy Minton rose and announced to the judge that the defense would have no questions of Betty Korndorffer on cross-examination.

Elizabeth Phiffer had seen it all. As records clerk at Autumn Hills in Texas City, she testified, "I have seen a medication aide take a narcotic sheet and write the whole thing because the narcotic count was off." Phiffer herself had, on numerous occasions, falsified records on behalf of the nursing home. Her testimony had a telling effect. Phiffer looked squarely at the jury as she made her admissions. Using body language, she demanded their attention.

Repeatedly, the prosecutors questioned Phiffer about efforts by the nursing home to meet the paperwork demands of the government. Phiffer testified that falsification of records did not stop with the pacification of picky bureaucrats but extended to actual patient records as well.

She further testified that many of the nurses' signatures on patient records were forged. Phiffer could be sure, because she had seen those signatures thousands of times since becoming records clerk in 1975. As Miguel Martinez, the young appellate lawyer questioned Phiffer about her own wrongdoing, she continued to look at the jury and confess what she had done. The articulate woman often emphatically answered, "I sure did!"

Marks followed Liz Phiffer with more Autumn Hills employees, but he was nearing what he believed was the heart of the case he had built against Autumn Hills. Though eyewitness testimony was critical to the case, much of David Marks's ego was wrapped up in the exhaustive studies he had conducted and supervised over the years before San Antonio. Essential to getting the studies into evidence and getting the jury to understand the complicated work he had done was to present expert witnesses who would be credible— and understandable.

First, Marks had to help the jury understand the complex medical problems facing the patients of Autumn Hills. In particular, he had to be certain that the jury understood that Elnora Breed did not die of cancer as the defense contended. To help him do that, he called Dr. William Steffee, a nationally known nutritionist, who testified that Elnora Breed died of starvation on the six hundred calories a day that her physician ordered for her. The portly doctor from Cleveland, Ohio, did his work well.

Steffee was the first of several expert witnesses who attempted to convince the jury that the Texas City home was a snake pit where even routine nursing and medical practice were the exceptions, not the rule. Nurse Sarah Burger of the Washington Home for Incurables presented Marks's highly touted bedsore study, in which he attempted to prove that the nursing home patients suffered from "an epidemic of rotting flesh" in 1978.

In cross-examining Burger, Sartwelle had his finest hour in the courtroom. He created doubt in the minds of the jurors by suggesting that Burger lacked the credentials to do such a study. His revelation of her failure to use the scientific method in the study created a serious credibility problem for Marks. Sartwelle convincingly showed that the state was counting every mark on the body of patients as a bedsore. "If I cross my legs for a period of time," he told the jury, "then uncross them, a red mark will appear on my thigh where one leg crossed the other, will it not? Is that what you count as a bedsore, Mrs. Burger?"

As the Texas autumn turned into winter, the jurors tired of the trial. They had tried to divert their attention from the boredom of the jury room, where they were confined during the countless in-chambers conferences that had punctuated the trial. Someone brought in a game of Trivial Pursuit that they played endlessly, the front row of the jury contesting the back row. Jurors brought food from home to sample with their new friends. Birthdays were celebrated, and cake was eaten. The jurors had been told they would be finished in three months. Now, as Christmas neared, they were restless. The beautiful Indian summer had turned wet and cold. The jury wanted to go home.

Guarino knew the jury wanted to go home. But he had a problem; Marks had done so much work on the case, had developed so much evidence, and he wanted to present it all. Morgan had knocked out a large portion of that work when he refused to admit portions of some studies Marks had prepared. In particular, Morgan had not allowed the state to introduce a large portion of the Ensure study, which Marks had hoped would prove that the penny-pinching administrators of Autumn Hills had starved patients to death by not supplying enough of the food supplement. In anger Marks said after court one day, "If I had known that [the study would be disallowed], I could have finished three weeks ago!"

The state's witnesses now came in rapid succession, each with a short story to tell to the jury. One such witness was Bob Yancy, a salesman who sold supplies to several Autumn Hills nursing homes. The 35-year-old man from New Caney, Texas, testified that most of the firm's seventeen homes were fairly good facilities. The Texas City home "really wasn't typical of an Autumn Hills facility," he said.

Yancy told of patients he had seen in the nursing home. "For the most part, they appeared to be unclean. . . . Most of the patients were unshaven. . . . I saw a patient in a geriatric chair with urine under the chair on the floor." Yancy said he passed that patient on his way to sell Sandy Canlas supplies. After spending quite some time with Canlas, he noticed the same patient on his way out. The patient was in the chair in the same condition as when Yancy came in.

Yancy and Canlas had become friends during her stay at Autumn Hills. Yancy described the supply situation on his first trip to the nursing home: "I didn't go down there and find the cupboards bare. When I initially went down there, it was below par."

Yancy testified that Canlas had tried hard to establish a system that would remedy the supply problems in the nursing home. Together, he and Canlas had worked to solve the problem. Still, under questioning by Vollers, Yancy said of Canlas, "She always tried to do the right thing and the best thing. The problem was that she was in over her head."

Later, during a break in testimony, Sandy Canlas stood next to a Coke machine in the courthouse basement, smoking a cigarette and crying because she had trusted Yancy. Though his testimony had not seriously damaged her case—it had, in fact, shown that she was trying to solve the problems of Autumn Hills—Canlas felt that Yancy had violated her trust and their friendship. "I'm learning that I trusted a lot of friends back then that I shouldn't have trusted. It hurts; it really hurts."

David Marks had struggled with the causation issue for years. What had caused the death of Elnora Breed, Edna Mae Witt, and the other patients? Marks had definite ideas, but his placing them before a jury was one thing, and an expert witness's saying them was quite another. And Marks was in the ideal city for his next expert witness, a man he had come to admire, Dr. Vincent Di Maio, medical examiner of Bexar County. Dr. Di Maio had examined the available evidence and had been present at the exhumation autopsies of Elnora Breed and Edna Mae Witt. As a forensic pathologist, he was convinced that both women had been murdered.

Marks asked Di Maio, "Did you arrive at an opinion regarding the manner of Mrs. Witt's death?"

"In my opinion, it was a homicide," Di Maio answered.

Morgan overruled the ensuing defense motion for a mistrial, allowing Di Maio to continue. Regarding Elnora Breed, Di Maio testified that medical records showed that Breed was relatively frail when she entered Autumn Hills in early October 1978. "But her medical history showed that she was a tough woman. She couldn't have been too frail. . . . She was naturally resistant to cancer."

"If the care had been provided, what would you expect to see in Mrs. Breed after 47 days at Autumn Hills?" Marks asked.

"She should have been up in a wheelchair, wheeling herself around, feeding herself."

The doctor testified that Edna Mae Witt had no bedsores when she entered Autumn Hills on August 29, 1978. By the time she entered the hospital on October 16, the woman had developed 22 sores, including one more than three inches across and more than an inch and a half deep, "extending right down to the backbone." Because of the sores, Di Maio testified that "bacteria had gotten into the blood, reproducing in the blood. . . . Essentially, you're being poisoned. . . . In my opinion, this was due to poor nursing care. . . . To go downhill like that in 47 days is unbelievable."

During cross-examination of Di Maio, Sartwelle forced the medical examiner to admit that he knew of no scientific study in which bedsores were shown to be the source of an infection that spread to the rest of the body. Sartwelle also brought out that during the May 1985 autopsy, it was discovered that Witt suffered from bronchial pneumonia on the day she died. Di Maio countered that, saying, "The way to prevent bronchial pneumonia is to sit them up and let them cough, get them up and sit them in a chair and let them cough up the congestion."

Di Maio also testified that Elnora Breed received a starvation diet of slightly more than six hundred calories a day for the first 41 days of her 47-day stay. "In my opinion, she starved to death, and her condition was complicated by decubitus ulcers and infection." Di Maio said that it was the obligation of the Autumn Hills nurses to notify Breed's doctor if they thought the woman was starving to death on the diet.

Regarding the maggots that so much earlier testimony had centered around, Di Maio explained, "A fly lays eggs on the surface, and they sit there for two days and finally hatch." Because the sore had been unwashed for 48 hours, the maggots were able to hatch. Simply washing the sore, he said, would wash out the eggs and there would have been no maggots.

Di Maio was then excused as a witness. At 11 a.m., Guarino stood up and announced, "The state rests, Your Honor."

CHAPTER THIRTEEN

"For every expert they presented, I will present three," Tom Sartwelle told reporters after the state concluded its testimony in the Autumn Hills case. Sartwelle had worked with his expert witnesses for almost as many years as David Marks had worked with his. Autumn Hills had spared no expense as its medical attorney searched the country and abroad for medical and nursing experts who would refute the allegations of the state. Sartwelle knew he must prove that nurses don't cause bedsores. He also must convince the jury that septicemia cannot be acquired through such a sore, even if the sore is open and has been exposed to urine and feces for hours, perhaps days. Finally, he must show that Elnora Breed, the frail 87-year-old alleged victim of starvation, bedsores, and septicemia, died of cancer, not neglect.

Prosecutors had presented 42 witnesses during two months of testimony. Those witnesses told a tale of horror unparalleled in the annals of American jurisprudence. Sartwelle was faced with defusing that testimony or, at the least, creating enough doubt in the minds of the jury to negate a conviction. It promised to be a monumental task for the insurance defense lawyer who was such a novice before a criminal jury. Yet, in his own way, Sartwelle was used to the strain of such an ordeal. He had actually run two marathons, despite his propensity for late nights and everything that goes with them.

Every day for years, he had been forced to live with the nightmare of death and dying. It was part of his job. Often he countered the problems of his work with his own brand of dark humor. Once, during the prosecution's case, he told reporters after court, "God, we tried to kill them. Some of those people just wouldn't die; they lived for months. Some of those people lived for eight weeks!" The press saw the humor for what it was and did not quote him.

He was equally quick to anger, both in the courtroom and out. During a long trial everyone—the judge, the attorneys, the press—comes to know one another well simply because they live in close quarters. Sartwelle had at first been shy of the press. During his career, reporters had seldom covered insurance cases in which he was involved. Now, however, the 41-year-old lawyer warmed to the constant presence of reporters, and even came to like a few of them. But when the press asked probing questions about bedsores, neglect, and the testimony developed by the state, Sartwelle often became angry, hurling questions back at the reporters to demonstrate their ignorance of medical issues. Sartwelle's knowledge of medicine was light-years ahead of the reporters'. Despite his passion and superior knowledge, he was seldom convincing. The state had presented a powerful and compelling case.

Sartwelle also displayed his anger and frustration in the courtroom, though not in view of Judge Morgan. During prosecution testimony, he would sit at the defense table shaking his head. During Elizabeth Phiffer's damaging testimony, he shook his head and muttered "Shit" under his breath. The other defense lawyers sitting near him merely laughed.

The defense of Autumn Hills was, in the technical sense, Sartwelle's case. Minton, Burton, Barrera, and Ramsey were top-notch criminal lawyers, but their considerable talents would be wasted if Sartwelle didn't do his job well. Sartwelle knew that, felt the pressure and responsibility that had been placed upon him. He was also frustrated by it. Gail Friend, Sartwelle, and the support staff of Fulbright and Jaworski had done a massive amount of research and organization, but now Sartwelle was tiring of that kind of work. He was also tired of working in a legal system he didn't believe in. As he stared at the jury across the room from the defense table, he wondered if they could possibly grasp the complex medical evidence and testimony that he was about to present. Sartwelle emphatically did not believe that his defendants were facing a jury of their peers. That was the problem with the system that most appalled him.

The system did not bother Mike Ramsey though. It was working for his client, Sandy Canlas, as the trial entered its second phase on a warm day in January. Canlas wore a brown print dress on the day the defense took the lead in the courtroom. The attorneys met in chambers shortly after Judge Morgan entered the courthouse at 9:15 a.m. Shortly thereafter, Ramsey entered the courtroom and whispered something to his client, who smiled back at him.

The jury came in next, followed by Morgan, who immediately announced that Canlas was being severed from the rest of the defendants and would have the opportunity to stand trial alone. For practical purposes, *State* v. *Autumn Hills* was over for the young nurse. There was little likelihood that prosecutors would be willing to spend another million dollars to prosecute Canlas, the least important defendant in the case and one who had possibly been indicted by mistake.

Canlas and Ramsey left the courtroom at the head of a column of reporters. Just outside the courthouse, Canlas broke down and cried, her relief evident as it became clear that her nightmare was over. Ramsey would let her say little, but she told the eager press, "I am excited about going back to Alabama, to my children, and to work."

Roy Minton stood before the jury that he had observed so intently for months. The defense phase of the trial was about to get under way, and in his opening statement the Austin lawyer would plot the course the defense would follow for the next few months. Minton, as always, wanted to look the jury in the eye as he addressed them. Eye contact was a trademark of his style.

Ordinarily a portly man, Minton had lost weight during the trial. The strain of constantly being in the courtroom takes its toll on almost all lawyers, but for Minton the strain had been worse; he had suffered with a gastric disorder for years. The rich food that he consumed on those evenings out with Morgan and the other lawyers simply wasn't good for him.

The anticipation of Minton's opening statement had produced a crowded courtroom, as people turned out to watch the great lawyer's opening performance. During the prosecution phase of the trial, Minton had occasionally demonstrated some of his much-heralded flair when cross-examining a witness. But more often, he played the fumbling, bumbling buffoon. His apparent vulnerability had endeared him, he hoped, to the jury. It had certainly worked favorably with observers who came to watch the trial every day.

But those observers were to be disappointed with Minton's opening showing. They and the press would have to wait to see him at full throttle. Known throughout the state for his oratory and skills in jury argument, Minton now eschewed that flamboyance and in reasoned tones gave instead a long history of the building of the Autumn Hills corporation by Bob Gay, a recitation of the American dream come true. Minton told the court how Gay had hired a young Ron Pohlmeyer away from his job as a state nursing home inspector to become administrator of Hermann Park Manor, a large nursing home in central Houston. He told how Mattie Locke worked with Pohlmeyer as his director of nursing at the home and stayed there six years. Minton described how the talented nurse was transferred to the Autumn Hills home office in 1974. And Minton told the jury that Locke put together a corrective plan when it became apparent that there was trouble at the Texas City facility.

In April 1978, Gay and Pohlmeyer were told that a special agent from the Texas attorney general's office was investigating suspected fraud on the part of Marie Ritchie, then administrator of the Texas City nursing home. Minton now attempted to show the jury that Gay and Pohlmeyer were responsive to the problem when they called Ritchie to the home office and put her on job probation.

Staring straight at the jury as he continued, Minton described how Mattie Locke had gone to Autumn Hills in Texas City and spent two weeks straightening out the problems, hiring fifty new employees in the process. Minton said that Gay and Pohlmeyer finally fired Marie Ritchie in a painful meeting at the home office in Houston. Ritchie had been a longtime employee of the corporation.

Minton also reviewed how Cassandra Canlas had worked sixty hours a week at the nursing home trying to solve its problems. "She would have personnel not showing up," he said, noting that when people didn't show up for work, Canlas went to the home herself to cover the shift. Of Virginia Wilson, Minton said, "Mrs. Wilson virtually lived at that nursing home."

Dr. John Konikowski had prescribed the six-hundred-calorie-per-day diet for Elnora Breed. Much of the prosecution testimony had been planned to show that the diet was certain to produce starvation. Minton knew that his fellow defender Sartwelle would work to show that Konikowski knew what he was doing by ordering the diet and would attempt to prove that Breed's body was in such a state of decline that she could not handle a more nourishing diet. Now Minton told the jury, "His clinic had been treating Mrs. Breed for almost thirty years. . . . This lady was dying and would be dead in a month or two months. . . . All of her organs were dying." Minton told the jury that the diet was changed shortly before Breed's death, but he noted, "The health department was raising Cain about her diet."

Minton's low-key opening argument was a disappointment to some in the room who were inexperienced at watching the evolution of criminal trials. But the Austin lawyer had been low-key on purpose, deliberately outlining the premise that his team was about to present, that Autumn Hills was trying, really trying, to correct the problems that existed in Texas City. Considering the restrictions of low federal reimbursement, the nursing home was giving the best care it was capable of.

Sartwelle now called his first witness. Dr. Paul B. Radelat served on the teaching faculty of the Baylor College of Medicine in Houston. He worked as a pathologist at the Diagnostic Center Hospital, and his most celebrated exhumation autopsy had come when he served on the team that carried out the exhumation of Joan Robinson Hill, the socialite wife and victim in the celebrated murder case of Dr. John Hill. Writer Thomas Thompson turned the case into the national best-seller *Blood and Money*.

Radelat set the stage for the nine other physicians who would come to San Antonio to testify that Elnora Breed had not died of complications caused by bedsores or of starvation. Radelat was one of the two defense pathologists who performed the autopsies on the bones of Elnora Breed and the intact body of Edna Mae Witt. Of Elnora Breed's diet, Radelat told the jury, "It was not a cause of her death." Of the bedsores he said, "They were more an effect of the dying process." Of the charge that Edna Mae Witt had died of blood poisoning, he told the court, "I think that she died fundamentally of renal failure. . . . We found no evidence of septicemia."

Sartwelle skillfully led Radelat through Elnora Breed's medical history, which many in the courtroom could almost recite from memory, they had heard it so many times already. At the prosecution table, Marks yawned as the pathologist used a pointer with the large, well-prepared charts Sartwelle had set up in the courtroom, showing the decline of Elnora Breed. Radelat had had little to work with when he performed the autopsy on her, only bones and a minuscule amount of tissue. Now Sartwelle had problems getting the doctor to be emphatic as Radelat described what he had found and the conclusions he had reached following that autopsy.

Radelat first described the diet order for six hundred calories and testified that Breed's doctor, Konikowski, had little choice. When Elnora Breed's caloric intake was increased, she died.

"Are these situations something that can be handled by nurses?" Sartwelle asked.

"These can hardly be handled by doctors because it is a situation that is doomed to failure," Radelat answered.

Radelat further testified, "Turning every two hours will not prevent decubitus ulcers. That's been demonstrated time and again."

Radelat then moved to the defense theory that blood poisoning could not be contracted through the exposure of open bedsores to bacteria. Because of scabbing and scar tissue formation, he said, the rest of the body is walled off from the invasion of dangerous fecal bacteria. He said that he had found no evidence of bacteremia or septicemia in the remains of Elnora Breed. Unfortunately, he had few remains to work with.

Radelat had much more to work with when the body of Edna Mae Witt was exhumed. He testified that the state pathologists who had attended the autopsy and looked over the shoulders of Sartwelle's experts "pretty much ratified what we were doing." That statement directly contradicted Di Maio's earlier testimony that both Breed and Witt had been murdered.

Regarding the condition of Witt at her death, Radelat revealed that she had lived her life with one kidney. "The laboratory work shows fairly unequivocally that her kidney had failed." He also testified that he had found bronchial pneumonia. In summary, he said, "We found absolutely no evidence of septicemia in Mrs. Witt."

In earlier testimony, the state had produced a blood culture showing the presence of fecal bacteria in Witt's body. Radelat said he believed it represented skin contamination on the needle when the culture was taken.

Sartwelle prodded the pathologist through his findings in endless detail, but he had a goal in mind. He was leading up to a smoking gun that he hoped would put a major hole in the prosecution case against Autumn Hills. The state had tried to show that the nursing home had abandoned its patients, giving little care to the epidemic of bedsores from which those patients suffered. Radelat now testified that in his autopsy of Edna Mae Witt's remains, he found, under the microscope, "an ulcer with an inflammatory base that showed some evidence of healing."

David Marks was waiting for Dr. Paul Radelat. He looked forward to cross-examining the Houston physician, just as he looked forward to taking his place in the pit opposite any of the doctors brave enough to risk their reputations in testimony favorable to Autumn Hills. Now the young prosecutor wasted no time. He quickly got Radelat to agree that the bones of Elnora Breed provided a very small thread of evidence on which to base an opinion.

Across the room, Virginia Wilson looked at Ron Pohlmeyer as Marks continued his questioning. She smiled, obviously relishing the fact that the defense was finally into its case. For years the defendants had wanted to tell their side of the story. For years they had been forbidden to talk to the press. Now Tom Sartwelle would show that they were not murderers. The disdain they felt for David Marks was difficult to contain; for Wilson at that moment, it was impossible.

Marks had little respect for any physician—either as expert witness or attending doctor—who had anything whatsoever to do with the defense of Autumn Hills. Radelat, despite his credentials, was only the first to feel the heat of the young prosecutor's questioning. Relentlessly, Marks drove a wedge in the testimony of the Houston pathologist.

There had been numerous references to blood in the stool of Elnora Breed. The defense contended that the blood was a manifestation of the cancer that they alleged was ravaging her body in the final days of her life. Shortly before the lunch break, Marks forced Radelat to try to support that contention from Breed's medical records. Marks knew those records better than anyone else in the courtroom, except possibly Sartwelle. And he knew he had found a chink in the doctor's armor. He would force Radelat to review the records. "I hate to destroy your lunch, but I'm going to ask you to do that," he said.

After the lunch recess, Marks honed in on the doctor, showing that a medication that had been administered to Breed caused a tarry stool. Marks also showed that the woman suffered from hemorrhoids and impactions that also might account for the blood. From the record he also showed that notations of tarry or bloody stools were not present on the chart every day. "Is cancer of the colon going to bleed one day and then heal itself and not bleed the next day?" he challenged.

He also got Radelat to admit that while she was a resident at Seabreeze nursing home, Elnora Breed was up and around and feeding herself two days before she was hospitalized. At that point, Marks had the doctor go to an easel and chart what a patient like Elnora Breed needed in the way of daily care. Most of the things Radelat wrote on the board the state had proved fairly conclusively had not been done at Autumn Hills. "Would you say that Elnora Breed received this basic care?" Marks asked.

"I would think, judging from the nurse's notes, that she received most of what is on that list," Radelat said.

"Did you form an opinion that she received good care?" Marks asked, still pressing what he regarded as an advantage.

"I would say that she received good care," Radelat said.

"Did you find that Elnora Breed continued to receive medications even after she was over at the funeral home?" Marks asked.

"I think that at least one person made a mistake."

Now Marks knew that he had Radelat in a difficult position. He continued by showing the doctor that 37 percent of the orders for Ensure, the food supplement that the state alleged was Breed's only nutrition, were falsified. He told the doctor that on her first day at Autumn Hills the frail woman could have received only 63 percent of the Ensure ordered for her. Finally, Radelat said, "If those assumptions were true, I would say that she did not receive good care."

Marks then moved through a litany of horrors in his questions of the doctor. Time after time, he asked the doctor to "assume with me that . . . the smell was of a rotting animal, it was so overwhelming." With each assumption the physician heard, Marks hammered home to the jury testimony they had heard months before, reminding them of what they may have forgotten during the trial's Christmas break.

Finally, the young prosecutor asked, "Doctor, based on these assumptions, do you have an opinion whether Elnora Breed received good care?"

"That's not good care," the physician reluctantly answered.

Tom Sartwelle had lost the first round.

Dr. Antonio Silvetti has been a physician since 1951. In that lengthy career, the Brazilian-born doctor has specialized in the healing of wounds. In particular, Silvetti has spent much of his career in the frustrating pursuit of a method for healing bedsores.

Silvetti, Sartwelle learned, had developed a technique for treating bedsores using polysaccharide powder directly on the wound after the rotting skin is cut away. Interestingly, Silvetti's technique has met with surprising success in the thirty-bed intensive care unit he runs. Sartwelle was so impressed that he traveled to Chicago and helped the physician produce a documentary videotape on his work that could later be shown as a fund-raising tool for the clinic. The tape could also be shown in San Antonio at the trial of Autumn Hills.

As Silvetti, dressed in a blue pin-striped suit, adjusted himself in the witness chair that first week in January 1986, Sartwelle asked, "Do nurses cause bedsores?"

"Absolutely not," Silvetti answered.

He then gave a brief history of how the ancients treated bedsores. He said that the wounds were treated with sugar by the Egyptians, vinegar and honey by the Greeks. He then went through a long list of outmoded treatments still being used in the United States, some of which, Silvetti said, actually aggravate the sore. Yet ill-informed physicians and nurses continue to use archaic topical drugs, he emphasized.

Silvetti then described how his treatment differed from standard practice. His staff irrigates the wound three times a day. Before treatment, they cut away the dead tissue. Finally, they apply the powder he has developed, which is used only in his clinic.

Silvetti also told the jury and audience, which were, after the long months of the trial, practically immune to shock, that medicare would not pay for prevention of bedsores for those most likely to get them, the aged and infirm. The prevailing interest of the federal government was to pay for treatment, not prevention, an attitude that was much more costly and sometimes fatal.

The physician told of new techniques that seemed more effective, such as an air mattress that cost only $47, and of corresponding techniques that he believed didn't work as well, such as the much-used egg-crate mattress. The doctor described a $47,000 bed that appeared to be quite effective. (In Texas, that bed rents for $90 a day.)

Sartwelle was making headway and he knew it, as the physician educated the jury with his testimony, the film he had made, and especially with snapshots of some of the patients the jury had been hearing about for months, including Edna Mae Witt. Canlas had taken the photos during her brief tenure at Autumn Hills. The state had introduced them as evidence earlier in the case. Now, Silvetti explained each type of sore the jury was seeing. Some of the sores, Silvetti said, were not bedsores at all, supporting Sartwelle's earlier contention that red spots don't constitute bedsores but were counted as such by the state in its bedsore study.

Silvetti showed pictures of some of his own patients who had suffered from sores the size of watermelons, far larger than any found on the patients at Autumn Hills. He concentrated on a woman who had come to his clinic from an Illinois nursing home with a massive sore. Silvetti's treatment healed her wound. The woman was released to the same nursing home and in a short time developed the same problem. Though that testimony did not apply directly to Autumn Hills, Silvetti was able to show that the treatment of bedsores is a highly specialized business that requires intensive care well beyond turning a patient every two hours. Silvetti said that patients who were likely candidates for bedsores should be turned every thirty minutes; those already suffering from bedsores should be turned every five minutes. In his facility, Silvetti employs one nurse for every two or three patients.

Silvetti estimated that there are five million bedsores at any given time in the United States. He said one million patients die each year with bedsores. He also told the jury that the populations of Japan, India, and the Philippines have fewer bedsores than people in the United States. He attributed that to the tendency of people in those countries to die younger and at home.

Silvetti also told the jury that only 3 to 5 percent of hospital patients develop bedsores, but 38 percent of patients in American nursing homes are likely to suffer from the ulcers, further supporting the contention that a nursing home probably is not the ideal place for patients who are acutely ill.

Sartwelle was in his element now, before a jury questioning a nationally recognized medical authority. He continued to press his points about the weaknesses of the state's case. For months, the jury had heard of a patient named Creasy Hill. The woman was named in the indictment that had been read to the jury. The state had accused Autumn Hills of, if not causing her decubitus ulcer, at least not treating it. With Silvetti, Sartwelle showed that the woman had suffered from a difficult-to-treat stasis ulcer for 34 years.

Marks did not like the testimony of Antonio Silvetti. He and the other prosecutors were soon busy on the phone checking on the doctor. Unless they did something to refute Silvetti's testimony, the physician would gravely endanger their case. Marks called a friend and physician in Galveston to see if Silvetti's treatments and success rates were possible. His friend's response was "You must be talking to God himself!"

Jim Vollers, the Autumn Hills special prosecutor, was also impressed with Silvetti. And now it fell to the Austin attorney to cross-examine "God." It was soon evident that Vollers and his colleagues had not neglected their homework.

Silvetti had testified that he had seen no evidence of poor nursing practice in the records he had been furnished on Elnora Breed and Edna Mae Witt. He had further testified that in 1978 "it wasn't the practice to disturb the doctor with such a little thing as a pressure ulcer." The bald Vollers repeatedly asked Silvetti if Edna Mae Witt and Elnora Breed had received good nursing care from Autumn Hills. "Do you still feel that there is absolutely no sign of neglect or poor care as reflected by these nurse's notes?" Vollers asked.

"I think that the doctor should have kept an eye on the patient," Silvetti answered.

Vollers then pressed Silvetti, using the assumptions that had proved so effective for Marks in his cross-examination of Radelat. "Assume with me, Doctor, that the patient was left in her own urine until it was dry, left in her own feces until it was dry, not bathed daily, not turned for hours, restrained and the restraints were not monitored, insufficient supplies to treat decubitus so that torn up sheets were used, that aides were not trained in turning and preventing contamination, that maggots were found in the bedsore, that there was insufficient personnel, that the sore was draining green purulent pus, that the dressings were urine-soaked and not changed for as long as 24 hours at a time. Is that good nursing care, Doctor?"

Silvetti responded, "Maggots were found to be used during the

Spanish[-American] War. . . . Maggots can produce certain en-
zymes, which help in healing."

But Vollers pressed the Chicago physician until Silvetti admitted
that if such conditions existed, then that would constitute poor
nursing care. Vollers then asked if sepsis could develop through the
line of infection caused by an open bedsore. Silvetti replied that in
rare instances, such a thing could happen but usually did not. Vollers pushed ahead and got a surprise not to his liking. "How long
would it take to develop maggots as big as your finger?" Vollers
asked.

"I've never seen maggots that big. Maybe here in Texas," Silvetti
responded. The Alamo City courtroom erupted in laughter. Vollers
had lost his moment. The rhythm was destroyed.

Vollers took a new tack, returning to Silvetti's contention that
systemic sepsis, or blood poisoning, occurred only occasionally. In
a brilliant piece of investigative effort, the prosecutors had contacted the Illinois attorney general's office, where Silvetti served as
a volunteer member of the nursing home task force. Illinois staff
members told the prosecutors about a patient of Silvetti's who had
died of septicemia and express-mailed the woman's death certificate
to San Antonio. Now Vollers handed the certificate, bearing Silvetti's signature, to the doctor. "How many death certificates have
you filled out?" Vollers asked.

"Not many. Not many of my patients die," Silvetti answered.

"Doctor, are you in the habit of making out a record, especially
an official record, that you don't mean?"

"No, I am not in the habit of falsifying documents."

All of the Autumn Hills prosecutors looked forward to cross-
examining the attending physicians of Elnora Breed and Edna Mae
Witt. None relished the thought more than David Marks. The
young attorney had spent years preparing for the moment. He had
even come within a hair's breadth of having two of the doctors indicted. When friends asked Marks why the physicians weren't
standing trial, he told them in confidence that Mike Guarino "had
just been elected. He believed that he had enough on his plate.
That's not taking anything away from Mike."

In particular, Marks looked forward to questioning Dr. C. Merrill Stiles, who had more patients in the Texas City nursing home

than any other physician. Marks had declared that Stiles ran a geriatric mill, showing little compassion for his patients. Marks told reporters, "When I get Stiles on the stand, I will not even give the man the dignity of calling him Doctor. Words cannot express the contempt I feel for C. Merrill Stiles."

Sartwelle, Minton, and the other defense attorneys were equally eager to put Autumn Hills attending physicians on the witness stand. Two strategies might work. First, the high regard most Americans have for the medical profession could overcome the charges that simple laypeople had made against the nursing home and its employees. The defense was betting that if a doctor got on the stand and swore before God that he had done all he could for his patient, the jury would believe him. Second, a long shot for the defendants, the prosecution would naturally be tempted to put the physicians on trial and might lead the jury to blame the doctors rather than the four defendants sitting tensely behind the bar.

Judge Morgan had a lot of experience putting physicians to the test in court. He had been a successful personal injury lawyer, so physicians were his specialty. Of cross-examining them he would say, "If you are going to fight the king, you have to kill the king." By that Morgan meant that the prosecution would have to utterly destroy the credibility of all four attending physicians that the defense planned to call.

Weldon Kolb began his practice of medicine in 1942 and soon moved to LaMarque, Texas, a bedroom community adjacent to Texas City. He spent a lifetime as a respected citizen there and for forty years treated the illnesses, major and minor, of the community. Among his patients was Elnora Breed; Kolb was her physician for 27 years. For 25 years he treated Elnora Breed's sister, who died in 1985 at College Park nursing home, the new name given Autumn Hills by Beverly Enterprises, which leased the home from Robert Gay after Autumn Hills' problems became public. Kolb also treated another sister, Ruth Linscomb; the first witness in the state's case had been to Kolb's clinic in recent weeks for treatments.

Weldon Kolb became medical director of Autumn Hills in Texas City shortly before the death of Elnora Breed in August 1978. The respect Kolb and his associates had built over the years was damaged by David Marks and the grand jury that named the physician in the indictment of Autumn Hills and its executives.

His credentials indicated that Kolb was uniquely qualified to assume the post of medical director. He had practiced in area nursing homes for forty years. Such experience is rare in the increasingly specialized field of medicine. Geriatrics is one of the profession's most unpopular areas. Only a handful of physicians carried on a nursing home practice in Galveston County in 1978. Even fewer do so today.

The evening before he was to testify, Kolb enjoyed a long dinner at Lela B's, the Crockett Hotel restaurant, accompanied by his associate Dr. John Konikowski, Dovina Gosnell, and Sartwelle. Gosnell, a nursing specialist from Kent State School of Nursing, was also an expert witness for the defense. They were meeting at Sartwelle's home base to discuss upcoming testimony. Sartwelle had sent each of the witnesses volumes of medical records that he had accumulated and assembled during his years on the case. With the exception of Gosnell, each was expected to study the data they had helped create so long ago.

In the hotel bar, the wives of Kolb and Konikowski waited for the meeting to end. They had accompanied their husbands to San Antonio to stand by them as they defended the treatment they had given Elnora Breed. Kolb had been Breed's longtime physician, and Konikowski had prescribed a diet of six hundred calories a day for the woman. Both wives knew that the next few days would not be pleasant.

When the meeting ended, their wives joined Kolb and Konikowski in the dining room with Sartwelle. It was now time for small talk and after-dinner drinks. The following morning, Weldon Kolb, respected member of his community, would testify in the trial of *State of Texas* v. *Autumn Hills*. For years, the Kolbs had lived under the pall of the nursing home scandal. After a few short hours on the stand, the ordeal would be over.

Weldon Kolb looked very much the trusted family doctor when he entered the courtroom the next day. He had a rumpled appearance, dressed in his gray suit and pullover sweater and carrying a large stack of records under his arm. Here was no smart-aleck Young Turk just out of med school. Instead, Kolb was everybody's family physician, the kind people remembered growing up with, the kind who delivered babies and then cared for them until they were adults, if they lived in small East Texas towns. He also enjoyed the respect of his colleagues, who had elected him president of the Texas Society of Family Physicians and 1983's Texas Family Physician.

Sartwelle wasted no time asking the physician Elnora Breed had trusted for 27 years what ultimately caused her death. Kolb was familiar with the recurring cancer that unquestionably had plagued the woman since the early sixties. Now he was prepared to testify that the cancer had finally defeated his small, slight patient. "I believe that Mrs. Breed died of three major cancers of the colon," Kolb flatly told the jury.

Kolb detailed the medical history of Elnora Breed, often using terms few in the room understood. Sartwelle often stopped the doctor and made him explain the medical jargon for the jury. Kolb's credibility increased with every question Sartwelle asked. When the Houston lawyer asked him about the diet his associate Konikowski had ordered for Elnora Breed, Kolb explained, "Under the circumstances of her general failure to accept nutrition, her failure to eat, it was appropriate."

The story Weldon Kolb told of Elnora Breed was a familiar one of aging and decline, unremarkable in the sense that as most people age, they suffer a decline in function of one sort or another. In Breed's case, the aging process included cancer as early as 1962, sixteen years before her death. In meticulous detail, Kolb told of scores of visits by Elnora Breed to his clinic, a typhoid shot after Hurricane Carla, stomach disorders, injections of vitamins, gastritis, and, as the aging process accelerated, signs of organic brain syndrome, or senility.

After Elnora Breed was finally placed in Seabreeze nursing home, Kolb allowed his associate Dr. John Konikowski to assume her medical management. "He was much more in that nursing home than I, and he took over her management for that reason," Kolb told the jury. The woman had little choice as to who her family doctor was once she was institutionalized. Although Kolb, the physician she had trusted for 27 years, saw her from time to time, it was John Konikowski who assumed her care in her final days. Kolb admitted that he seldom saw her after she entered Autumn Hills. "I do recall one occasion looking in on her because I had known her a long time."

Kolb further testified that he was not particularly alarmed by the diet Konikowski had ordered for the 87-year-old woman. And he said he witnessed no neglect or nursing malpractice with any of his patients at Autumn Hills. The physician was performing exactly as Sartwelle had hoped he would. He was telling the story of a dying patient suffering from the irreversible effects of cancer that had ravaged her body for years. The fact that Kolb saw the woman only once in the nursing home was easily explained. He said he couldn't have done anything different for Elnora Breed if he had seen her every day at Autumn Hills; the woman was in an irreversible decline. Kolb said he saw no value in daily visits to nursing home patients.

The LaMarque doctor described his role as medical director at the Texas City facility. State law mandates that every Texas nursing home must have a medical director. In 1978 Kolb was paid a small monthly stipend of $200. He testified that he took patients when there was no attending physician and no known local doctor for the patient.

Kolb said he saw no problems at Autumn Hills. "I continually recommended to my families that they admit my patients to that home." But he admitted that he did not place his own mother in Autumn Hills. When she finally needed nursing home care, he sent her to nearby Manor Care because, Kolb told the jury, the wings were segregated from each other and there were fewer problems with odors for that reason.

Finally, Kolb testified that he was never notified of any neglect, abuse, or other problems during the time that Betty Korndorffer and her team were inspecting Autumn Hills. He minimized the nursing home inspector's findings. "I can go into any nursing home or any hospital and I can find little problems to pick at." Sartwelle was pleased with Weldon Kolb when he passed the witness to the prosecution.

An angry Mike Guarino faced a rumpled, benign family physician on the witness stand as he began his cross-examination of Weldon Kolb. The doctor, accustomed to a lifetime of respect from colleagues and patients alike, would for the first time be confronted with an individual who held little esteem for his position or accomplishments. Guarino opened with a bang; before he uttered his first question, he asked the court to issue a Miranda warning to Kolb from the bench. And though Morgan declined, the message was clear. In the eyes of the prosecution, Kolb could be implicated in the murder of Elnora Breed.

The Galveston County D.A. moved immediately into Elnora Breed's medical record. He zeroed in on the absence, in the last year of her life, of any notation in the record of cancer. "They put it in when they even suspect cancer! They put it in to guide you, don't they, Doctor?" Guarino shouted. Kolb continued to read from the record as the district attorney stood by impatiently. "Are you through, Doctor?" Guarino said, disgust in his voice. Then he accelerated again. "The diagnosis has absolutely nothing to do with cancer, does it, Doctor?"

Kolb had done little to interpret the complicated medical jargon he used and that filled the medical records. In particular, he had mentioned that Breed was on a medication with a long and complicated name. Guarino helped him along, brought the testimony down to street level. "Isn't that kind of like a Rolaid, Doctor?" Kolb's body language showed that he was getting angry. No one had ever spoken to him like that before. Mike Guarino was accomplishing one of his goals. He was rattling the witness. He pressed on.

"That's pretty plain English, isn't it, Doctor?" he asked as he read from a chart. "Are you reading something there now that you didn't see back in 1978?" he asked sarcastically at another point. "There are no findings in the progress notes on the May admission on cancer, are there, Doctor?" he continued. "The nursing records regarding her activity are in contrast to your testimony," Guarino said, challenging the doctor.

He then read from the Seabreeze notes on the progress of Elnora Breed just before her transfer to the county hospital and then to Autumn Hills. Kolb had testified that Breed was not capable of activity during the final months of her life, but the Seabreeze progress notes told a different story. "Up in wheelchair," "Out in hall," "Rolls self around," "Wheels self around facility," "Up in wheelchair and rolling down the hall," "Able to stand and pivot to transfer." Then Guarino produced a form, signed by Kolb, that was the short-term goal for Breed in the nursing home. The form said, "Will attend exercise classes in the morning, will attend music program."

Guarino continued reading from what the nurses had charted. "Twenty-two times in a good mood, seventeen times in a pleasant mood, two times in a nice or cheerful mood." In fact, Guarino pointed out, Elnora Breed was in fairly good health for a woman her age until she had a flu shot just before entering the county hospital. It was the state's contention that an adverse reaction to the shot, not recurring cancer, led to Elnora Breed's final hospitalization.

But Kolb refuted Guarino, saying that the woman couldn't have had a negative reaction between the shot on September 26 and her entry into the hospital on the following day. It was just too quick.

Guarino then moved to the diet prescribed for her by Konikowski. "She was released on a 636-calorie-a-day diet?" he asked Kolb.

"In the condition and weight of this patient and her reduced metabolic weight, I don't think this was a starvation diet," Kolb responded.

Shortly before the morning break, Guarino asked Kolb, "You don't believe, Doctor, that daily visits or frequent visits would have made any difference?" Kolb answered by noting that there were eleven telephone communications between his clinic and Autumn Hills regarding the patient during the 47-day period Elnora Breed was in the nursing home's care.

During the break, Kolb walked to the far side of the rotunda around which the three large federal courtrooms were scattered. He was clearly shaken. His wife rushed to his side to calm him. Sartwelle looked at nearby reporters and said, "I don't know what Mike is getting so mad about," referring to Guarino's surprising anger in questioning the doctor. Before cross-examining Kolb, the D.A. had been the quietest lawyer in the case.

He was just as aggressive after the break, to the delight of the state's attorneys. Guarino seemed relentless in his attempt to crack the defense contention that Elnora Breed had died of cancer. Here before him was the woman's longtime doctor; here, too, was the medical director of the nursing home that had been named in the indictment. Guarino wanted to remind the jury of that connection. "Although you are not a defendant in this case, you are named in this indictment that you recklessly tolerated the commission of murder. . . . In your grand jury testimony did you invoke the Fifth Amendment?"

Minton, Burton, and Sartwelle were immediately on their feet, shouting motions for a mistrial. "Right now!" Sartwelle shouted at the judge. Calmly, Morgan instructed all the lawyers to approach the bench. Everyone in the courtroom was quiet in an attempt to hear what the judge was telling the attorneys. There was no question that this was a serious, not frivolous motion. Morgan and the lawyers adjourned to chambers.

Ten minutes later, David Marks returned to the courtroom. He was alone. The young prosecutor sat at the state's table, shuffling papers, doing busywork to keep his mind off the threat to his case. Marks did not think there would be a mistrial, but the possibility was there. He had been disturbed and amused by the theatrics going on in the judge's chambers. "There's a lot of posturing going on in there. I'm hearing lines like 'I'll bet you ten thousand dollars.'"

Morgan knew he wouldn't declare a mistrial. There was far too much investment in the case. He did, however, have to have case law to back up his decision. Miguel Martinez, the state's appellate lawyer in the case, would have the weekend to find the needed cases. In the meantime, everyone would have to wait, wondering how the judge would rule.

As he walked back to the Menger Hotel, Morgan looked at the birds in the trees. He prided himself on being able to identify the wild birds of Texas. "An Inca dove," he said, looking up. "A mourning dove. A whitewing dove." The serenity that Morgan felt, looking at the birds, was felt by him alone. The rest of the legal minds in the case would spend a weekend of white knuckles, sweaty palms, and sleepless nights.

CHAPTER FOURTEEN

San Antonio in the winter can be one of the most delightful cities in the country. Usually blessed with mild, clear days and cool nights, couples, families, and an occasional loner can stroll the sidewalks of the Paseo del Rio, the Riverwalk built alongside the San Antonio River where it meanders through the heart of the city's downtown. A tourist mecca year-round, the Riverwalk is studded with restaurants, clubs, and hotels. On January 20, 1986, the city was enjoying a weekend bonanza in the tourist trade; the date marked the first Martin Luther King Day in the nation's history. But the new national holiday did not delay the ongoing drama of the Autumn Hills trial.

Judge Don Morgan was beginning to feel pressured about the length of the trial. Some—the judge included—estimated that longevity and endurance records had already been shattered. It was established fact that Morgan was presiding over the longest criminal trial in Texas history. The strains imposed by that length were wearing on judge, jury, lawyers, defendants, press, and the most casual observers alike.

Word of the possible mistrial following Mike Guarino's questioning of Dr. Kolb had spread. Both the Associated Press and United Press International had been carrying the case on the national wire. Now, on the warm winter day of January 20, the press returned to the courtroom in force. But they were to be disappointed. Morgan ruled that the trial would continue. There would be no mistrial for the Autumn Hills defendants.

A more subdued Guarino reopened his cross-examination of Dr.

Kolb. "In your mind, what would be evidence of neglect to a geriatric, bedfast patient?" Guarino asked.

"Documented failure to turn the patient. Documented failure to
not clean up excreta for hours on end. Documented failure to bathe
and clean," Kolb answered.

Guarino was again making headway. He told Kolb of the bed
buzzers placed out of reach of patients. Kolb responded, "One
would have to know if the patient was able to handle the buzzer
even if it was right in their hand."

Guarino then began to read from the Texas Department of
Health reports on Autumn Hills, which were available to Kolb in
his position as medical director of the facility. As Guarino questioned him regarding the specifics of the reports and letters from
the inspectors, Kolb said, "I would need to read the complete
record."

"Did you take the time, Doctor, in 1978, to sit down and review
this five-page letter?" Guarino snapped back at Kolb. "These reports had to do with the flesh and blood of these patients. . . . Did
you refuse to face the fact that there was poor patient care? . . . Is it
all kind of hazy now, Doctor?"

"I was there periodically every few days. I knew what went on,"
the doctor answered.

"Did you also bill the patients?" Guarino asked contemptuously.

"The patients I wrote progress notes on," Kolb answered.

John A. Konikowski had inherited the care of Elnora Breed from
Weldon Kolb when the elderly woman arrived at Seabreeze nursing
home. Now he found himself testifying in a murder trial. For months
the prosecution had contended that Konikowski's diet order, combined with neglect, had killed Elnora Breed. Now Konikowski
would have an opportunity to answer those charges. His wife, Jan,
was in the courtroom audience as he approached the witness stand.
She had witnessed the testimony of Kolb and knew how brutal the
cross-examination of her husband was likely to be. Jan Konikowski
had braced herself, smoking cigarettes, smiling, talking.

"Dr. Konikowski, did you prescribe the six-hundred-calorie-a-
day diet?" Sartwelle asked the dapper physician.

"Yes, I did," Konikowski answered.

"Did she starve to death, Dr. Konikowski, on that diet?" Sartwelle continued.

"No," Konikowski responded.

Sartwelle then led the physician through his qualifications and credentials, showing the jury a highly educated, competent doctor. Konikowski testified that he still had thirty patients in the nursing home that had once been called Autumn Hills. He said that twenty percent of his practice involved elderly patients.

Konikowski testified that he first saw Elnora Breed in May 1978. He had attended the woman because his associate, Kolb, was going out of town. Konikowski told the jury that he had believed at the time that Elnora Breed had inoperable cancer. "She would not have survived any kind of treatment we could have given her."

He also told the packed court that Elnora Breed wouldn't eat, that she clamped her mouth closed. "A patient becomes more and more unmanageable," he said. Sartwelle meticulously led the doctor through the medical aspects of Elnora Breed's final months of life. He had Konikowski interpret his notations on Elnora Breed's chart, as well as notes by other doctors and nurses.

From the defense table, Roy Minton carefully watched the jury. Konikowski was a key witness. If Sartwelle could convince the jury that Konikowski's diet order had not starved the woman to death, a major hurdle in the defense team's case would be overcome. Was the testimony of the doctor appealing to the jury, Minton wondered. He often thought no lawyer could really read a jury, but he watched them anyway, twirling his thin mustache, his hands constantly in motion. And Konikowski was smooth on the witness stand; there was no evidence of nervousness on his part as Sartwelle questioned him.

Now Sartwelle asked the physician about the order on Elnora Breed's chart that she be permitted to participate in activities at Seabreeze. "That was an optimistic goal but not very practical," Konikowski responded. He went on to clarify. "She probably could not support her own weight."

Konikowski admitted that he often forgot to make entries on a patient's chart. He said that it was a bad habit of his.

"Don't you make a charge to the patient when you see them?" Sartwelle asked.

"Like I don't always write notes, I don't always write charges."

The prosecutors were delighted with that answer from the doctor. They hoped that the memory of the jury and common sense would at least hint that Konikowski's credibility should be questioned. Who had ever been seen by a doctor and not charged for the visit?

Konikowski next testified that he judged the progress of his patients "mostly from what the nurses were telling me." He then said that Elnora Breed had good days and bad days. "That's fairly common with organic brain syndrome," he continued. "I doubt very much that she was capable of wheeling herself around in the hall and know where to go."

The doctor said that in late August 1978, Elnora Breed experienced a sudden change in her condition that could be attributed to either a mild stroke or a small heart attack. By September 6, Konikowski said, the woman's legs were a mottled color and she had a purple bruise, her extremities were cold and her ears were dirty, but he could find no heart problem. "She was certainly much deteriorated at that point."

Konikowski continued to read from Elnora Breed's patient record. He noted that Dr. Kolb had ordered the flu shot.

"Did she get that vaccine?" Sartwelle asked.

"Yes, she did," Konikowski answered.

"Did she get the flu?" Sartwelle pressed.

"No," the physician responded, then added that flulike symptoms would occur several days later. "That shot the previous day could not possibly have caused her to have enough symptoms to warrant me to be concerned about it."

The following day, Breed had been hospitalized. Konikowski testified that his diagnosis was cancer of the colon, a urinary tract infection, and diarrhea. He testified that Breed was semicomatose and dehydrated and her blood pressure was 96 over 60. She wouldn't eat.

Elnora Breed was an 87-year-old black woman. But on her record Konikowski had described her as a white female. During prosecution testimony, the mistaken description had been repeated again and again for the jury. Now, Konikowski said that it was a typographical error or a mistake in dictation from force of habit.

Sartwelle asked Konikowski about further problems that the doctor believed the woman suffered from. The doctor said that her pupils were sluggish and poorly responsive to light, that she had fluid in the chest and possible congestive heart failure.

"Do you necessarily put all of that down in these records?" Sartwelle asked.

"No, I'm a notoriously poor record keeper."

Sartwelle then asked the physician detailed questions about the diet he had prescribed for Elnora Breed. He also went through lab tests that Konikowski said confirmed Breed's cancer of the colon. On September 29 a nasal gastric tube was installed for feeding. "She was very ill. She would not take any oral feedings. . . . She was going to die if I didn't do something," Konikowski said. At 1 p.m. that day, Elnora Breed was lying in a fetal position.

Konikowski testified that he was worried about fluid overload, which could put the woman into congestive heart failure. Sartwelle pressed that point, asking, "Did you intend to give anything other on the order than precisely what is written here?" Konikowski said that he intended for the nurses to follow his orders.

"If you read the nurse's notes, you will find that she was very debilitated and an uncooperative individual," Konikowski said. He also told the court that just because his name wasn't on the nurse's notes did not mean that he wasn't present in the hospital.

By October 1 Elnora Breed was again awake and complaining. The following day, Konikowski ordered that the woman could have a liquid lunch. On October 3 the nurses noted a small decubitus ulcer on the bony prominence of the ball of the foot; Konikowski did not enter a note about the bedsore. He also told the court that he does not make nurses who work with him note small skin breakdowns.

As they read through the volumes of notes on the care of Elnora Breed, Sartwelle and Konikowski came to a troublesome item that would have to be addressed. If the woman was in fact in her final days and not recovering, why, on her discharge from the hospital, was there a notation saying, "Recovering nicely with antibiotics and IV fluids. To be followed in clinic." Konikowski said that he made the notation out of force of habit.

Sartwelle turned again to the diet that Konikowski had prescribed for Elnora Breed. "This diet has been labeled as a starvation diet and a death sentence. Do you agree with this?" the Houston lawyer said.

"The death sentence was the disease," Konikowski answered.

By mid-November of 1978, Elnora Breed was dying, hell was being raised by the inspectors, and her case was under close scrutiny. Konikowski's associate, Dr. Sullivan, changed the woman's diet order, increasing her calorie intake. After that increase, Elnora

Breed became swollen, suffered congestive heart failure, and died.

Sartwelle had one final bit of testimony he wanted from Konikowski. Did the doctor know of conditions at Autumn Hills and their effect on his patient Elnora Breed? "Did anyone ever call you and tell you before this good day about maggots in Elnora Breed's bedsore?" Sartwelle asked, trying to shift the blame to the state inspectors.

"No," Konikowski answered.

Guarino wasted little time in demonstrating for the jury the contempt he apparently held for Konikowski. Again an angry prosecutor shouted his questions. "When did you visit Autumn Hills in 1978?" Guarino asked.

"I don't recall the days that I was there," Konikowski answered.

"You've had ample time to review your records," Guarino said pointedly. He then brought up the earlier testimony of eyewitnesses and followed that by challenging Konikowski about his record-keeping habits and the lack of records of visits he claimed to have made to Autumn Hills. He then turned to the diet order, which the state contended was paramount in the death of Elnora Breed. Flustered, Konikowski answered, "She was not on a starvation diet. She was on a starvation diet that she was doing well on."

The next day, Guarino pressed the doctor on his unawareness that the bone was exposed through the bedsore on Elnora Breed's foot. The prosecutor also pointedly called attention to the medication used on the sore: Toughskin, a painful preparation known in every athletic training room in the state. To the men on the jury, that name struck home.

"You don't drop Toughskin in on muscles or tissue or on bone, do you?" Guarino asked.

"No," Konikowski answered.

Guarino again pressed the point that Konikowski didn't know that Elnora Breed's bone was exposed.

"Are you approving the type of nursing activity when the bone is exposed?" Guarino asked, referring to a November 14 nurse's note.

"I'm certainly not beyond making mistakes," Konikowski responded.

The prosecutor returned to the condition of Elnora Breed in Seabreeze nursing home. He made Konikowski read a nurse's note stating that the woman was out of bed, in a wheelchair, and eating in the dining room; Elnora Breed, the note said, "appears to be in good mood, lunch in dining room."

For months, the state had attempted to put Tom Sartwelle and Gail Friend on trial along with the defendants for coaching their witnesses. Guarino now attempted to show the jury that Konikowski was just such a well-coached witness. "When did you first meet the defense attorneys?" Guarino asked.

"About a year ago," Konikowski answered.

"Whom did you meet with?"

"Mr. Sartwelle," Konikowski said.

"How many times did you meet with him?"

"About ten," the doctor answered.

"How many hours did you meet with him?" the prosecutor asked, pressing.

"Twenty hours, thirty hours, twenty-five hours," Konikowski answered.

Sartwelle followed Konikowski with Robert Sullivan, the physician who changed Elnora Breed's diet order shortly before her death. Sullivan testified that he spent a great deal of time in nursing homes, that he had pronounced Elnora Breed dead, and that Autumn Hills gave its patients good care.

Sartwelle then did something strange. He called to the stand Dr. John Reeves, who had once owned a nursing home in Texas City. Born in Oklahoma and "reared in the fields of West Texas," Reeves had a down-home quality in his speech and manner, and for three decades he had attended to the medical needs of the working people of Texas City.

Reeves had no patients in Autumn Hills in 1978, but his practice with older people was substantial. From the witness stand he said that he had one basic philosophy in caring for his elderly patients: "Don't overtreat them."

Reeves described his experiences as a nursing home owner. "In a moment of insanity I conceived and built and operated Fifth Avenue Nursing Home. . . . It was an unrewarding, overregulated, depressing business." The Texas City doctor then told of the disdain of most physicians toward long-term geriatric care. "You couldn't take a pitchfork and drive some doctors into a nursing home," he drawled.

Reeves further testified that nursing home owners and staff are "scared to death of lawsuits." He said that some of the conditions on which the state was basing its case against Autumn Hills were common to almost all nursing homes. "I can take you to a nursing home in San Antonio or Galveston and I can show you an old man or an old woman sitting in urine." He further said that he treated a woman whom he wouldn't catheterize because she always pulled the catheter out. It was better to let her urinate on herself, Reeves contended.

Reeves had attended the bedsore seminar that Sartwelle had arranged for local physicians. "I didn't know one third as much about the care of decubitus ulcers as I do now," he said of the seminar. Regarding turning the patient, Reeves pointed out to the jury, "If you have them on the average hospital bed, you could turn them like a shish kebob. . . . I can cure a bedsore with them lying on it now."

Reeves had provided the courtroom a moment of comic relief, and Guarino had few questions on cross-examination. But his last question to the doctor was no throwaway. "You told the jury that you are a former nursing home owner like Mr. Gay . . ."

The testimony of Dr. Merrill Stiles was not limited to the questions Tom Sartwelle asked him and the answers Stiles gave in return. Stiles was smooth on the witness stand as he described why his patient, Edna Mae Witt, died. To no one's surprise, Stiles did not attribute her death to septicemia caused by lying in her own urine and feces. Instead, Stiles contended, the 78-year-old grandmother died from chronic renal failure. He said that fifty percent of his practice was with geriatric patients and that he had become Edna Mae Witt's doctor because he had previously cared for her son.

Sartwelle again questioned the physician in laborious detail. Stiles, more than the other physicians, had become the focus of gossip when the Autumn Hills case surfaced. He and his wife, Carolyn, were well known in Galveston and moved in the best social circles. When the physician's name appeared in one of the earlier indictments and was reported by the local news media, it created quite a stir. Now Stiles was on the stand, and Tom Sartwelle was letting him tell his side of the story for the first time.

Stiles was a good witness, perhaps the best in the entire case at explaining complex medical concepts to the jury. Tall and thin, Stiles spoke softly and looked the jury in the eye as he addressed them. He sounded credible when he said that Edna Mae Witt's "rehabilitation potential was extremely limited." He also estimated, contrary to the state's contention, that the Autumn Hills staff had called him nineteen times about the condition of Edna Mae Witt.

Stiles told the jurors that older people often eat little, not because they are being starved to death but because they say, "I'm never hungry." They often refuse lunch and dinner. "It's a very common problem."

Sartwelle moved on to Edna Mae Witt's bedsores. "What would prevent the bedsores?" he asked Stiles.

"Youth," Stiles answered, then added that Edna Mae was extremely heavy, and "she gave no assistance in trying to get her up."

Sartwelle produced a notation from a social worker: "Mrs. Witt is responsive today." Stiles questioned the note. "It is never the way I would describe her on either of my visits in the nursing home."

As he chronicled the decline of Edna Mae Witt, Stiles said that on rounds he always dictated his progress notes. The state had earlier tried to show that Stiles made infrequent visits to the nursing home, didn't return calls from the families of patients, and that a rubber stamp had been used in place of his signature. Stiles admitted that he dictated and had given the nursing home a stamp with his signature imprinted on it.

He said that Edna Mae Witt had been taken to the county hospital, on the orders of his associate Dr. Louis Leon, because she was in her final decline. On that day, Stiles was not on call. As he reached the final days of her medical record, Stiles told the court, "Basically, she's dying at this point."

And at that point in the testimony, Sartwelle and Stiles were confronted with objective, verifiable evidence that Edna Mae Witt had septicemia. A blood culture had been ordered by a county physician on duty at the hospital to determine if, in fact, the dying woman was suffering from sepsis. The results, which did not come back until after Witt's death, were positive. Stiles offered the explanation that the doctor had used a long spinal needle to obtain the blood from a thigh artery after he couldn't secure the specimen any other way, and the thigh was contaminated with feces that produced a positive culture.

Stiles also referred to the autopsy report prepared seven years after the death of Edna Mae Witt and paid for by Sartwelle and the defense team. He said that it showed no evidence of septicemia. He said that there was evidence that Witt suffered a cardiopulmonary arrest on October 16, 1978. "She's just a terribly sick, dying lady. This is what happens to all of us. The heart stops."

As Edna Mae Witt lay dying, Merrill Stiles found himself with a problem after he returned to his patient. The woman's son, Charles Witt, had told Stiles that there were to be no heroics performed on his mother in her final hours. In medical shorthand, Edna Mae was a no code. But Leon, Stiles's associate, had ordered heroic measures in Stiles's absence. To further complicate things, the family members were arguing among themselves. Stiles had dictated a memorandum into the hospital progress record to protect his position, and he now read that memo to the court: "In view of this apparent family conflict, it makes it somewhat difficult to please both mutually exclusive sides of the family, and for the time being we will try to do what can be done towards the care of a generally impossible situation in this lady. Her condition has been one of gradual progressive decline at the home, related primarily to her unresponsiveness, diabetes, anemia, tremendous obesity, and progressive skin care problems, including a significant sacral area decubitus, which has defied improvement, although considerable attention has been directed toward its care there at the home."

Stiles explained to the jury that a nursing home is the end of the line. Staring straight at the jury, he explained that documentation is a problem in a nursing home. "There are more arms and legs and fingers and eyes to do that in a hospital. It's just a different expectation." The physician also told them that he had been medical director of Autumn Hills from January 1976 to May 1978; for those services he was paid a monthly salary of $2 per patient by the home.

The prosecution had presented a great deal of information about falls by patients, and Stiles and Sartwelle now wanted to show the jury that falls are a commonplace problem among the elderly. "I get called at least once a day about someone falling in a nursing home," Stiles said, adding that often the patients don't complain of pain immediately. He further testified that doctors rely on nurses' observations after a fall. Often patients walk around on a fracture for days.

Finally, Sartwelle needed to refute months of testimony that depicted Stiles as conducting blitzkrieg visits through the hallways of the nursing home, stopping, looking in a patient's doorway, and dictating as he went. "When you examine your patients in a nursing home, how long does it take?" asked Sartwelle.

"You see them for one main reason. The government says you have to see them every thirty days. There is really no other reason. It is really a social visit. . . . Those visits don't take very long at all. . . . The patients who are sicker, we will spend more time with that patient."

David Marks had been waiting to cross-examine Merrill Stiles for the better part of a decade. For Stiles, the young prosecutor had been a bad dream. The doctor, a respected member of the community, had suffered the indignity of being called before a grand jury, having his name on an indictment and in the newspaper, and having to hire an attorney to protect himself. The contempt that Marks felt for Stiles was mutual.

Marks opened his questioning with an edge of contempt in his voice, but he moved in on the doctor slowly, asking him about staffing, supplies, accurate information, basic criteria for any nursing home. But he soon moved to more volatile areas, such as the amount of time Stiles spent at Autumn Hills. And Marks brought up Pauline Goodwin Kaper.

"She was there forty hours in one week. How many years would it take you, sir, to accumulate forty hours in a nursing home?" Marks asked acidly.

"It wouldn't take very long," Stiles answered. It was evident he was beginning to feel his own hostility.

Repeatedly, Marks asked Stiles the same questions, questions about strong urine odors and slimy water pitchers. Stiles' patience was wearing thin; he interrupted his testimony to ask Morgan, "Do I have to answer this question over and over again?" The judge answered, "Yes."

The jury now came to life. Even those jurors who seemed to sleep through the redundant medical testimony were now alert as they watched the personal duel going on before them. Much like the gallery at a tennis match, their eyes moved to and fro from the witness to the young lawyer seated before them.

Marks soon went into the issue of shortages and filth to which previous eyewitnesses had testified. He spoke of aides who did not know how to take vital signs, failure to reposition patients often enough, filthy bedding changed only rarely, sediment in water pitchers, an aide who couldn't read or write but was taking vital signs, no Telfa pads, few heat lamps, few sheepskins, few bandages, and aides doing laundry instead of caring for patients.

"Sir, does this testimony in any way affect your opinion?" Marks asked.

"No, sir."

Marks went right back to the same theme, describing the testimony of aide Carol Josey Oliver. He recited her charges about the shortage of Ensure, dressings that were unchanged and dirty with drainage, frequent lack of bandages, soap, lotions, and even linen, aides watching TV, aides hiding linen, dirty water pitchers, patients lying in their own dried waste.

Stiles had heard enough. "Those conditions which you described are so foreign to what I saw at Autumn Hills that I question the credibility of the person saying it."

Marks turned to pressing the doctor about his failure to return phone calls from patients' family members. "Would observations of family members be important? Would they be important enough for you to accept phone calls when these people are desperately trying to reach you?" Marks continued.

"There is never a sun that sets that we don't try to return phone calls to family members."

Marks countered by citing specific family members who had tried to reach Stiles but could not. He also did not miss the opportunity to recite again the problems that were behind those calls. "Assume with me . . . that Brenda Di Cristina came to Autumn Hills to visit her grandmother for one week from 8 a.m. to 5 p.m. every day and found dried urine, reeking of urine, lying on her back all day. . . . She found her in the morning with her hair greasy and wet." He said that others found the woman much the same way at night. "Assume with me that they saw an aide trying to take your patient's temperature in her vagina. . . . Doctor, if you had received this information in 1978, would it have been of help to you?" Marks asked.

"It doesn't help me a bit. It just defies all credibility. . . . To say that nobody came in the room for eight hours' time just defies all."

Marks turned next to the testimony of Mary Utley and Laurie Montaign, the family members of Mary and Amelia Sarich. Both women had told horror stories to the jury. "I guess you would discount that," Marks said.

"I certainly would. If those statements were true it seems incredible that these families weren't just beating on my door," Stiles responded.

"The question is, Doctor, where were you?" Marks pressed.

"I was there," Stiles snapped back.

"Because you would not return phone calls that these families made, they called the Texas Department of Health," Marks said.

Marks kept up a barrage of baiting questions designed to provoke the already angry Stiles. "Doctor, are you aware of how many times TDH received complaints from the families of your patients?" Marks asked.

"No," Stiles answered curtly.

"Part of your opinion is based on your limited exposure to Autumn Hills nursing home," Marks continued.

"I thought that you were never going to get to that," Stiles responded, aroused now by Marks's questions and vicious style. Marks had maintained that Stiles was running a geriatric mill, seeing patients on a wholesale basis, making it on volume. Now he pressed that point.

"Give the jury an idea what your practice was like in 1978. How many patients did you see in a day?" Marks asked.

"About forty," Stiles answered.

Marks homed in on the numbers, showing that in 1978 Stiles was practicing in three clinics, four nursing homes, and three hospitals. Stiles would see twenty patients in Autumn Hills on his visits. He made rounds in 45 minutes to an hour.

Marks then did what he said he was going to do in his questioning of Stiles. The attorney called the doctor Mr. Stiles. Sartwelle immediately objected, and Marks angrily stood, saying to Morgan, "I didn't know that he came in here with a title, Judge." Marks knew that he was on safe ground here; Morgan's disdain for most doctors was well known to Galveston County attorneys. Minton, on the sidelines, smiled at the youthful Marks, watched the jury, and twirled his mustache.

"Of that 45 to 60 minutes that you are out there, how much of that time is spent with you communicating with the nurse?" Marks continued. "What percentage of your time is related to communication as opposed to observation?" Marks asked.

"A lot of time is spent with communication, with the patient, with the nurse. It is not unusual for a family member to be there,"

Stiles responded.

"Do you always go into the room, Doctor?" Marks asked.

"Not always," Stiles answered.

"Do you always lift up the sheets and examine the patients?" Marks continued.

"Not always," Stiles said.

"Do you ever examine a patient from the doorway?"

Marks pressed, his contempt barely contained. "One sign of neglect of this type of patient can be a bedsore, wouldn't you agree with me?" he asked.

"I think we ought to discuss that a little," Stiles answered, his own contempt for Marks evident.

"A bedsore provides a route for systemic infection to the body," Marks continued.

"The facts show that is a very uncommon cause of infection," Stiles answered back.

Marks then dropped a bomb. There was nothing in the record to support Stiles' testimony that the blood culture taken from Edna Mae Witt just before she died had been drawn with a spinal needle. Marks's hands shook as he held the record before the jury. He went on to show that the woman's veins had been easy enough to find to insert intravenous needles for feeding and fluid intake. He also showed that Witt was on an antibiotic, to treat the septicemia that Stiles had testified she didn't have. "There is a reason for you not to remember that antibiotic. The reason is that you prescribed the wrong antibiotic. This is another lab test that you don't believe," Marks said.

"I didn't say that. Don't you listen?" Stiles retorted.

"Doctor, your opinion about Edna Mae Witt has vacillated over a period of time," Marks said. He charged that in an earlier affidavit Stiles had said that a cancer might have caused the woman's death.

"How do you presume to say that?" Stiles shot back at Marks.

Marks then asked if the Galveston doctor had thought of the possibility of losing his license. "My license is on the line every time I go to work," Stiles responded.

"If you were to testify that any of these things constituted neglect that you were aware of, would it jeopardize your license?" Marks asked.

Sartwelle was nearing the end of his case before the jury. He had placed the attending physicians before them and felt that they had all done a credible job for his clients. Now, he must refute the testimony of the nurses, nurse's aides, and family members that had been so effective for the prosecution.

But Roy Minton was troubled that the case was taking so long. He knew that the long and technical examinations of witnesses that was Sartwelle's style must be wearing on the jury; it certainly was tiring almost everyone else in the courtroom. Minton also knew that Morgan was getting impatient with the length of the trial. Unfortunately, Minton also knew that the job Sartwelle had before him could be critical to the case. The nurses and nurse's aides that Sartwelle was about to call to the witness stand were also eyewitnesses who could refute some of the powerful testimony of the state's in-house personnel.

Sartwelle had also worked over the years with family members who were satisfied with the treatment their loved ones had received at Autumn Hills. After all, not everyone in the home had died of abuse or neglect. The attorneys had to make their point to the jury that the nursing home was competent and often a pleasant place for its elderly residents.

Both Minton and Burton knew that although patience was wearing thin, they would have a difficult time getting Sartwelle to abbreviate the testimony of his remaining witnesses. And Minton and Burton had crucial tasks of their own that they were eager to begin; within a week, they would call the defendants to the stand in a final effort to show the jury that the people on trial before them were not murderers and did not knowingly cause the death of Elnora Breed.

Judge Morgan was faced with a problem too. His trial had overstayed its welcome in Judge William Sessions' federal courthouse. The borrowed room that contained the Autumn Hills trial was needed for pressing federal business. The trial would have to move at the end of January. The logical choice for an alternate site was the already crowded Bexar County Courthouse, on the other side of downtown San Antonio.

Roy Barrera had been helpful in obtaining the borrowed federal courtroom, and now he would again have to use his personal influence to obtain a place to finish the trial. His first choice was the lecture room at St. Mary's University that had been unavailable in the fall. Frantically, Barrera began phoning his friends.

Again, his luck didn't hold. He would not be able to obtain the room at the university. But his connections in the courthouse came through for him. At the beginning of February, the Autumn Hills trial would move to the small courtroom of Republican judge Tom Rickhoff. The change would be a stark contrast to the grandeur of the huge room in which the case had thus far been conducted.

Tom Sartwelle and Gail Friend sat in the rented back room of the Stockman Restaurant on Commerce Street in downtown San Antonio. A few other diners were enjoying their meal in the front room of the eatery on a cool January night. Surrounding Sartwelle and Friend were the nurses and aides of Autumn Hills that they had brought to San Antonio to testify. In a forceful voice, Gail Friend, a nursing instructor turned lawyer, talked with the nurses in their own professional language.

The nursing personnel were being prepared for their time on the witness stand. Some of them had been named in the indictment or barely escaped being indicted themselves. Others had family members who had been named. The message that Friend and Sartwelle had to convey to the women was that neither they nor Autumn Hills had done anything wrong. That message must come through loud and clear in front of the jury.

There had been conflict between some of the women now seated in the Stockman Restaurant and the state's eyewitnesses. Some of the prosecution witnesses had been fired from Autumn Hills. It was important that that information be brought out. Furthermore, it was more important that the women seated around the lawyers, eating catfish and steak, be shown as compassionate, competent workers. Sartwelle and Friend were earning their fee in the shirt-sleeve skull session.

Nettie Gage worked at Autumn Hills as an aide from 1976 until 1981. The single, unemployed mother of one now lived in the small Louisiana rice-farming community of Jenerette. She had come to work at Autumn Hills from a sugarcane factory. Now Tom Sartwelle called the young woman to the witness stand, following a fairly unproductive defense witness named Jeanine Soloman, a former Autumn Hills medication aide. Soloman testified that she had seen none of the abuse and neglect that the prosecution witnesses had described in such detail. "All I did was pass my medication," she said.

Sartwelle led Nettie Gage through the daily routine she had followed at the nursing home. She said that there was plenty of help available to turn bedfast patients, the food looked and tasted pretty good to her, and in fact, staff members were permitted to purchase a tray for fifty cents. She never had to work in the laundry room when she needed to care for patients.

Minton interrupted Sartwelle to ask Gage, who was named in the indictment, a question that he knew would not be lost on the jury. "Mrs. Gage, you know that there is no statute of limitations on murder, and if evidence comes out in this case, you could be charged with murder. Have you or any of the ladies in the indictment done anything to knowingly cause the death of anyone?" Minton asked. He knew the jury remembered that Gage had been given a Miranda warning from the bench.

"No, sir," Gage answered.

"Pass the witness, Your Honor," Minton said, satisfied with the one question that he would continue to ask almost every witness to come.

Jim Vollers, the Autumn Hills special prosecutor and former appeals court judge, now had his opportunity to question Gage. He quickly established that Gage did not remember Elnora Breed. Vollers also showed that Gage had worked regularly at the nursing home during the 47 days Breed was there and that the woman was probably one of Gage's patients. Gage did remember Edna Mae Witt but could not remember that the elderly woman had any bedsores. Nor did she remember that any of her other patients had sores. "Did any of your patients have decubitus ulcers in 1978?" Vollers asked.

"I don't remember. . . . I imagine there were some there."

The former nurse's aide did remember that Edna Mae Witt was a heavyset woman. "It took two of us to turn her." Gage said that she gave Witt bed baths and that, in fact, she gave five or six bed baths on each shift she worked. She described her procedure for washing the patient's face and genitalia, cleaning the mouth, changing the sheets, and placing the call light next to the bed. Gage also testified that she had reported red spots on the body of Edna Mae Witt to the charge nurse.

"How often did you report to her that you found red spots on Mrs. Witt?" Vollers asked.

"Whenever I had her," said Gage, who had already testified that she didn't remember any bedsores on the elderly woman.

Gage then said that she had never bathed patients with dried feces on them, had never seen dried rings of urine on the bed linens. "The whole time you worked at Autumn Hills?" Vollers pressed.

David Marks knew the patients of Autumn Hills as if they were part of his own family. Now, he whispered questions to Vollers as the older attorney continued his questioning. The aide did not remember Pearl Creighton, who had suffered from multiple bedsores, did not remember Frank Coss, whose genitalia had swollen to the size of a cantaloupe, did not recall Guadalupe Martinez or her bedsores, did not remember Betty Cappony, who suffered from a decubitus ulcer with foul, thick drainage and whose left shoulder was partially necrotic, rotting, and open. "Would you recall if you saw that?" Vollers asked.

"No, sir," Gage answered helplessly.

Vollers continued, knowing that he was successfully destroying the credibility of the witness. He asked Gage if she recalled patient Fannie Burns, whose whole toe was reported rotting off by a nurse on May 5, 1978. Gage couldn't remember the woman.

Unlike Guarino and Marks, Vollers was never harsh with a witness. But his quiet competence could be equally devastating. He now asked Nettie Gage if she remembered the names of 26 patients who had suffered from bedsores and about whom the jury had heard months of testimony. Some of the patients had suffered from bedsores so large that the bone was exposed. "Do you recall if any or all of those patients had decubitus ulcers?" Vollers asked.

"I'm sure some of them had them, but I don't remember who at the time . . . whatever," Gage answered.

"If a decubitus ulcer went down to the bone, would you remember that?" Vollers continued.

"Yes, sir," Gage answered.

At the defense table, Tom Sartwelle shook his head in open despair. The Autumn Hills staff members he had so carefully cultivated over the years were not working out for him. At the table where the prosecutors sat, David Marks smiled at Vollers's apparent success in destroying the credibility of Nettie Gage. The only salvation available to the defense was to play a numbers game and show how many patients Gage had dealt with over the years. Minton did the best he could, but the damage was already done.

CHAPTER FIFTEEN

In the course of the trial Don Morgan warmed to Tom Sartwelle, and the successful Houston attorney warmed to the volatile judge. The two met by accident in the Crockett Hotel restaurant late one evening, when Morgan joined two members of the trial press corps for a nightcap. Morgan and Sartwelle had not met socially since the trial got under way in San Antonio. In fact, Sartwelle held traditional views about the propriety of attorneys' meeting trial judges in social contexts.

But on this night Morgan and the reporters joined Sartwelle at his table. Sartwelle was at first ill at ease, but as the evening wore on the Houston lawyer began swapping legal war stories with Morgan, who was always ready to tell a tale on himself or a colleague.

Morgan and Sartwelle had much in common and shared numerous friends. Morgan had faced men like Sartwelle throughout his legal career, when he represented clients who were suing insurance companies. And though Morgan had been an adversary of such lawyers, he recognized and respected their talents.

Sartwelle in turn had appeared before many tough judges in his career. He knew that his style was often abrasive and that he had been on thin ice with Morgan. But now he warmed to the judge who months before had humiliated him in front of the jury. In the Crockett Hotel bar that night, the wall between the two men came down, and Tom Sartwelle found himself liking Don Morgan.

Sartwelle's nurses and aides had been a disaster for the defense, although Sartwelle didn't see it that way. Of the fifteen brought to

San Antonio to testify, two thirds actually reached the witness stand, as the defense found itself in the uncomfortable position of having to cut its losses. Perhaps family members would present a more credible story to the jury. They too had been eyewitnesses.

Minton and Burton were intent on moving the case along. They were ready to put the four defendants on the witness stand. Morgan knew the effect such a move could have on a jury. The people on trial for murder in his court were well-dressed, attractive, above-average Americans. From their appearance, it was difficult for anyone to believe that these people had willfully killed anyone. Now it was time for them to swear that they had not.

The Bexar County Courthouse is a busy place at the best of times. It can be a frenzied place, where lines of prisoners in gray prison garb and handcuffs are paraded in human chains through the hallways on their way to court. During the first week of February 1986, the contrast between the pristine federal courtroom and the noisy, crowded county courthouse was dramatic. Now in another borrowed chamber, the lawyers, defendants, judge, and jury of the Autumn Hills trial were all within a few feet of each other.

Morgan now sat behind an antique golden oak bench, actually enjoying the new surroundings. In the federal courtroom, there had been no windows. A cold, prisonlike atmosphere had pervaded the modern, spartan surroundings. But in the county courtroom the surroundings were much like those Morgan had spent most of his adult life in. He felt at home.

Nor was the small courtroom a new experience for the lawyers in the case. They were all experienced men who had practiced in the lower courts of the judicial system, where the dignity of the court is not measured by the size of the room. Tom Rickhoff's borrowed facility on the second floor of the Bexar County Courthouse would do just fine to wind up the case.

At 3:05 p.m. on Tuesday, February 4, 1986, Mattie Locke, nervous but eager to testify, walked through the bar to the witness stand. As she had throughout the trial, Mattie Locke was smiling. She carried a large notebook pressed to her chest as she sat down. Her hand was steady as Morgan swore her in. Unknown to Locke, Morgan thought that she had more problems than the other three defendants. He had told friends early in the trial, "It might do her some good to spend some time in jail." Watching Mattie Locke from the bench, Morgan had developed the impression that she was an arrogant, corporate automaton, perhaps even lacking in intelligence.

Minton was worried about Mattie. At first she had been difficult, but as the years went by, the nurse smoothed herself out as she grew more accustomed to courtrooms and their procedures. But Minton was also worried because during the trial Mattie's health had been in decline. Always tall and thin, Mattie Locke was almost frail as she took the witness stand.

Minton began his questioning gently, in a soft voice yet with the staccato style he always used. Court reporters often had difficulty keeping up with Minton, he spoke so fast. Minton began by asking Locke about her life with her husband, Virgil, and she described how they had built their life together. Mattie had worked her way through college, then worked in a doctor's office, and later became a head nurse at a hospital in Beaumont. Virgil had opened a meat market in nearby Silsbee. Mattie spoke of how she had worked in her first nursing home as director of nursing and how she then moved to Houston and went to work at Hermann Park Manor, which Bob Gay eventually bought to add to his growing chain.

Ron Pohlmeyer came to work for Gay in 1969. Mattie Locke was nursing director at Hermann Park Manor when Pohlmeyer arrived as the new administrator. She described for the jury the growth of the small nursing home chain. Mattie was on hand throughout that growth period, working to make things better for both the patients and her superiors.

"Truthfully, do you think you were good at it?" Minton asked her.

"Yes, sir, I do," Mattie Locke answered forcefully.

She worked directly with Pohlmeyer after he moved up in the corporate hierarchy. He was a busy man, a hard worker who, she said, would act on her recommendations. Pohlmeyer was constantly on the phone to the other nursing homes in the chain. "We used to tease him about having a telephone ear," she said.

In the nursing home business there are constant problems to be dealt with. Mattie eventually moved up to the post of nursing consultant for the chain, a position that made her the chain's troubleshooter. "That was very much a part of my function," she told Minton and the court.

Minton had Locke describe in detail the state inspection process that all nursing homes in Texas must undergo. Through her, he attempted to show how Autumn Hills was responsive to correcting problems that arose in the corporation's seventeen facilities.

At that point, Minton homed in on a major problem that the state had for months identified as one of Autumn Hills' great sins. He entered into evidence letters that had come to Mattie Locke's desk identifying problems in the Texas City facility. Locke said the letters spoke of charting problems, which are common when a new director of nursing takes over a nursing home.

Mattie Locke spoke directly to the jury when she answered Minton's questions. She had almost the quality of a little girl smiling on the witness stand, yet demonstrating that she was not the mindless automaton Morgan had thought during the months he had observed her. Instead, she quickly established herself as an articulate professional who was at home in her work. And shortly she demonstrated that she was either very well coached or possessed almost total recall.

Tom Sartwelle was relieved. For months, he had carried the complexities of the trial almost alone. It had fallen to him to handle the majority of the witnesses, digest the difficult medical aspects of the case, and fend off assaults on his witnesses from the zealous prosecutors. Now, he had little left to do in the trial; there were a few minor witnesses left for him to put on the stand, but the major part of his task was over.

For months reporters covering the trial had urged Sartwelle to go out on the town with them. Some of them lived in San Antonio and knew well the variety of the city's nightlife. Now it was a relaxed Tom Sartwelle who met them in the Roosevelt Bar of the Menger Hotel. Gone was the attire of the courtroom. Instead, Sartwelle wore a sport shirt and slacks. In front of him was a longneck beer, an established trademark of San Antonio and certainly appropriate for the Menger's antique saloon.

Sartwelle ate and drank long into the night with the reporters. For the first time they were able to see him as just another human being who could joke, tell stories, and be sociable. Sartwelle, in turn, saw the press in a new light. In his insurance defense practice he had little contact with newsmen. He had held a basic lawyers' distrust for the fourth estate. Now he warmed to them, even admitting that coverage of the trial, much to his surprise, had been fair.

The following morning, a tired Tom Sartwelle walked in the hallway outside the Autumn Hills courtroom. It had been a rough but

well-deserved night of revelry for the Fulbright and Jaworski lawyer. To one of his companions from the previous evening he said, in
jargon appropriate to the trial, "I feel like I've been tube-fed and
rolled."

In the courtroom, Minton continued his questioning of Mattie
Locke. She needed little prompting, often digressing as she answered in endless detail. For years she had wanted to tell her side of
the story. And for all those years, the attorneys had told her not to
talk to anyone about the case. Now she could speak freely, and she
was making the most of it. Finally, Morgan was forced to instruct
her to answer only the questions that were asked of her, without
digression.

Mattie Locke traced the state inspections of Autumn Hills from
the first time she had heard there was a problem. Minton then read
from the correspondence of Betty Korndorffer to show how extensive the state inspector's efforts had been in launching the Autumn
Hills investigations. Locke knew little of that. "Again, were you
ever informed that Mrs. Korndorffer had initiated an investigation
of fraud?" Minton asked.

"No, I was not," Locke answered.

Mattie Locke was reassured to see members of her family enter
the courtroom. All of the Autumn Hills defendants had enjoyed
support from their family and friends. Bob Gay's friend and business
associate, wealthy Houston oilman George Mitchell, had spent an
entire day watching the trial from the front row. Ron Pohlmeyer's
family made frequent visits. Virginia Wilson's husband, Lynn, was a
frequent visitor to the San Antonio trial. Now, members of Mattie's
Sunday school class came into the room. She was not alone in her
time of trouble.

Mattie Locke explained how Autumn Hills had begun using a
new computer system in 1978. She said the system had operating
flaws that made it "appear that we were giving medications without
doctors' orders." She said she had investigated and determined that
medicines were being given according to doctors' orders, but the
computer's documentation did not reflect that.

She answered the state's contention that Autumn Hills often did
not have medication on hand by explaining that patients' families
often wouldn't pay for it. The state required that the facility pay for
the medication in such a case. Locke testified that she had sent a

note to Marie Ritchie, at that time the chain's administrator, saying, "If the family will not purchase medication, the facility must purchase the medication."

Mattie Locke knew that there were problems with the patient progress charting done by her nurses. "They had developed kind of a negligent attitude about charting every day," she told the jury. She also said that she held an in-service training program to correct that problem. She described one nurse as "one of the most caring nurses I have ever encountered. However, her ability to document it on the printed page did lack."

Locke told the jury that she had made rounds with the facility's director of nursing. She knew that the state would attempt to make an issue of whether she was aware of the bedsores of the patients. "I did not turn back the covers and look at them unless [the director] requested that I do so." It was a damaging admission, but at least Mattie Locke and Roy Minton, not David Marks and the other prosecutors, had brought it to the attention of the jury.

Minton then approached the difficulties Mattie Locke said she had with Betty Korndorffer. "Over a period of time, did you and Mrs. Korndorffer have differences on charting?" Minton asked.

"Yes, very definitely, we did."

Minton drew a large calendar for the jury on which he targeted the month of May 1978. He checked off the days on which Locke worked to correct problems in the nursing homes of the Autumn Hills chain. It was a full and busy schedule. He also had her describe Marie Ritchie's final days as administrator, following the initial fraud investigation. Locke described the woman as visibly upset and totally withdrawn. "My recommendation was that we needed some administrative assistance," she said. She returned to the nursing home in June, after Ritchie left, and hired between thirty and fifty people. Many employees loyal to the administrator had left with Ritchie.

Mattie Locke testified that she had had problems with Betty Korndorffer when she worked at the company's Friendswood nursing home, shortly before Locke was promoted to the home office. Now she told the jury, "It was obvious that Mrs. Korndorffer didn't like me. . . . She likes confrontations. I don't like confrontations."

Locke also described the training of nurse's aides. Throughout the trial, the defense had contended that the nursing home gave extensive training to the aides who worked for it. Locke confirmed that, saying, "We would do this so that we could give the facility the best chance in the world to go on."

Mattie Locke was indeed well prepared for her testimony. For years she had been able to think about what she would say on the witness stand and had studied the documents and her own notes of the period to refresh her considerable memory. Now, when Minton forgot to ask about a particular fact or incident, Locke would interrupt and force him to deal with an area she wanted to talk about.

Cassandra Canlas had cried when she saw Edna Mae Witt's bedsores while on inspection, Betty Korndorffer had testified. Mattie Locke had also examined the 78-year-old woman in the company of Canlas. "Did either one of you ladies cry?" Minton asked.

"No, sir, we didn't," Locke answered.

"Did Mrs. Canlas exhibit any kind of emotional outburst when you examined Mrs. Witt?" Minton continued.

"No, sir, she did not," Locke said.

The following day, Mattie Locke was again on the witness stand. The defense attorneys were pleased with her as a witness. Minton said, "I was planning on putting Bob Gay on first, but now I'm glad that I didn't." Morgan was also impressed with the woman. Her performance was not at all what he had expected. "She's a smart woman," he said.

Mattie Locke told the jury that she would have questioned the six-hundred-calorie diet prescribed for Elnora Breed and would have called the doctor about it, but she did not because, she said, "I've had a lot of doctors tell me to mind my own business."

Minton then led Locke through a list of nurses and aides who had been blasted during the prosecution phase of the trial. Locke was generally complimentary of the women, but she noted that many had problems documenting their work. Minton then asked Locke if any of the nurses and aides he had mentioned would knowingly kill a patient. "Absolutely not!" Locke answered. "They would have done everything in their power to take care of them."

Finally, Minton asked Locke if any of the other defendants would knowingly harm a patient. She described Pohlmeyer as fair, interested, and dedicated. She said he was interested in community problems in Texas City. Locke said Virginia Wilson was "very interested in doing the best job she possibly could." Locke said that she had known Autumn Hills president Bob Gay since July 1968, and she described him as involved and interested. "All of us had a profound respect for Mr. Gay," she said in answer to Minton's final question.

In the audience, Bob Gay's wife, Joyce, could contain her emotions no longer. She cried at Mattie Locke's description of her husband, while Gay himself sat dry-eyed next to her, patting her arm. Ron Pohlmeyer walked to a courtroom window and wiped tears from his face. Virginia Wilson sat stoically. It was the first time in years that anyone had said anything good about the defendants in a public forum.

As he had with Merrill Stiles, David Marks looked forward to facing Mattie Locke in his own arena. For her part, the nurse could barely conceal her contempt for the man who had made her life so complicated for so long. Marks knew that before a jury and a packed courtroom, Mattie Locke was a time bomb set to explode. He knew that if he could make the woman angry, he just might be able to discredit her testimony.

Mattie Locke had turned in a stellar performance under Minton's expert questioning. But her cross-examination would not be so pleasant. Could she face down Marks? Could she convince the jury under his brutal questioning that she hadn't killed anyone? Tension filled the room as Marks began to question the first of the people he was trying to send to prison.

He opened by saying that the nurses should have called the physician about the Elnora Breed diet.

"I don't agree with that," Locke answered shrilly.

Marks repeated himself; the nurses should have called.

"I don't agree with that statement," Locke said curtly. "Nutrition was not one of the areas that I have specialized in, in my nursing home experience. I would have called a nutritionist."

Asked to reevaluate that answer, she said, "That is not my training, Mr. Marks."

Marks hammered at his point that the nurses failed Elnora Breed. "That cost Mrs. Breed her life. That's enough, isn't it?" Marks continued.

"I don't agree with your statement," Locke again answered.

Word travels in the press corp when something dramatic is happening at a trial. Now, as Marks continued to question Mattie Locke, reporters began to slip silently into the courtroom. Just as quietly, they watched the contest between Marks and Mattie

Locke, waiting for the one moment of confrontational high drama that would become their lead paragraphs under the morning's headlines or on-camera stand-ups for that evening's news. Locke's performance was as poor in front of Marks as it had been superb for Minton. Repeatedly, she did not answer his questions or elaborate on the issues that he was raising. She simply limited her responses to "I disagree with your statement."

"Autumn Hills had a long history of dietary problems," Marks pressed.

"I disagree with your statement," Locke answered.

"This was not a strange type of report for Autumn Hills nursing home?" Marks asked of an inspector's report.

"I disagree with your statement," Locke said.

"These same findings were made time and time again, weren't they, ma'am?" Marks questioned.

"I disagree with your statement," Locke answered shrilly.

During her direct examination by Minton, Locke had maintained good eye contact with the jurors, often smiling at them. Now she looked at the jurors again. Perhaps they would see David Marks as she saw him, as the tormentor who had disrupted her life and was trying to destroy her. But the jurors did not return her stares or maintain eye contact as they had during her earlier testimony. Instead, they watched David Marks.

Marks now launched into a nutritionist's report that was critical of the nursing home. He spoke of meat that patients couldn't chew. "That's a lack of nutrition, ma'am, isn't it?" he asked Locke.

"I disagree with your statement" was her only reply.

Marks turned next to Locke's earlier testimony that most of the charting failures in the nursing home were documentation problems, the failure of nurses to maintain notes. She had told the jury that those failures did not seriously compromise patient care. Marks calmly but repeatedly asked Locke, "Does this appear to be a documentation problem?" as he described nightmare events in the home.

During the course of each trial day, Morgan habitually gave the jury four recesses. Now, as the afternoon wore on, the defense attorneys looked forward to the next one. Mattie Locke was not holding up well under cross-examination. She needed to calm down and conceal her hostility toward Marks, and her attorneys felt it was their job to calm her down. But Minton knew that only his client could do that. "That's something that they have to do for

themselves," he said philosophically. In the hallway of the courthouse, with her attorneys and reporters surrounding her, Mattie
Locke asked Minton, "Do I have to look at him?" Minton paced
the hallway, nervous that the client who had done so well was now
her own worst enemy.

Mattie had not understood Minton's instructions to her as he prepared her for the cross-examination. The veteran lawyer had told
her to keep her answers short and not give away anything. She
knew that she was coming across to the jury and the audience as
shrill, and she resolved to change her approach.

Back in the courtroom, a different Mattie Locke resumed the
witness stand. She was still an angry woman, but she was more responsive. Rather than refusing to answer Marks's questions, she decided to fight back as he attempted to prove that the nursing home
corrected problems only when its funding was at stake.

Turning to the nursing home staff, Marks asked, "Did it appear
to sink in? Did they appear to understand the problems the TDH
found?"

"They were very responsive. They did their best," Locke said.
"Mr. Marks, I took corrective action. . . . Yes, I did." She smiled,
looking at the audience. "I went to the facility, I worked in the facility, I spent time in the facility." As Marks pressed the issue, she
fired back, "As I have told you, Mr. Marks, we have a recurring
problem with documentation."

Marks then questioned the nurse about the nursing home's alleged failure to use sterile techniques. Locke responded that there
was a problem with only one nurse, whom she fired after she served
as acting director of nursing in Texas City for a brief period. Marks
then charged that Autumn Hills did not meet minimum staffing requirements, but Locke countered that with "I don't recall that we
left any shift uncovered." The prosecutor next asked Locke about
unsanitary conditions in the nursing home. She admitted that "was
a realistic problem with the dishwasher. We got it fixed."

The next morning, as Mattie and Virgil Locke prepared to go to
the Bexar County Courthouse for another day of testimony, tragedy struck their family. Mattie's sister Sue Lenamond had often
come to court in support of her sibling. At night, Sue stayed in the
condo on the river, giving Mattie the comfort she needed during
her testimony. Sue awakened that morning complaining of a head-

ache but soon could not speak, the victim of a stroke. Mattie and Virgil rallied to Sue's side as the loving sister was taken to nearby Baptist Memorial Hospital, but within days she would be dead.

The jury noticed that Mattie Locke did not return to the courtroom and suspected that something was wrong in her family. Juror Linda Peña, a secretary with San Antonio's Datapoint, had overheard someone on a pay telephone say that Mattie's sister had suffered a heart attack and Mattie wasn't taking it very well. Peña told the other jurors the news. None of them knew that Mattie's sister had died.

David Marks thought he was doing a good job of destroying Mattie Locke's credibility. Now he wondered if this new interruption and the reason for it would become known by the jury. Would the jury find out that Mattie's sister had died? Would they have sympathy for the woman he thought had been responsible for the deaths of Elnora Breed, Edna Mae Witt, and other Autumn Hills patients? David Marks was a profoundly troubled prosecutor at this point in the trial.

The defense team now scrambled to keep the long-running trial going without having to take a break. They had a series of witnesses to present to the jury, and each would take only a short time on the stand. That group included patients' family members, a nutritionist, and a seventy-year-old patient who had lived in the nursing home since 1977.

All those witnesses did little to bolster the defense position. From the family members Sartwelle brought to San Antonio, little could be learned, except from the relatives of Carrie Bacon. They refuted prosecution testimony that had declared that maggots had been found in the patient's shoe. Carrie Bacon's family had never heard of such an event. In fact, they testified, their frequent visits to the nursing home never revealed anything wrong with the care Carrie was receiving.

Other patients' families may have done more harm than good to the credibility of the defense case. One woman, a relative of a long-time Autumn Hills patient, told attorney Roy Barrera, "I don't go there more than once a year now. I'm still struggling with my guilt feelings."

Ron Pohlmeyer took the witness stand ready to confront his accusers with the facts as he knew them. Pohlmeyer had not visited the Texas City home often; he was a corporate man, a home office man, an expediter. Pohlmeyer got things done. That he was standing trial for murder in San Antonio, for the deaths of people he had never seen, was still astonishing to him. During the 47 days Elnora Breed had been a patient in a nursing home he helped run, he had never heard the woman's name.

Pohlmeyer was also a profoundly private man. The other defendants, Gay, Locke, and Wilson, were giving interviews to television and print reporters. Pohlmeyer had shunned publicity throughout the trial, embarrassed, some said, by the predicament he found himself in. Now he had another piece of business to attend to, to expedite, to make work. He would finally tell his story, what there was of it, to the judge and jury.

Charles Burton, the sphinxlike law partner of Roy Minton, had not said more than a hundred words since the trial began in September. Even away from the courtroom, Burton was generally quiet; it was his trademark. Some said that though the tall attorney was a miser with words, his mind was always at work; Burton was regarded as a legal genius, perhaps the real power behind Minton's success. Now, facing Ron Pohlmeyer, Burton needed to show the jury that the man before them was not the cruel creature portrayed to them for months.

Calmly and in quiet tones, Burton questioned Pohlmeyer about his work as a nursing home inspector before he joined Autumn Hills. Burton led Pohlmeyer through the inspection process, attempting to show that what Betty Korndorffer and her fellow inspectors had done in Texas City was out of the ordinary. He next introduced Pohlmeyer's nursing and medical experience. Pohlmeyer testified that though he had served as administrator of a nursing home, he had no nursing training.

Pohlmeyer also detailed for the jury the business end of the nursing home industry. "You can't be successful unless you have all of those rooms and all of those beds filled," he said. When he went to work for Gay at Hermann Park Manor, the nursing home was losing money. Pohlmeyer said that he contacted churches and doctors' offices to solicit business. He invited those he contacted to visit the home. "The image, unfortunately, of nursing homes is not that good. . . . I wanted them to come and see what we had." Soon after

Pohlmeyer's arrival, the home was showing a profit.

Burton led Pohlmeyer through the difficulties of running a nursing home, citing in particular the problems of dealing with the government. "Today, there are some two thousand rules and regulations that nursing homes have to comply with," Pohlmeyer testified, describing for the jury the bureaucratic maze he dealt with every day. He said that when he was a nursing home inspector, the inspection process took only hours. Now, he said, it took days.

Pohlmeyer described how Bob Gay had built his business. In the early days, most nursing homes were mom-and-pop operations, often functioning out of converted two-story houses. Pohlmeyer testified that Gay had a different concept. He built his nursing homes from the ground up. Many smaller operations closed in the face of increased regulation, Pohlmeyer said.

Much of Autumn Hills' success came when the chain instituted performance reports, which aided the corporation in containing costs by identifying problem areas. Pohlmeyer said the system worked because the report was so detailed. For example, an administrator knew precisely how many scoops of laundry detergent to use. He described the Texas City home as a well-run operation, "a cost-effective nursing home."

Early in the trial, the state had charged that Pohlmeyer and Locke went to Betty Korndorffer's superior in an attempt to have her removed from inspecting the Texas City nursing home. But now Pohlmeyer said he knew that there had been trouble between Locke and Korndorffer when the inspector had worked for Autumn Hills at its Friendswood facility. He testified that Locke stopped visiting that nursing home on her rounds because of the conflict. Pohlmeyer explained that he and Locke went to Korndorffer's superior "to make him aware of the personality conflict of two or three people."

Pohlmeyer said he was shocked when news of the vendor hold on the Texas City nursing home appeared in the *Galveston Daily News* and the *Texas City Sun.* "This was the first time a vendor hold was released to the press. . . . We had never had anything like that happen to us at Autumn Hills. . . . We had great concern about Mrs. Korndorffer inspecting one of our facilities." Pohlmeyer said that he and Locke asked that Korndorffer inspect both of the Galveston County nursing homes or neither. They were refused.

Pohlmeyer also testified that when the fraud investigation of

Marie Ritchie began, it totally disrupted the operation of the nursing home. When he and Gay ultimately dismissed the longtime administrator, "it had a tremendous impact. She had been there many years. She had a very loyal following of employees." Marie Ritchie and her husband had been involved in running the home for years. "They had no children. They devoted their entire lives to running this nursing home."

Now Burton confronted the problem that David Marks had made so much of during the trial. Studies done by the state showed that in 1978 Autumn Hills in Texas City ran as much as forty percent short of food supplement requirements. The state contended that Breed, an Ensure patient, had starved to death, among other things. Part of Marks's motive theory was that Autumn Hills starved the patients in order to make a profit. Now Burton and Pohlmeyer confronted that issue head on. Pohlmeyer testified that although the corporation wanted its homes to purchase the food supplement through the chain's central purchasing department, each facility had the authority to purchase Ensure from local vendors. "There is no reason, absolutely no reason, for a shortage of Ensure in any of our facilities."

Finally, Burton reached the question everyone in the courtroom knew he would ask. "Did you knowingly kill . . . or cause the death of anybody in that nursing home?"

"Mr. Burton, I've been in nursing homes for twenty-one years," Pohlmeyer said, now crying. "I've inspected nursing homes; I've been a general manager. I cannot believe that I'm sitting here indicted for murder." Sobbing, he said, "I would never have harmed Mrs. Breed in any way."

An angry Mike Guarino confronted Ron Pohlmeyer on the witness stand. The Galveston district attorney said he had listened to the Autumn Hills administrator for three hours and never once did Pohlmeyer mention patient care. "Patient care doesn't show up in the performance report, does it?" Guarino asked pointedly. "Do you feel patients in Autumn Hills, Texas City, received adequate patient care?" Guarino asked next.

"I certainly do," Pohlmeyer responded.

"They certainly paid for it, didn't they?" the district attorney snapped back. Guarino then produced checks that Ruth Linscomb, the sister of Elnora Breed, had written on Breed's savings to pay the nursing home for her care. "Mrs. Breed was the picture of neglect in a nursing home, wasn't she?" Guarino asked.

"I would have no knowledge, sitting in the central office, of a particular patient," Pohlmeyer calmly answered.

Guarino moved to the issue of the state inspections that had caused Autumn Hills so much trouble. "You put the best foot forward that y'all could put because you certainly knew they were coming," Guarino charged.

"You don't run a nursing home just for the state inspectors," Pohlmeyer shot back.

"The only time ya'll ever did anything was when you were about to get your medicaid money cut off, isn't it, Mr. Pohlmeyer?"

Guarino then moved to the testimony of the patients' relatives who had appeared for the state. He confronted Pohlmeyer again with the assumptions that had so characterized the state's questioning of defense witnesses. "Assume with me, Mr. Pohlmeyer," Guarino would say as he listed the horrors that previous witnesses had testified to. "Was that good patient care?" he asked.

"If I have to assume those facts, that would not be the very best of patient care," Pohlmeyer said.

"One of the first things that you did after they put you on vendor hold was not to address the problem but to try to get the inspector removed," Guarino angrily pressed.

"That is not true at all. In the sixteen years I have been at Autumn Hills, I have questioned an inspector one time," Pohlmeyer responded.

Concerning the patients at Autumn Hills in Texas City, Guarino savaged Pohlmeyer. "Those patients were suffering, suffering greatly, weren't they?" Guarino shouted.

"I can't agree with that," Pohlmeyer answered calmly.

The district attorney knew that Pohlmeyer ran the day-to-day operations of the nursing home chain. He also knew that during the system-wide administrator's meeting, Pohlmeyer and Gay had been effective motivators of their employees. "The bonus system was a motivating factor," Guarino stated.

"Oh, yes, by all means," Pohlmeyer responded, almost proudly.

"Were you present when stacks of hundred-dollar bills were put on the table?" Guarino continued.

"Yes, I was," Pohlmeyer answered.

"Mr. Pohlmeyer, y'all used cash, not a check, in 1978 to get their attention, didn't you?"

"I would agree with that. It was an incentive," Pohlmeyer answered.

"Could an administrator be on vendor hold and still receive a bonus?" Guarino asked.

"In all honesty, yes. The system was not based on punitive action," Pohlmeyer responded. Guarino was gaining ground.

Guarino then demonstrated for the jury that in February 1978, the administrator of the Texas City nursing home received a $200 bonus. He further showed that the administrator of the Conroe, Texas, home got a $300 bonus while the facility was on vendor hold.

"It was devised to promote good management. Certainly, it was to benefit the corporation, it was to benefit the administrator, it was to benefit the patients, it was to benefit everyone," Pohlmeyer said.

Guarino continued to press Pohlmeyer to admit that the home had not paid overtime, had not maintained adequate staffing, and had padded the levels of care so that the facility could make more money. Pohlmeyer had had enough. Completely ignoring Guarino, he turned to the jury and delivered a long lecture on how he would rather double staff than not have coverage. "Many days, Mrs. Ritchie would be overstaffed," Pohlmeyer said, looking straight at the jury.

"She is your kind of administrator, isn't she, Mr. Pohlmeyer?" Guarino said cynically after the witness finished his lecture.

In the audience Joyce Gay was sitting on the front row, next to her husband. She was becoming increasingly agitated by Guarino's questions. Finally, she turned to her husband and in a stage whisper said, "They can't deal with facts." As the D.A. continued, she couldn't believe that he was asking such questions of the man who had worked with her and her husband for so long.

"After you passed that September 19 inspection, you did like you did all along. You stopped giving the home support," Guarino charged Pohlmeyer.

"It's not the role of the central office to run the nursing home," Pohlmeyer responded.

"Patients in your nursing home aren't just sacks of rice, Mr. Pohlmeyer. They are human beings," Guarino shot back as he finished with the witness.

Charles Burton knew the value of courtroom theatrics as well as any lawyer. So he had one more question for Ron Pohlmeyer on redirect. He asked his witness to describe his mother. Pohlmeyer said that when he was ten years old, his mother suffered a massive stroke that affected her side and her speech. Ron Pohlmeyer and his two sisters had to take care of his handicapped mother as they were growing up. Even as he testified, Pohlmeyer told the jury, his mother was in a Brenham, Texas, nursing home.

Roy Minton is handsomely paid because he can create reasonable doubt in the minds of jurors. Part of that process depends on his ability to discredit witnesses. Occasionally, Minton is able to destroy a witness utterly. Such was the case with Howard Johnson, an investigative auditor with the Texas attorney general's office.

A significant part of the state's case centered on Marks's contention that patients were shorted care, food, medication, and supplies because of the personal greed and opulent lifestyle of Bob Gay, the corporation's founder and chief executive officer. Marks contended that if the money spent on Gay's perks had been spent on patient care, there would not have been so many problems at the Texas City nursing home.

Throughout the case, the defense contended that Gay was entitled, as the top executive in the chain, to live as he saw fit. The defense also minimized the amount of money involved. Now Minton was charged with proving that the state had played fast and loose with the figures to show that Gay and his family had personally received salary and benefits totaling $527,756, as Johnson had testified early in the trial. Minton was right. Marks and the auditor, Johnson, had indeed massaged the numbers to make Gay look bad in front of the jury. In the prosecution phase of the trial, the press picked up the numbers that Johnson supplied to the jury. Minton reserved the right to cross-examine the auditor later in the trial. Now, as the jury was about to hear Bob Gay tell his story from the stand, Minton called Johnson.

On a chart displayed before the jury, Minton noted each sum the state was attributing to Gay: a salary of $97,230, dividends of $6500, an $18,000 bonus, an $18,000 salary to Joyce Gay, car expenses of $1252, a deer lease at $2028, medical bills of $1584, a trip to Vail, Colorado, for the relatively modest sum of $390, an investment in Villa Northwest of $25,000, insurance totaling $38,197, profits on Diamond Construction Company of $13,500, a trip to

Vancouver, British Columbia, for $5800, investment property on Galveston's Seawall Boulevard worth $132,345, a certificate of deposit collateralizing a loan of $150,000, and an investment in an Austin shopping center worth $13,000.

Minton quickly established that Johnson had not used accepted accounting principles in developing his audit. Johnson, in turn, said that he had done an investigative audit, which had its own procedures. Minton pointed out that those procedures did not constitute acceptable business practice. Yes, said Johnson, "Mr. Gay couldn't go to a bank and borrow money on the basis of my audit."

"I'm not an accountant. Can you tell me where we can find investigative audit principles?" Minton asked.

"There are no principles," Johnson answered.

Minton pressed the point. In the case of Diamond Construction Company, Minton demonstrated that because Gay owned 75 percent of the small in-house corporation that worked on his nursing homes, the state had indicated that 75 percent of the benefits from the company accrued to him not in the form of dividends but in cash. Minton also showed that Johnson had worked only with gross figures, not net gains after taxes and overhead. He concluded his questioning by showing that the $13,500 in Diamond Construction Company invoices included a 20 percent markup for labor and materials. Johnson had listed the markup as a profit, disregarding expenses that the company had incurred in doing the work, and credited the amount to Gay personally.

From his seat at the prosecution bench, David Marks watched the picture he had painted of Bob Gay's lifestyle destroyed before his very eyes as Minton discounted almost every category on Johnson's list. Later, Marks would say, "I'm not happy. I am a perfectionist, and I don't like to see things crash down, but I take full responsibility." What he took responsibility for was either an incredibly sloppy job or outright dishonesty on the prosecution's part.

Later in the day, the defense put yet another witness on the stand who further discredited Johnson's accounting study. Harry Mishra, an Asian-born CPA and Bob Gay's personal accountant, testified that Gay didn't receive anything from Diamond Construction in 1978. In addition, Mishra discounted most of the state's investigative audit. By late in the afternoon, David Marks felt "lower than low, more down than down."

CHAPTER SIXTEEN

Almost one week to the day after the debacle of Howard Johnson's cross-examination by Roy Minton, and almost two weeks since her last testimony, Mattie Locke returned to the witness stand. She had buried her sister. She could resume the nightmare of standing trial for murder. Now she would again have to face the relentless questioning of David Marks.

For Marks, finishing the cross-examination of Mattie Locke was his penultimate act in *State of Texas* v. *Autumn Hills*. After that, there remained only a short final argument to convince the jury that a corporation could commit murder and that its top executives should go to prison. Marks had to put everything he could muster into breaking the corporation's director of nursing. It was his last shot in the consuming task he had set for himself seven years before.

When Mattie Locke took the witness stand this time, the strain of the past year was evident in her face. But as Marks began to review her previous cross-examination testimony, she summoned unseen strength and was again reserved in her answers, not giving an inch to the prosecutor. She repeated that most of the events she and the other defendants were on trial for were evidence of documentation problems. Marks began once more to ask rough questions. He did not know if the jury knew of the death of Locke's sister. He did not know if there was sympathy for her in that jury box. He only knew that he had to undermine the credibility she had apparently built during her testimony under the able guidance of Roy Minton. Marks hoped before it was over he would see Mattie Locke cry on the witness stand; he thought she deserved to cry, just as the relatives of the patients entrusted to her company's care had cried.

Roy Minton watched carefully as Marks plunged ahead. He had observed the young lawyer throughout the trial, and from a purely professional point of view he thought he detected the development of Marks into a trial lawyer. He still believed that Marks had done terrible things to his clients, and he would not hesitate to crucify Marks in court, but Minton also felt a grudging admiration for the young man he had come to know over the years. In his own career, Minton was proud of what he could get away with in the courtroom. Now he saw in Marks some of the same qualities. "David wants to cheat. . . . He's learning," Minton said to a reporter.

As Marks grilled Locke on the pages and pages of inspector's reports, he repeatedly asked her, "Just another documentation problem, right?" appropriating the answer she had so frequently given in her testimony and almost turning it into a sad joke. But Marks hadn't counted on one thing that Locke was prepared to say. Unlike many of the witnesses before her, Mattie Locke was willing to admit that there were serious problems in the Texas City nursing home. She honestly believed that those problems were not created by the corporation she served as director of nursing and that they certainly were not willful neglect, but problems they were. It had been her job to correct them, and Mattie Locke believed she had done her job.

Marks next moved to the physicians who practiced in the nursing home. "The physicians were practicing medicine over the phone, is that right?" Marks asked.

"There were physicians through that facility almost daily," Locke answered.

Marks then read from her grand jury testimony: "'Accurate documentation is necessary for legal purposes, and it doesn't add to patient care.' That's the attitude you communicated to the nurses down there," Marks said.

"Absolutely not," Locke responded.

Marks pointed out that to document what is going on with a patient, a nurse must get up and go to the room and examine the patient. "Is it important for the nurse to examine the patient? . . . Is it important for her to lift up the sheets and look at the patient?" he continued.

"It's not the practice," Locke responded, adding that the aide's job was to care for the patients and to look under the sheets.

Marks moved on to the attempt by Locke and Pohlmeyer to get Betty Korndorffer removed from her position as an inspector of the Autumn Hills facility. "Your purpose was to get rid of Betty Korndorffer, wasn't it? . . . Isn't it true that you and Mr. Pohlmeyer could not show that Betty Korndorffer had anything but the best interests of those patients at heart?" Marks continued. "You went [to Korndorffer's superior] to play a personality game. . . . Mr. Danial told you on several occasions in the past that you had come up with the same excuse you were coming up with now. . . . On several occasions in the past you and Mr. Pohlmeyer tried to manipulate the inspection process."

Marks's assault succeeded in making Mattie Locke angry. She responded that she wasn't aware of any attempts in the past, but Marks fired back that her grand jury testimony had indicated that she had tried to get inspectors removed in 1977. "I have no way of knowing that," she answered, the strain evident in her voice.

That shrillness continued as Marks pressed her, but Mattie Locke recognized it and fought to regain control. As the prosecutor moved to the subject of the training that Autumn Hills employees received, she recovered. "I taught a lot of people in my life. I can't be sure that they understood." She said that she had been one of the most adamant people in her profession about preparing care plans for patients. Unfortunately, she said, that feeling wasn't shared by others; "I wish it were."

Now, just as Marks had used her redundant "documentation problem" response to his advantage, Mattie Locke answered all his questions the same way, saying, "No, Mr. Marks, that's not right." Marks was getting nowhere in his cross-examination. He had taken the witness too far, had gone on too long, and now arrived at a point of diminishing returns.

But he still had work to do. Marks had attempted to get two letters into the court record throughout the trial, one from Cassandra Canlas, the other from Mary Wagner, a director of nursing in the Autumn Hills chain. In a letter to administrator Paul Smith, Wagner wrote, "Mrs. Locke feels that 21 patients have died because of lack of good nursing care." Marks believed that the letter, written in June 1976, would devastate Locke's credibility. But he had not found a way to enter the letter as evidence. So he pressed on, trying to show the jury that Locke lacked compassion.

"Do you lift up the sheet and look at the skin of the patient?" he asked.

"In 1978 it was not my practice to look at the skin of the patients," Mattie Locke answered.

Marks next cited notes from the state inspection reports that the jury had been hearing about for months. Locke gave in on small items, such as patients' fingernails not being clipped, but gave little on matters of a more serious nature. She responded briskly on the issue of call lights left out of the reach of patients: "That's probably a very astute observation. We put the patients in the doorway where we could watch them."

As he had done so often, Marks questioned Locke about the testimony of such former Autumn Hills employees as nurse Jurline Boone and aide Pamela James. "Mrs. Boone was a hospital nurse and oriented toward hospital nursing," Locke pointed out to Marks. She added that she would have reported Pamela James for abuse and neglect had she known what was going on.

Marks then touched on the strong odor in the Texas City nursing home. "I never smelled that in Texas City," Locke testified. Marks pressed, repeating that patients stayed soiled and wet for long periods. "Patients left that way have a urine burn. There is no indication that we had that," Mattie Locke said.

"In September, were you aware of the maggots found in one of your patients?" Marks continued.

"I was aware of the maggots in Carrie Bacon's shoe," Locke answered.

Marks then asked Locke if she remembered the drainage and foul odor of Edna Mae Witt's bedsore. Witt had died of renal failure, the defense contended. "Mr. Marks, in the years I have worked in long-term care I have see many persons die of renal failure. It is not a pleasant death. They inevitably develop decubitus." Locke also said that she remembered Elnora Breed. She and Canlas had discussed the Breed case. "Yes, I do remember that particular patient." But she had not reviewed Breed's diet order. "The number of draining, oozing decubitus was no different than in any other skilled facilities," Locke estimated.

"Then that was the standard for Autumn Hills," Marks shot back.

"Absolutely not!" the nurse retorted.

Marks was approaching the point that he hoped would cap the cross-examination of Mattie Locke. In his hand was the letter that

Cassandra Canlas had written to Bob Gay. In it, the former director of nursing had blasted Autumn Hills' policies. In particular, the young nurse had castigated Virginia Wilson, then administrator of the nursing home. Marks thought that the letter was a crucial piece of evidence because in it a defendant, whom the jury had observed before them for months, indicated that all was not right in the Texas City nursing home. Morgan permitted the letter to be read to the jury.

The letter was like so many that administrators find on their desks, from a bitter former employee venting the frustrations accumulated as high expectations were dashed by overwork, unfulfilled promises, and the unresponsiveness of supervisors with problems of their own. But Canlas did point out specific instances that were helpful to the state's case and damning to certain defendants.

Canlas complained about often being shorthanded, to the point of working many shifts herself when she couldn't find help. She complained that her efforts to find help were sometimes frustrated by Virginia Wilson, the administrator. She also said that she was reprimanded because her medication aide had accumulated too much overtime. Canlas further wrote that she had received complaints about the quantities of supplies she ordered and added, "We have 13 decubitus ulcers in the facility and the nurses must have something to work with if they are to treat these sores as the doctor has ordered. Dressings are expensive!"

She blasted Virginia Wilson, writing, "Our dear Mrs. Wilson is very shortsighted." Canlas said that she had twice requested that Mattie Locke visit the home in October. Locke hadn't responded to either request. Canlas's venom increased as she wrote, "I enjoyed working for Autumn Hills until I found out that everything you're told when you begin working is a lie, and no one is behind you when you try to do something different that has worked somewhere else. The only informative discussion I've had with anyone concerning the problems in this home has been with Betty Korndorffer. She is the only person that seemed to care that I was working my rear end off and nothing seemed to get any better."

Mattie Locke sat motionless and stoic as Marks read the letter, then passed it to the jury. On the oak bench in the front row of the courtroom, Virginia Wilson had an unpleasant look on her face. Gay and Pohlmeyer showed no response to the reading of the letter, which was Marks's last evidential thrust at what he alleged they had done.

Roy Minton now had to offset the damage done by Sandy Canlas's letter. He wasted no time. In her letter, the young nurse had repeatedly pointed out that she had asked for a raise and hadn't received it. Now, Minton would turn the tables on Marks. "Would it have made any sense to have given this lady a raise when you are about to fire her?" Minton asked.

"Absolutely not," Locke replied.

"Do you know of any lie that you or Mrs. Wilson ever told to Sandy Canlas or anyone else?"

"Absolutely not."

Minton had just one more question of Mattie Locke: "Do you know of anything you would have done differently?"

"There is not anything I would do. I may not have done it perfectly, but I tried."

The ordeal of testimony was finally over for Mattie Locke. Her lawyers thought she had performed perfectly on the stand. As the court recessed, Minton hugged the woman he had worked with for so many years. Pohlmeyer also embraced her. At last, Mattie Locke cried from relief, not because David Marks had broken her on the witness stand.

Roy Minton was feeling the pressure of his position. An attorney doesn't charge a client more than a million dollars and lose the case. Minton was paid handsomely for one reason. He had considerable clout in state government circles, and he knew how to make a trial work. The strain of the longest criminal trial in Texas history was taking its toll, though. Minton always lost weight during a trial; in this one, he had lost thirty pounds.

Minton had one, possibly two, witnesses left to present before he rested his case. Mattie Locke had done so well that he might only lose ground by doing more, yet Bob Gay had to face the jury and tell his story. As February ended, an exhausted Roy Minton fell ill. Morgan delayed the trial for eight days until the lead defense attorney could return to the courtroom.

During that same period, tragedy again struck one of the Autumn Hills defendants. The brother of Virginia Wilson was found dead of natural causes in his home.

Until 1978, Bob Gay had lived the American dream. He was a self-made man and justifiably proud of it. He had a beautiful family, a successful business, and all the bounty such a life could offer. Gay, too, had found it hard to believe that he was in San Antonio standing trial for murder.

He had sat in the courtroom for months, watching the trial unfold, the analytical mind of an executive at work. In his spare time he read James Michener's *Texas*, a cumbersome novel of more than a thousand pages that had been widely anticipated but was a disappointment to many Texans. It was the first novel he had read in years, he said.

Gay had mortgaged property and dickered with banks to get the money to keep the defense alive. He had paid for his and the other defendants' lawyers, and now he could finally take the stand in his own defense.

Minton did not have high hopes for Gay. There was no smoking gun that the president of Autumn Hills could offer the jury. Mattie Locke and Ron Pohlmeyer had provided all the answers. Gay had simply been the executive, the top man. Locke and Pohlmeyer were the worker bees, the expediters, the can-do team for his nursing home chain. Yet Gay had to face the jury and convince them that he never killed anyone through neglect as the state charged.

Roy Minton, his voice hoarse, led Gay through the history of how he had built Autumn Hills into a chain of seventeen nursing homes. The 59-year-old executive spoke with pride of how he had built the business. He described how he spent his time: "Most of the time, I was working on financial matters, acquiring nursing homes." He spoke of the Galveston project that Howard Johnson had tried to prove was Gay's personal asset, not the corporation's. "It was slated to be the nicest nursing home in Texas," Gay said.

Gay detailed the banking relationships he had developed and pointed out that despite the corporation's growth, the banks still forced him to guarantee loans personally. He also spoke of his friend George Mitchell: "I've known him since I built the first nursing home. . . . He helped with the original financing." Gay went on to say that he constantly consulted Mitchell on financing. He told the jury that in 1978 Mitchell was worth $500 million.

Gay described the acquisition process, saying that the right in-
gredients had to be there. He had looked at 170 nursing homes in
order to buy the 17 he owned. Effective operation of those homes
depended on nursing care. "You have to deliver a product the cus-
tomer wants." Gay said that ninety percent of the homes he had
acquired were in trouble when he bought them because their owners couldn't budget.

Minton knew he must confront the Autumn Hills bonus system
head on. He had to show the jury that the display of $100 bills that
Gay and Pohlmeyer placed before the administrators was standard
business practice, an incentive program much like those practiced
in sales departments everywhere. Gay began by saying that the
homes were not profitable before he came up with the idea of incentive bonuses based on profits. At the time, none of his administrators were paying any attention to the carefully prepared performance reports. He had placed the stacks of money in front of the
administrators and didn't mention them during the meeting. Finally, one administrator asked what they were for. Gay said to the
court, "Four hundred dollars in a stack of hundred-dollar bills is
pretty impressive." When he explained the bonus system at the
meeting, something changed for his company. "Instead of wanting
to leave my office, they wanted to sit around and talk about accounting again," he told the court. "For every dollar we were
spending, we could make it go twenty-five percent farther than in
the past."

As Gay testified, the jury saw a corporate executive, a businessman, a numbers man, a man whose primary concern was the bottom line. Bob Gay ran his business properly. The exteriors of his
nursing homes were attractive and blended into the neighborhoods.
The brochures his company passed out to prospective clients were
well designed and colorful.

From the audience, the Gay family watched as the paterfamilias
continued his story under the careful guidance of Minton. Bob
Gay's family was well dressed, looking as if they felt at home at
Lord and Taylor, Neiman-Marcus, Saks Fifth Avenue, or on Rome's
Via Condotti. They wore their success like a badge for all to see,
proud of their status in life. The prosecutors were secretly delighted with the way Gay's family dressed. Could the blue-collar
workers on the jury possibly relate to them?

Gay's testimony was remarkably short. Minton knew that his client had little knowledge of what had gone on in Texas City. Pohlmeyer and Locke were the hands-on people. They made the wheels of the company turn, handled the day-to-day business Gay had long ago stopped attending to. When he finished, Minton was elated with what he had accomplished in Bob Gay's short testimony. "I didn't open a single fucking door" for the prosecution, he would later say.

It fell now to Jim Vollers to administer the final cross-examination in the Autumn Hills case. He moved slowly at first, testing Gay to see if the man would easily blunder into an area where his credibility could be challenged. The prosecutors had been preoccupied throughout the case with Autumn Hills' practice of passing out $100 bills to its administrators. Now Vollers confronted the paymaster. "As a matter of fact, it was standard procedure for Mr. Pohlmeyer to stand up and pass out hundred-dollar bills," Vollers began.

"It never was done that way. It might have been dramatic, but it was never done that way," Gay responded.

"Never?" Vollers pressed.

"I was there! It never was done that way," Gay repeated angrily.

Vollers went on, charging that Pohlmeyer forced administrators who hadn't earned a bonus to stand up before their more successful colleagues and explain why. Gay fired back, "That was never done!"

But Vollers stayed on that tack, grilling Gay about padding level-of-care reports to increase the amount of government money the home would receive for more seriously disabled patients. He then asked Gay if he had read the state inspectors' reports. "I read over them very fast. I then got a report from Mr. Pohlmeyer and Mrs. Locke."

Vollers turned next to the cash-flow problems that the state alleged were caused, in part, by Gay's extravagant lifestyle. Vollers pointed out that on some occasions Gay had been forced to borrow money to meet his payroll. But Gay skillfully defused that charge by answering, "I think I've had a cash-flow problem since my first date in high school, but not a serious cash-flow problem." The capacity crowd in the courtroom erupted in laughter.

Gay then pressed the point that he, as an executive, wanted to make. He had experts working for him that he expected to take care of the daily operations of his nursing homes: dietary experts, nursing experts, the gamut of health professionals in the extended-care field. He went on to say that deficiencies in his homes were very disturbing to him. "It means that I have to have someone go down and take a look at every one of those deficiencies. It means that something is wrong and I don't like it! . . . Any of these things that are written up as deficiencies means something bad to me."

Vollers now moved to the tactic that had been so effective for him and the other prosecutors throughout the case. He began to read from the reports the horror stories that the jury had heard repeatedly for six months. "What does that mean to you regarding patient care?" Vollers asked.

"It doesn't sound good to me," Gay answered disarmingly.

Vollers pressed but could not get the answers from Gay that he wanted. Gay sounded too reasonable, too agreeable, often admitting that he didn't know what had gone wrong. "It sounds like it's not good here, but I really don't know," Gay answered again and again as Vollers tried to box him in about the problems in Texas City.

Vollers asked Gay about the food that was served in his nursing home, citing testimony that meat often wasn't cut for patients. Again, Gay answered, "It doesn't sound good to me. I would want it changed." Vollers then asked Gay to judge the efficiency of his administrators. "When you are dealing with human life, as you do in a nursing home, did it ever cross your mind that an efficient manager could be shortcutting on supplies to obtain a bonus?" Gay admitted that such a thing was possible but unlikely; it was his opinion that such an administrator would not last long in his operation because he would quickly be found out.

"Have you described Betty Korndorffer's inspection reports as horrible inspection reports?" Vollers continued.

"I don't know if I described it that way, but that wouldn't miss it much," Gay answered calmly, drawing smiles from the other defendants, Autumn Hills staff members, and the defendants' families. "I was in that facility many times, and it looked good. The patient care was good; it was probably the best nursing home in Texas City. I never felt that the health of any of the residents was in jeopardy in that nursing home."

Vollers then asked Gay if he had read the reports that cited Elnora Breed's diet. Gay answered almost frivolously. "Reading over the report there was some concern, but not a whole lot. If it didn't excite an RN, it would be lost on me."

The special prosecutor continued to pepper Gay with questions, but it was evident that he was not getting anywhere. Finally, he asked Gay about the availability of medications, and the nursing home owner answered that when the family wouldn't pay for the medication, it was unavailable. Vollers then struck pay dirt when Gay's next answer demonstrated a lack of compassion for the patients in his facilities and their families. "We tell the family if they are not going to take care of their obligations and buy them, they need to take their family member to another nursing home or take them home."

Vollers then brought up Betty Korndorffer, the woman who had meant so much to the state's case. He asked Gay about Mattie Locke and Ron Pohlmeyer's attempt to have Korndorffer removed as inspector of Gay's nursing homes. Gay had sat through six months of trial and heard almost a hundred witnesses, many of whom agreed with what Betty Korndorffer had reported, yet he minimized her findings. "She went into such detail in her reports. I had never seen anything like those reports. . . . I don't think that the lady was outright lying. I just think she was making a mountain out of a molehill in many cases."

That marked the end of Gay's testimony. There were no more witnesses for the defense to call. At the bench, in front of Judge Don B. Morgan, Minton and David Marks smiled at one another. At 2:09 p.m., March 11, 1986, the defense and state rested in what had become the longest and most expensive criminal trial in Texas history.

It took another full week for the attorneys to fight out what would be contained in the charge that Morgan would read to the jury before they retired for deliberations. In general, the lawyers had gotten along remarkably well throughout the case. Certainly, animosity remained between Marks and Sartwelle. The Fulbright and Jaworski lawyer had repeatedly said that when the case was over, he would attempt to have Marks disbarred.

But Sartwelle's relationship with Morgan had continued to improve as the two men came to know each other on a social basis. Over dinner, good wine, and good talk, the two found that they had much more in common than either had believed. Morgan even joked with Sartwelle that whoever had called him a prick was really paying him a compliment with a grudging sign of respect. The only fireworks during the days of charge conferences came because of Minton's habit of nicknaming people around him. He had called Miguel Martinez "Santa Anna" throughout the case. Finally, the Mexican-born Martinez responded angrily, telling the famous attorney not to call him that again.

The product of their week of intense work was a compromise document that would take Morgan four full hours to read to the jury. At the end of that time, Morgan was hoarse and his throat raw. The charge on the corporation and the four remaining individual defendants ran to 106 intensely legalistic pages. Most observers believed that the document would be incomprehensible to the jury. And the charge favored the defense, for while Guarino and Marks had to convince twelve people to vote guilty, Minton, Burton, Sartwelle, and Barrera had to convince only one juror to vote for acquittal and stick with that vote to the bitter end. All the attorneys, prosecution and defense, knew that the state would never spend the money to retry Autumn Hills. It was an all or nothing case.

The small courtroom in the Bexar County Courthouse was filled to capacity as Miguel Martinez began his final argument to the jury. Morgan had allotted each side four hours to convince the jury to convict or acquit. Now Martinez told the jury, "That Mrs. Breed was dying of cancer is what is called a courtroom diagnosis. Mrs. Breed was not dying of cancer until these defendants were called upon to answer for her death. . . . A sick life and a healthy life have equal value. . . . They are not entitled to hurry up their death."

David Marks had worked seven years to reach the point of addressing the jury in this case. Slowly, Marks told of a Yellow Cab that had taken Breed's sister Ruth twice daily to the nursing home. He told of what Mrs. Linscomb had seen, and he told how nice the outside of the building had looked to Mrs. Linscomb, but then he reminded the jury of the trust that all people put in doctors and nurses. "How many times have we turned our lives over to what is represented by a white uniform in a clinical setting?" he asked the jury.

Marks told how Linscomb had paid the nursing home "a check

representing a portion of the life savings of Elnora Breed, representing the careful planning of her earlier years." Marks went on to describe in scathing terms the nursing home industry. "Contrary to what Mr. Gay says, the nursing home industry is not the competitive model of the free enterprise system. You don't change a nursing home like you change a grocery store." Furthermore, he said, "The duty of a nursing home operator is as strong as the duty of a parent to a child. . . . They owed a duty to Elnora Breed to maintain her in comfort.

"On October 4, 1978, at 11:30 a.m., a trusting Ruth Linscomb walked into the administrator's office and handed them a check. Twenty minutes later, Elnora Breed arrived, and thus began her exposure to the Autumn Hills brand of care. . . . She was to receive her reward, a reward for careful planning." Marks pressed on, hoping that the jury would realize that Elnora Breed had paid part of her life's savings for the right to die in a state of degradation in Autumn Hills.

Finally, Marks concluded by telling the jury that every one of the eyewitnesses to the events in Texas City had cried before him. "My role over the past years has been to bring this matter to justice." Tears came to Marks's eyes as he closed his seven-year crusade by calling each witness by name for the jury.

"Does it really make a difference that Mrs. Breed had cancer?" Vollers asked as he spoke to the jury. "Does it give them the right to kill them?" He went on brutally, describing Breed and other Autumn Hills patients. Then he talked about each of the defendants and was particularly devastating to Bob Gay. "Does Robert Gay have a reason to lie?" Vollers said. "I think you know that Mrs. Breed was wronged. Mr. Gay is out for the almighty buck. . . . You cannot allow these people to take advantage of little people like Mrs. Breed, . . . that a shark does not get in among the elderly." That metaphor brought an immediate motion for a mistrial from Barrera, but Morgan overruled it.

Barrera opened the final arguments for the defense and presented the argument that has sounded in American courtrooms for two centuries. A verdict, he reminded, must be unanimous, "but you are an individual." He then proceeded to put the Texas Department of Health on trial: "Why didn't they do something about it?" he asked the jury. "If Elnora Breed smelled like a rotting animal, the state health department was aware of it." He asked why that agency didn't close the place down. The jury hadn't heard of the intervention of two powerful legislators in the early days of the case.

Barrera also reminded the jury that the state had not done an autopsy on Elnora Breed at the time of her death. "It was the defendants who disinterred that body," he went on. "If you have pictures of decubitus ulcers in this courtroom on any of the patients at Autumn Hills, it was the defendants who brought them in." Barrera then attacked the idea that a conspiracy went on at the nursing home. "Read those indictments. . . . Ten people at a hands-on level, . . . all of those people developed a necessary state of mind to kill Elnora Breed?"

More than eighty people filled the tiny courtroom as Tom Sartwelle rose to speak. They stood, knelt, or squatted, but all eyes were trained on the lawyers inside the bar. Sartwelle rose, nervous, saying that he had been given one and a half hours to sum up the medical testimony of the last six months. "That is an impossible task," he said. "I'm not going to call anyone a liar. If anyone should call a witness a liar, it should be you."

Sartwelle returned to Ruth Linscomb, Elnora Breed's sister. "Mrs. Linscomb put another sister in that same nursing home under the care of the same doctor." Sartwelle asked the jury why they had not heard from Betty Korndorffer's husband, the Galveston County medical examiner. "He was the medical examiner then; he is the medical examiner now." He asked why the jury hadn't heard from expert medical witnesses from Galveston County. He mentioned the University of Texas Medical Branch, less than twenty miles from Autumn Hills. "There Autumn Hills sits in one of the world's largest medical complexes."

Sartwelle read to the jury a long list of the ailments of the 87-year-old widow. Guarino immediately rose and objected, shouting, "She was dependent like an infant child." But Sartwelle continued, waving the Breed medical record at the jury and telling them that every page said cancer of the colon.

Next, Sartwelle spoke of Dr. Antonio Silvetti. "I hope that his pictures said more than his testimony did," Sartwelle said, referring to the videotape the defense had paid for that showed Silvetti's work. "Dr. Silvetti told you that medical science doesn't know much about bedsores. What knowledge they have gained, they have gained in the last five years."

As he continued, Sartwelle's parents watched their son, while from another row Marks's parents stared at the man who wanted to end their son's career. Both families watched as Sartwelle discussed the diet that Marks and the other prosecutors contended had starved Elnora Breed to death. "Were the nurses obligated to follow that order? . . . A nurse is supposed to countermand that order? . . . Is there some kind of Betty Korndorffer exemption? . . . There are doctors all over Galveston County; couldn't she have got one of them to call Dr. Konikowski and say, 'Hey'?"

Now Sartwelle faced the problem of refuting the testimony the state had presented on the horrors of bedsores. He had, throughout the case, contended that turning does not necessarily prevent bedsores. He believed he had proven that the turning procedures still used by nurses across the country were antiquated. Of the nurses in the state's case, he said, "Those nurses want to bury their heads in the sand." He attacked the state's contention that Autumn Hills nurses had not followed proper documentation procedures. "If it's not documented, it's not done?" Finally, Sartwelle brought the reality of a nursing home existence home to the jury. "Among the people in this room, some of us are going to die with bedsores. . . . You know, you go to a nursing home to die, you don't go to be rehabilitated."

The audience could barely hear Charles Burton as he spoke to the jury. But Burton didn't care if the audience heard him; he was concerned only with the twelve people who counted. Burton spoke of the law, reminding the jury of Vollers's closing argument. "He told you that you were here to see that little people like Elnora Breed are protected, . . . to see that we have not spent six months here for nothing. A trial in our system of justice is not a political rally or a pep rally. . . . You do all of those things in a polling booth, but not here. Can you imagine anyone with that concept of our system of justice, that if you don't come to a guilty verdict, your time is wasted?"

Finally, Charles Burton attacked the press. He told the jury that what they had seen in the courtroom was not the same as what their neighbors were reading. He said that when it was all over they, the jurors, would go home and read the papers about what had gone on. He told the assembled group before him that they would say to their neighbors, "That's not the same trial I saw."

Roy Minton stood before the jury and spoke the language of the streets tó make his plea. None of the other lawyers had really pleaded with the jury. Minton pleaded, prayed, cajoled, argued, harangued, begged, beseeched, entreated, implored, solicited, supplicated, adjured, petitioned, and finally simply requested that the twelve people before him find his clients not guilty. He had sat for months twirling his mustache and watching the jurors. He knew that some of the jurors felt warmly toward him. Throughout the trial, he had cultivated those jurors, maintained eye contact with them, spoken to them as they passed in the hallway of the courthouse. He had, in fact, infuriated the prosecution with his warmth to the jurors.

Minton had studied the jurors as individuals. He knew that of the men on the jury, three were in their fifties and sixties and might feel warmth for a man their own age. He knew, for example, that he and juror Sherman Miller had both served in the armed forces and had even been stationed on the same base. Would Miller respond to that? Minton believed that he would.

Before a jury, Minton was mass in motion, but the once-portly attorney was now almost thin. Because of his round face and balding head, he still looked like an aging cherub with a mustache, and he always simply looked larger than he really was. As he addressed the jury, Minton paced back and forth, using his hands as he spoke.

"Each one of those people look to me and Mr. Burton as their lawyer," he said, then went on to explain that for the jury to find his clients guilty of murder, it would have to determine that they had knowingly caused the death of Elnora Breed.

"I guess I've tried as many murder cases as any man in Texas today except Jim Vollers, who has probably prosecuted as many." Minton didn't mind giving a member of the prosecution a mention. Throughout the trial, and usually in front of the jury, Minton would smile at his opponents, laugh with them, appear to be friends. Whenever a prosecutor dropped a piece of paper on the floor of the courtroom, it was Minton who politely picked it up and handed it back to the man who was trying to put his client in jail. Minton wanted the jury to believe that he was the nice guy, the man they could trust.

But now he shot from the hip as he spoke, telling the jury of his past cases and describing those former clients and their problems in phrases familiar to the hardworking people on the jury. "This guy jacks him around," Minton would say; every member of the jury had been jacked around at least once and knew what the term described.

For months the jury had seen Mattie Locke writing in a large notebook. Now Minton turned those observations to his advantage, as he said, "If you have not learned anything in this lawsuit, you have learned that Mattie Locke will write a note on anything around." Although some of the audience laughed, not one of the jurors so much as smiled. They were now feeling the full weight of their responsibility.

Minton spoke of Mike Ramsey, Sandy Canlas's lawyer, who had departed three months before. "I was so sorry to see Mike go, toothpick and all." Ramsey had sat for hours at the defense table chewing a toothpick. A few jurors laughed at Minton's reminder.

Minton talked about the mass of numbers Mattie Locke had been faced with every day of her professional life. "If Mattie Locke had the primary responsibility for Elnora Breed, she had it for two thousand patients!"

Of Pohlmeyer he said, "He was raised the way I wish my boys had been raised, raised out on a ranch, raised in a country town. He said, This is what I did and I did it the best way I know how."

Of Bob Gay, Minton said, "I suppose that the state is attempting to show that Bob Gay is money-hungry, that he has no feelings. . . . He was building a chain of nursing homes because he wanted to. He wanted to for years." Of the bonus system, Minton continued, "I don't know if you think that was a good idea or a bad idea. I have been listening to it for five years. All I know is that it worked." Of making money, he said, "God, I wish I had that ability."

About Virginia Wilson, who had not testified in her own defense, Minton told the jury, "The problem I have with Virginia Wilson is that there was no evidence against her." Minton was right, the state clearly had not presented much of a case against the former administrator. She had run the nursing home only a short while in 1978 and before that had worked there as a secretary.

Minton again used the street language that some of the jurors were sure to understand. He told of barroom brawls, imitating a street fighter using a pool cue as a weapon. It made no difference that such assaults had little to do with the passive murder his clients were charged with; the theatrics were there and counted as he spoke to the twelve jurors. .

Then, in a strange and offhand way, Minton attempted to transfer guilt from the defendants to the attending physicians of Elnora Breed and then to the charge nurses who had direct responsibility for her care.

I don't want anybody to cause any harm to Dr. Konikowski or Dr. Kolb or Dr. Sullivan, but doggone it, I'm representing four people right here who are charged with murder. And the theory of the state's case, is it not, is that Elnora Breed was starved because she was put on a six-hundred-calorie diet and that those charge nurses should have known when they saw that diet that that was a starvation diet. . . . Now, who of you knows why Elnora Breed died? Knows, bet your home on it? Not me. I don't know why Elnora Breed died. I'm not about to tell you that I know why she died. I will tell you this. There is nobody, that's who, who knows why she died.

I'm not confident six hundred calories is starvation. They've put me on it at fat farms several times, and I'm here. They put me on it during this trial, incidentally. Lost forty pounds in six months. I'm afraid I'm going to dry up and blow away.

I don't understand how they take the position, the theory, that Konikowski does it and somehow it's a mistake, and we move from there to the position that we're on trial for murder. Get me, we're on trial for murder because some charge nurse, it is alleged, did not snap to it and say, Hold it, this is a starvation diet. Golly, that does not make any sense.

Next Minton spoke of some of the lawyers in the case. He spoke of Vollers, an old friend. He spoke of Sartwelle; "I hired what I believe is the best medical lawyer in Texas. He's a bit of an arrogant old boy sometimes, goes on a little bit too long on some of those questions, but I believe that he demonstrated to you people that nobody knows why that lady died."

Returning to Vollers, Minton said, "Any time a lawyer will stand up in a room with eight other lawyers and call a person a shark, he's got guts!"

Sounding like a tent-show evangelist, Minton finished his final argument. "I'm proud to represent these people. . . . When you tell a man you are going to dig someone up and it might be a problem, they might have septicemia. . . . Bob Gay said, 'Dig 'em up. I'm not afraid of the truth.' Go out there, folks, please, God, please, look at that evidence, read that charge! Best of luck, Godspeed."

Minton had been awesome. Mike Guarino, the prosecutor who would make the final argument, said, "It's time to holler," as he walked down the hallway of the Bexar County Courthouse and into the courtroom. After the jury was brought back in and the packed house settled to hear the final words said about Autumn Hills in the trial, the prosecutor who had shown so much fire in his questioning began. He began quietly; there was no fire, none of the anger that had characterized so many of his cross-examinations.

"I don't think that the state can get up and be as glib, be as funny as some of the defense attorneys. . . . Let the evidence be your guide. Before you start going down some rabbit trails, remember that good defense attorneys can put up a smoke screen." Guarino then told the jury of a fundamental reason Autumn Hills was in business. "Each of the defendants has a primary responsibility to deliver patient care. . . . That's why the corporation existed."

The district attorney continued, saying, "You take an old lady and stick rags and soap in her mouth and then you laugh—that's the kind of home that you have." He also reminded the jury that the defense didn't cross-examine two key witnesses, Betty Korndorffer and Jurline Boone. "It's interesting to note that some of the finest defense attorneys in the country did not choose to ask them a single question. They would not dare ask them a single question." Of Sartwelle, Guarino said, "He knows the answers to those questions. It is damning."

Guarino attacked the expert witnesses Sartwelle had carefully selected over the years. He compared the nurses and physicians the state had presented with Sartwelle's health care professionals. He called Sartwelle's witnesses arrogant, then asked the jury whether they would rather be cared for by the state's witnesses or by Sartwelle's witnesses. Finally, Guarino stood before the jury and said, "It is a unique and rare opportunity for you to enforce this law."

Pohlmeyer began to wipe tears from his eyes as the district attorney concluded his argument. Then, as the jurors filed from the room and Morgan left the bench, a flood of tears engulfed the tall defendant. Mattie Locke also cried. Virginia Wilson, who had endured dry-eyed throughout the case, broke down as the knowledge that her ordeal was almost over shattered her enforced calm. Only Bob Gay showed no emotion in the still-crowded room.

Of reporters and friends, Roy Minton asked, "What has God done to me, putting David Marks into my life everywhere I turn?" as he looked across the room at the young prosecutor who had started the case and helped bring it to its conclusion.

In his closing argument, Minton had been awesome. Later some jurors would say that the prosecution was outclassed by the highly paid, experienced defense attorneys Gay had hired. They knew in advance that Minton would bring fireworks to his final appearance before them, and they were not disappointed. David Marks had tried with every fiber of his being to bring the case to a successful conclusion. Now it was in the hands of the jury; he had nothing left to do but wait.

CHAPTER SEVENTEEN

After six years of investigation, six months of trial, and six days of jury deliberation, the Autumn Hills case came to an end on a warm March day. During the six days, the jury voted again and again but without a unanimous decision. They had sent out notes to Judge Morgan that they were hopelessly deadlocked. Barrera, the San Antonio lawyer most familiar to the local press, repeatedly told reporters as each note came out that the defense had called for a mistrial. Just as repeatedly, Morgan denied the motion and told the jury to continue its deliberations.

As each day passed, tension mounted among the attorneys, the defendants, and the press from across the state and nation who stood watch in the hallways of the courthouse. For some, the tension and boredom of the wait became too much. Sartwelle and two friends he had made during the trial, Renee Haines of UPI and freelance writer Lynelle King, played dominoes sitting cross-legged on the floor of the hallway outside the courtroom. A photographer walked by, snapped a photo, and it looked like the Fulbright and Jaworski lawyer would appear in the morning papers in a less-than-dignified position. But Sartwelle, exhausted and grateful that his ordeal was nearly over, didn't care. If the firm didn't like it, too bad; besides, Sartwelle was winning at dominoes.

As the jury remained deadlocked, the lawyers often retired to the judge's chambers, where they and Morgan passed the tedious hours telling and retelling stories of past glory and occasional bitter defeats in the courtroom. On Saturday, Barrera raised the specter of religious coercion, since the following day, Palm Sunday, was a high holy day in the Catholic faith. Morgan decided to allow the jury to attend church services. Shortly thereafter, the jurors sent Morgan a note saying that they all wanted to go to church in a body. One of the jurors, Janet Barse, a 37-year-old housewife who also worked with her husband, was not Catholic, but she remembered later that she "would have done anything to get out of there." Barrera again told the press, "It is not only physical coercion, but it is also religious coercion."

Gay, Locke, Pohlmeyer, and Wilson occupied a long bench outside the jury room. As the twelve individuals who would decide their fate left for meals or returned to the hotel where they were sequestered, they had to pass the four defendants, their families, and their friends and coworkers. The jurors always averted their eyes; they were taking their responsibility seriously.

At one point in the waiting ordeal, Virginia Wilson walked over to a group of reporters just as Jimmie Woods of the *Houston Post* began an account of what was going on in Morgan's chambers. Woods, who had spent many evenings with the judge, had easy access to the bull sessions taking place in Morgan's office. When the reporters suddenly noticed that Wilson was standing with them, the defendant told them, "I've been with you guys so much I feel like one of you." Tactfully, the reporters moved away to continue their conversation.

By Monday, the people occupying the hallway of the Bexar County Courthouse resembled a deathwatch in a hospital corridor. All were tired, impatient, and ready for the ordeal to end. At 4:37 p.m., a note was brought into Morgan's chambers by the bailiff, known only as Sha Na Na. The note said, "We, the ladies and gentlemen of the jury, cannot reach a unanimous verdict. We await further instructions." The jury was hung and had been for days. Morgan brought the jurors back into the courtroom and polled them. The group was deadlocked, and several told Morgan that a verdict was unlikely. But Morgan ordered them to deliberate further.

David Marks knew it was over. There would be no verdict in the Autumn Hills case. A reporter asked, "Now that it appears that your years of work are crashing down around you, what are your feelings at this moment?" Tears filled Marks's eyes as he struggled to answer. Finally composing himself, he said, "I feel disappointment. I had higher expectations as to where it would be right now. The likelihood of a decision is growing dimmer. I have worked in black and white as opposed to grays."

Across the bar, Bob Gay told reporters, "A mistrial is a hollow victory, but it is a victory that at this time I am glad to accept." The president of Autumn Hills said that no verdict would leave a cloud over his company for some time. "I think that the entire industry has been on trial here, and I think that we have come up with no answers." Gay then said he thought that "many nursing homes are going to shy away from skilled care," an ominous possibility for the thousands of nursing home patients facing the end of their lives.

Morgan, Minton, Burton, and one reporter crossed the street to the bar in the Travel Lodge Motel after the jury was released for the night. More war stories, refreshing beer and drinks, and relaxed conversation took the edge off the four men who had come to know each other so well. Minton had another funny story; he related how Frank Erwin, the longtime chairman of the University of Texas Board of Regents, had come to him after receiving a drunk driving charge. Erwin told the lawyer, "I want you to understand one thing. I don't have any more principles than you do." The judge and lawyers laughed. They all needed it.

The following morning at 11:32 a.m., Judge Don B. Morgan granted a defense motion for a mistrial. The Autumn Hills case had come to an end. As the defendants embraced their lawyers, free for the first time in almost a decade, knowing that the case would not be retried, the press corps poured into the hallway to interview the jurors. There they learned that Marks had almost secured his conviction for corporate murder. The vote had consistently been nine to three in favor of conviction of the corporation, at one point stretching to ten to two. Marks had been denied outright victory, but he could walk away from the courthouse with his pride intact.

Some jurors were angry. Linda Aldridge, a clerk at San Antonio's Kelly Air Force Base, had been a stalwart for conviction. When the final note was sent out, she had believed that the foreman was only asking about what to do with six days of dirty laundry. She and her friend and fellow juror Linda Peña shed bitter tears of anger as they talked to reporters. Nine of the jurors would meet a week later, still angry that they had not been able to persuade the remaining three jurors to convict at least the corporation. Most of the jurors had not wanted to see the individual defendants go to jail.

The Cadillac Bar sits a block from the Bexar County Court-house. The white limestone building is a blend of the rich Mexican culture of San Antonio and the Western flavor of the Texas Hill Country. There tables sat on an outdoor patio, filled with trays of Mexican food, a glorious display of San Antonio's culinary art. Around that feast the defendants, their families, and some long-time employees of Autumn Hills gathered after the trial. Many were drinking beer and cocktails. As three of the jurors who had heard their case walked in with Burton and Barrera, applause erupted. One of the jurors had voted to convict the corporation, but at that moment it did not matter; the longest murder trial in the state's history was truly over.

Attorneys and defendants quickly surrounded the jurors, asking questions, their natural curiosity aroused. Clinton Jenschke, Jr., who worked with boiler plant equipment, told listeners that the biggest doubt in his mind was why Betty Korndorffer hadn't closed the nursing home down. Of Dr. Merrill Stiles, he said, "If I was sick, I would go talk to him." Sherman Miller, the veteran whom Minton had counted upon to at least relate to him, wondered aloud, "Why didn't they have an autopsy before the woman was buried?"

The group's festive mood lingered well into the afternoon, the partiers filing out one at a time. Finally, only the lawyers were left. Morgan had joined them. Minton said that his fee would total $1.3 million; Fulbright and Jaworski had received $1 million for Sart-welle's contributions.

Morgan sipped his usual Dewars and soda; Minton, a Carta Blanca beer. Burton and Sartwelle, in the spirit of San Antonio, en-joyed a longneck Lone Star, while Barrera drank the single mar-garita he allows himself daily. He was the first to leave, hugging his fellow lawyers as he went. Minton and Burton left next, embracing Sartwelle, who had cried as he told the defendants good-bye. Min-ton had an appointment with a former federal judge in Austin the following morning. There would be no break in his practice.

Minton turned, his coat thrown over his shoulder, and waved at Sartwelle and the judge. Morgan said, "Talent whips truth every time."